THE 9TH GRADE

150 YEARS OF FREE CLIMBING

© 2015, LES ÉDITIONS DU MONT-BLANC
WWW.LESEDITIONSDUMONTBLANC.COM
CATHERINE DESTIVELLE, DIRECTOR OF THE ÉDITIONS DU MONT-BLANC

OTHER TITLES IN THE MONTAGNE-CULTURE COLLECTION:
REGARDS SUR LES ALPES, JACQUES PERRET, 2011.
MONT-BLANC, PREMIÈRES ASCENSIONS, MICHEL JULLIEN AND JACQUES PERRET, 2012.
LA MONTAGNE À LA UNE, PHILIPPE BONHÈME, 2013.
ALPINISME, LA SAGA DES INVENTIONS, GILLES MODICA, 2014.

ISBN: 978-2-36545-022-5

— DAVID CHAMBRE —
FOREWORD BY JEAN-BAPTISTE TRIBOUT

THE 9TH GRADE

150 YEARS OF FREE CLIMBING

les éditions du
MONT-BLANC

'MAN NEEDS PASSION TO EXIST'

ÉRIC TABARLY
MEMORIES OF THE OPEN SEA

CONTENTS

—

PREAMBLE

——

It is almost 30 years since Jean-Baptiste Tribout and I wrote *Le 8ème degré* (The 8th Grade). We wanted to take stock of the situation of the latest developments, mainly in France, which had swiftly transformed an activity that was still closely linked to mountaineering into a new sport in its own right.

Clearly the title was a tribute to the book *The Seventh Grade* by Reinhold Messner. Besides arousing our interest and motivating us in our youth, he had in his time, from the mid-1960s, broken down first, the mental barriers of rock-climbing, then of Alpinism and, finally, Himalayan mountaineering. Although rock-climbing had already been practised for almost a century, it needed a manifesto such as this to liberate it from the conservative and often reactionary attitudes of traditional Alpine circles.

At the time we were young and impatient. Writing together in our Paris hovels, our daily life was carefully planned and very repetitive: two hours writing, two hours training on our 'home' beam which filled most of the room, writing... Until death do us part... But in three months we had done it, the only price we had had to pay being a few stubborn bouts of tendonitis.

Then followed nearly three equally busy decades in which, despite the various inevitable distractions of life, our passion remained intact. Surprisingly, no one picked up the baton of writing a book covering the new developments of rock-climbing which had now become even more global.

Then, recently, two conversations stirred me from my natural laziness to write again. While visiting my usual indoor climbing centre, I started chatting with a strong young climber. Continuing my train of thought, I mentioned the word 'Yosemite' and, seeing his blank expression, I realised with dismay that he had absolutely no idea what I was talking about. A little later, talking to another kid, I mentioned Patrick Edlinger and the response I had was: "Who's he?"

From this came the idea, after Jibé (Jean-Baptiste Tribout) had freely expressed his caustic opinions on what climbing had become in the 21st century, of going back in time, resurrecting a few ghosts, doing justice to those who have been forgotten, glorifying the icons and, above all, making people want to go rock-climbing.

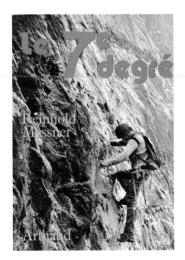 

THE 7TH GRADE, PUBLISHED 1975.

THE 8TH GRADE, PUBLISHED 1987.

—

PAGE 10:

JIBÉ TRIBOUT GIVES HIS BEST ON *FAKIR*, F7C+, BUOUX, 1984.

FOREWORD

—

First of all, before I start, I want to thank David Chambre for giving me a little place in this book: Originally, the idea had been that we would write this book together, as we did with *Le 8ème degré (The 8th Grade)* over 25 years ago but, David was so quick and so motivated by research and writing that he had already written his part before I had even begun. The conclusion was obvious: he must write the book on his own. And our long friendship saw to the rest. Here then is *The 9th Grade*.

Since 1987, when our original book came out, David and I have often discussed how rock-climbing has progressed and this book is the perfect opportunity to share with you the incredible developments which have taken place; I can assure you, they were mostly unimaginable at the time but now they are quite normal for the climbers of today.

These developments are on three levels. The first is from the point of view of achievement with a fantastic increase recently at the highest level; grade F9a on-sight and F9b+ redpoint, longer routes focusing on F8c and F9a pitches and boulders which verge on the impossible. This was predictable but not to this extent. Recently I was so impressed when the Czech climber, Adam Ondra, came to Volx and completed *Super Plafond* (F8c+, 1992) on-sight, placing quickdraws as he climbed. I had made so many attempts at this route, I had wanted to reach this level so much, that seeing Adam do this on-sight shocked me but in the best sense of the word; such was the class performance of his technical mastery and fluency. This man is a phenomenon, undoubtedly the best climber in history and I am happy that 'my' sport should produce such a prodigy. He is the embodiment of what today's rock-climbing is about as well as of its amazing technical evolution; today's rock climbers know better than we did where to put their feet, they are faster, physically stronger and above all proceed with an enormous fluidity which enables them to overcome difficulties as well as jumping many moves which would have been impossible to overcome when climbing at the rhythm common in our time. The other key factor in this evolution is the density of today's rock-climbing community. There has been an incredible internationalisation of climbing which has brought in new talents and also new styles of climbing. For instance, there is the remarkable contribution of Asian climbers whose style is fluid, attractive and not at all jerky; completely controlled. Watching Jain Kim in competition, soaring up the routes apparently without effort, or seeing Sachi Amma climb an F8c+ at Margalef, as I had the chance to do, is a real feast for the eyes, a surreal ballet and that is a real contribution to the sport. It also marks the end of Western supremacy in the world of rock-climbing and demonstrates how universal it now is.

The second development, in my eyes the most unexpected and the most important, is the relentless growth and popularity of indoor rock-climbing on artificial climbing walls; the first of which appeared in the early 1970s more than 40 years ago and which were in rather bleak, unwelcoming gymnasiums. Those days are far away from the current revolution with private centres which have created new disciplines with their own rules, its own special milieus and its own patrons for whom the rock-climbing of the past is almost unknown. They are fans of a kind of vertical fitness which shapes the body but even more the mind. But, how sad it is to climb indoors without experiencing the most important aspect of our sport, of actually climbing rock faces in breathtakingly beautiful landscapes with the overwhelming presence of the cliffs themselves. It is sad to miss the experience of your fingers making contact with the mineral of the rock, with the fine grain of sandstone, the aggressiveness of granite or the richness of limestone. To experience the incredible verticality of the Gorges du Verdon, the majesty of rock faces throughout the world, is not just a physical act, it is also a communion between nature and a human being. Indoor climbing is great fun and I love doing it but it must be said that without knowing and experiencing outdoor climbing, it is no better than any other sport. The spread of climbing is also a business revolution. Private centres attract more than two million visits annually in France alone and 30 million throughout the world, while companies specialising in rock-climbing are flourishing; whether selling equipment, clothes or walls. There are training programme apps for downloading to your Smartphone and, of course, rock-climbing has created many related services and facilities such as hotels, restaurants and so on. Taking everything into account, it is estimated that climbing is now responsible for the astronomical turnover of a billion Euros a year. For me, who started taking part in a relatively unknown sport in the early 1970s when it was seen as rather an eccentric thing to do, it is surreal and a little disconcerting to see what it has now become but it is also proof of its incredible richness which today is appreciated by so many. And, this is good, because I still believe that most climbers are people with an extra large soul.

The third development, a revolution of recent decades, is that of competition rock-climbing and its organisation. From a minor sport groping for a set of rules in the 1980s, it has now become a discipline which sought to be accepted as a sport in its own right by the Winter Olympic Games of Albertville in 1992, then again more recently for the 2020 Olympic Games. These requests were turned down but, they show how far the sport has come in only 30 years. Today there is a well-established official circuit including levels of difficulty, bouldering and speed climbing with World Championships and many official titles but all this has somehow developed ad hoc. Indeed, as time goes by it has become increasingly obvious that there is a gap between, on the one hand, the representatives of 'official' rock-climbing, the Federations and, on the other hand, people wanting to enjoy themselves in rock-climbing centres and on outdoor sites, who are also looking to achieve the best performance outside of any official or government control.

It is interesting that the international stars who appear in this book have seldom come from the world of competition. Although they have taken part in competitions as Edlinger, Destivelle and, more recently, Sharma and Ondra have done, their fame has arisen from their performances on rock and through films of their outdoor activities. By contrast, the impressive achievements of winning competitors such as François Legrand, Alex Chabot, Ramón Julian and many others receive much less media coverage, which seems a little unfair. This inability to make stars from the competition world confirms that the existing organisations and management of competitions is not in tune with these rock-climbers and this is something which both the specialists and non-specialist public feel as well. It is the authenticity of our sport and its values which attract media coverage but the format of competitions has not managed to integrate them and create this indispensable alchemy. I believe this is the greatest failure in the development of our sport. It is such a pity. From the sport's point of view too, it is clear that the present format needs to be updated. With their innate pragmatism the Americans understood this when they created Deep Water Soloing competitions at swimming pools, which provide a great spectacle while also requiring the highest performance. It is important to explore this kind of approach to ensure that competitions reflect the rich complexities of climbing.

Another fascinating aspect of delving into the history of rock-climbing is finding out about the people who have been involved in it. I was lucky enough to know many of them when I was part of the tribe and several of them made a lasting impression on me. Some of the close friends who come immediately to mind are the brothers Marc and Antoine Le Menestrel, David Chambre of course, Alain Ghersen and Laurent Jacob. What wonderful days we spent climbing rock faces together, encouraging each other with our shouting. It was a healthy competition, with the hope of being the best in the group always in mind. This happened to each of us at one time or another, depending on our form. Then there was the travelling round the world, hoping to repeat previous exploits or exploring some of the toughest routes. I can still see Antoine at the foot of *Revelations* on Raven Tor, in England in 1985, starting his incredible solo, casting a last glance at me who was stressed by the challenge he was facing, yet confident that he would succeed. What a perfect climb – and that's an understatement. Then there was the wonderful feeling of togetherness afterwards, before the English arrived and saw what had happened. The beer in the pub that evening was so good.

The other significant person I met at that time was Patrick Edlinger. Much has been said and written about him but it is all hot air. The truth is completely different. At that time Patrick was almost a god in the eyes of both climbers and the media but I knew that I was as good as him, if not better. He had a very personal climbing style, supple and technically expert but he also included unnecessary moves just because they were so attractive, hence the public's fascination with him. Our rivalry came about by accident, simply because I had said that our first ascents were more important than Patrick's routes. I should add that as well as being rather rebellious, I was not very tactful. I became a target and was accused of jealousy which was very hard for me but the funny thing is that this rivalry pushed me to prove myself even harder. It helped me become a better climber. It was some time before things got back to normal with me in relation to the media and the world of rock-climbing. In fact, it was my first ascents of *Just Do It* in the USA and of *Super Plafond* which really settled the debate. I remember Patrick getting ready next to me when we were in the final of a major event in Germany. I can still see his face, hard set, his body rigid, looking almost haughty but that day I knew that we respected each other as athletes. His death greatly affected me, he was a brother-in-arms who died much too young. I cried on that day.

Besides my fellow Frenchmen, I also had a special relationship with British and American rock-climbers. The Brits, Ben Moon and Jerry Moffatt for instance, who were so very competitive, so very British and who thrashed us in a major way several times in the Verdon and in Buoux. Jerry with his on-sight ascents such as *Papy on Sight* was impressive but he was also much more than that; a free spirit who enjoyed solo climbing in Joshua Tree and who was happy to share some magic mushrooms with us – which some of us tried, of course, always smiling, always ready to climb. Then he won the 1989 World Cup event in Leeds which he had been looking forward to so much. That day he had the world of rock-climbing at his feet: it was beautiful to see. As for Ben, he was more reserved but so powerful, certainly the best climber at the time, crazily strong. Only his rough technique and lack of resilience limited him slightly. His ascents of *Azincourt* (always recorded as *Agincourt* in English) and the *Maginot Line* in France impressed us all. But, besides the talent of all these climbers, what struck me was their common understanding, their sharing, their same desire to climb, to train. This year I happened to bump into both Ben and Jerry and even 20 years later they still have that same passion in their eyes.

As for American climbers, I have known several generations of them. Some of them settled in Provence at the time when it was akin to an international centre of high level rock-climbing; Lynn Hill being one of them. She was incredibly talented with an ego to match. Extraordinarily ambitious, she always climbed for herself but, at the same time, she was always determined to show that she was better than everyone else. In spite of her accusing me of misogyny, I have always thought she was by far the best climber of her generation. It is her determination which has always fascinated me; she was literally 'hooked' onto the rock face, using the flimsiest of holds. Her free ascent of *The Nose* did not surprise me. It was made for her and on that day she achieved what she had wanted all her life; to win ahead of the men.

The other American who has impressed me enormously is Chris Sharma. I met him when he must have been about 16 years old. It was at the X Games in San Diego and he suddenly turned up, looking cool, climbing barefoot on the warm-up wall with little technique but breathtaking brilliance. As soon as I saw him I knew that he would consign the rest of us to the history books. Later I came to know him personally and found that as well as being sensitive and ultra-accessible, the routes he climbed showed that he was also a creator. He is famous for *Biographie*, of course but for me *Es Pontàs* on the rocky island outcrop in the sea off Mallorca, remains *the* route which symbolises him. It has everything: grade F9b or perhaps more, never repeated, requiring ruthlessness and the conquest of mental uncertainty to succeed, with the added danger of climbing alone above the sea, topped off by the wild beauty of this route. For me it is the symbol, the quintessence of our sport and if I was still capable of it, it is this route I would most like to do.

Climbers meeting at the foot of cliffs, by boulders or in competition halls all have one thing in common: passion. They all live, eat and organise their lives around climbing; some living on the very fringes of society, so driven are they by their passion for climbing. As for me, I can say that rock-climbing has defined my life, it being more than an activity but a philosophy of life, a way of looking at the world. This is what distinguishes it from other sports. Climbing has been the school of my life. I remember the day when, as a little boy of nine, I suddenly discovered this passion. I was at the foot of a slab in Fontainebleau, alone, in the cold and I felt this desire fill my entire being. Since then I have never stopped and I will not stop until I take my last breath. It is not easy to explain but it is the gesture which fascinates me, the body language enabling one to solve the equation set by the rock. This equation is always changing: it evolves with time, with the grade, with the support but there is always the hope that you can solve it and that is the magic of rock-climbing.

Good climbing and good reading to you all.

JEAN-BAPTISTE TRIBOUT

01

THE
TIME
OF
ADVENTURE

CLIMBING,

THAT IS, ASCENDING STEEP OR EVEN VERTICAL TERRAIN USING JUST YOUR HANDS AND FEET, IS PROBABLY AN ACTIVITY AS ANCIENT AS HUMANITY ITSELF. GATHERING FOOD, HUNTING, SPIRITUAL AND RELIGIOUS QUESTS AND, MORE MUNDANELY, THE NEED FOR PROTECTION FROM WILD ANIMALS, BAD WEATHER AND HOSTILE GROUPS HAVE, SINCE TIME IMMEMORIAL, LED PEOPLE TO SEEK OUT HIGH PLACES THAT ARE DIFFICULT TO REACH. FROM FUNERAL SITES PERCHED HIGH UP CLIFFS IN AFRICA, SUCH AS THOSE OF BANDIAGARA, TO THE ANASAZI AMERINDIANS AND THE GATHERERS OF SWALLOWS' NESTS OR HONEY IN ASIA, THE BOLDNESS WHICH DROVE THESE PIONEERS AND THE CLOSE RELATIONSHIP THEY HAD DEVELOPED WITH THE ROCKS IS STILL ASTONISHING.

PAGE 14:

RUDOLF FERHMANN ON THE *THREE FINGERS TOWER*, ELBSANDSTEINGEBIRGE, 1917.

—

PAGE 16:

LEFT: OWEN GLYNNE JONES ON DERBYSHIRE, GRITSTONE, 1888.

CENTRE: JAMES W. PUTTRELL (1868–1939), GRITSTONE PIONEER, 1885.

RIGHT: BOULDERING SESSION, FEET LEADING! MOSE-DALE, LAKE DISTRICT, UK, 1890.

Free climbing was defined 30 years ago in our book *Le 8ème degré (The 8th Grade)* in words which still apply: 'When the climber uses only their hands and feet on the unevenness of the rock to progress. The protection points are only there for the climber's safety in case of a fall but they are not used as an aid to progress and stopping or resting on them is forbidden. It is up to the climber to make the most of what the rock offers. The term 'forbidden' indicates that free climbing does not mean climbing without rules. There are rules and they should be obeyed. From being just a physical activity, in this way, free climbing has acquired the status of a sport'.

The birth of rock-climbing as a leisure and sporting activity goes back to the late 19th century, originating in Europe in various locations far apart from each other. In those 'heroic' times equipment was rudimentary and often cobbled together, so rock-climbing was a dangerous passion attracting bold, adventurous people.

THE ENGLISH GENTLEMAN ALWAYS CLIMBS FIRST.
CLIMB WHEN YOU'RE READY.

EARLY BRITISH CLIMBERS RELAXING AT A GRITSTONE CRAG.

The British had been visiting the Alps throughout the 19th century and it was during the Victorian period that rock-climbing first became popular. In the north-west of England, then still a wild and unfrequented region, the new middle and upper classes discovered the pleasure of outdoor activities during their summer holidays. The Lake District and the Peak District (both National Parks today) were the birthplace of British rock-climbing. Though at first this was simply a matter of clambering about on the outcrops, some of these adventurers, most of them young, soon became much bolder. From 1880, the number of climbs (naturally they were all first ascents) gradually increased, with or without a rope. That said, the almost complete absence of protection made it very dangerous for the leader, even when roped.

At the same time and in the same place, a charismatic character emerged: Oscar Eckenstein. Looking like a cross between an old sea-dog and an Old Testament prophet he was a man of many talents and an adventurous explorer. In 1902 he led the first serious expedition attempting to climb K2, the second highest mountain in the world, accompanied by his friend, the occultist Aleister Crowley who was also a bold climber on the chalk cliffs of the Sussex coast. Eckenstein was the inventor of crampons and the modern short ice axe. Extremely strong (he could do one-arm pull-ups), he was one of the founders of bouldering, a form of rock-climbing requiring balance and a command of footholds and grips on boulders a few metres high and in this respect was several decades ahead of his time. The volcanic rocks of the Lake District and Wales were ideal for this type of climbing.

W. P. Haskett-Smith was an undergraduate at Oxford University who first visited the Lake District in 1881 with some university friends. Being athletic, he enjoyed climbing the rocks in the vicinity without any equipment, notably without ropes. He must have enjoyed the sport because he returned year after year, tackling increasingly daring climbs in which there was no room for error. His moment of glory came in 1886 with *Napes Needle*, a sharply pointed arrow-shaped rock which had defeated so many attempts that some compared his eventual conquest of it to that of the Matterhorn two decades earlier. In the end, without any artificial aid and without any belaying, Haskett-Smith reached the summit, where his photograph was taken in the traditional manner. As a result he was hailed as the founder of British rock-climbing, 'by fair means', a reasonable description since it really was free climbing with bare hands.

A few years later, the technical level was raised further by a London professor, Owen Glynne Jones. Having all the qualities of a modern climber, strength, agility and daring, he preferred to focus more on the intrinsic difficulty of a route than on the conquest of a new peak. In this respect he was similar to Eckenstein but he was very different when it came to talking about it. For 'OG', climbing was a perfect opportunity to publicise himself, while Eckenstein, like his friend Crowley, saw it mainly as an inner, personal achievement. In 1897 OG set his heart on a wide crack some 20 metres high, the *Kern Knotts Crack*. In order to climb it free, he chose to practise it on a top-rope. This new technique enabled him to master it very quickly. It is interesting that even then, some people were already condemning these practices as unfair, because they deviated from tradition. Today the crack is rated MVS (Mild Very Severe), the equivalent of a good French 5. Owen Glynne Jones was the inventor of this English adjectival grading system and he published one of the first rock-climbing guidebooks to this region which did much to popularise this new sport.

In 1885, James W. Puttrell was the first climber to venture on to the Peak District gritstone cliff of Wharncliffe Edge on the outskirts of Sheffield. On these cliffs, seldom more than 15m high, he developed 'outcrop climbing', in contrast to the objectives of Victorian climbers. Because it was easily reached by public transport, Wharncliffe was probably the most popular crag in the world on the eve of the 20th century with already over 100 routes. Progressing with limited safety measures and sometimes even on his own, he explored the most obvious cracks, free climbing our present day fifth grades and was also a pioneer of caving. He subsequently spread his wings, climbing in Wales, the Lake District, Scotland and as far as the Alps. Today he is recognised as one of the founding fathers of climbing as a sport.

The other great legend of the period was Siegfried Herford. His was another meteoric rise, brutally brought short by the First World War. Born in 1891, he was a disturbed child who would probably be described as hyperactive today but he was extremely good at science; studying physics and mathematics at Manchester University and becoming one of the first engineers specialising in aeronautics. At the age of 20, with his friends John Laycock and Stanley Jeffcoat, he 'reinvented' gritstone climbing, leaving the cracks and venturing onto the much more dangerous slabs. Like Paul

ABOVE LEFT: *PINNACLE RIDGE* ON AMPHITHEATER BUTTRESS, CRAIG YR YSFA, WALES, UK, 1905.
ABOVE RIGHT: THE FAMOUS NAPES NEEDLE, LAKE DISTRICT, PICTURED HERE IN 1961. HIS FIRST ASCENT IN 1886 BY WALTER PARRY HASKETT SMITH WAS A MILESTONE FOR CLIMBING IN BRITAIN.
BELOW, FROM LEFT: WALTER PARRY HASKETT SMITH (1859–1946), ONE OF THE FATHERS OF ROCK-CLIMBING. / JAMES W. PUTTRELL (1868–1939). / OWEN GLYNNE JONES (1867–1899). / OSKAR ECKENSTEIN (1859–1921).

Preuss, the practice of down-climbing, which seemed to him a guarantee of safety in the event of it being impossible to move forward, would be carried out with just a piece of rope round the waist or, often, even solo.

A remarkable photograph taken in 1912 by the famous mountaineer Geoffrey Winthrop Young shows the young man, Herford, accompanied by George Leigh Mallory, who 12 years later would be part of the greatest mystery in the history of climbing when he and Andrew Irvine vanished near the summit of Mount Everest. The pinnacle of Herford's career was the *Flake Crack* on Scafell, the second-highest 'mountain' in England, in the Lake District which, today, still has a local grade of E1 5b, equivalent to a modern F6a; this was comparable to the maximum difficulties found in Saxon Switzerland at that time and by Paul Preuss in the Dolomites (see further on). Then in July 1914, the First World War began and Herford, in the uniform of the Royal Fusiliers, was killed by a shell in 1916.

In 1913, John Laycock wrote *Some Gritstone Climbs*, a rock-climbing guidebook focusing on the best climbs in the Peak District. In it, he described for the first time the incredible potential of climbing on gritstone which would be the cradle of the best British climbers of the 20th century and the local city of Sheffield became the spiritual capital of British rock-climbing. Thus, one of the strongest rock-climbing traditions was born which, with its strict ethics, continues today under the name of 'trad' (traditional). In contrast with more ruggedly mountainous countries, in the United Kingdom it is normal to start with rock-climbing and then to move on to mountaineering.

ABOVE LEFT: SIEGFRIED HERFORD (1891–1916) ON CASTLE NAZE, GRITSTONE, UK.
ABOVE RIGHT: SIEGFRIED HERFORD, DURING THE FIRST ASCENT OF *THE GREAT FLAKE*, LAKE DISTRICT, 1914.
BELOW LEFT: SIEGFRIED HERFORD AND GEORGE MALLORY AT PEN Y PASS, 1912.
BELOW RIGHT: SIEGFRIED HERFORD CLIMBING *THE MANTELSHELF*, SCAFELL PINNACLE, 1914.

CLIMBING ON GRITSTONE

Rock-climbing pioneers also appeared in less obvious, more remote places such as Saxon Switzerland near Dresden, in what would later be the former East Germany. The Elbe Sandstone Mountains or Elbsandsteingebirge are magical formations which continue to fire the imagination of many a rock-climber of today. This forest of sandstone towers has attracted lovers of active rock-climbing since the end of the 19th century and it is estimated that it attracted about 500 excited rock-climbers in 1900.

In 1892 the young Oskar Schuster climbed an intimidating chimney crack (which was later named after him) where the smallest mistake would result in a fall. Paradoxically it was an American, Oliver Perry-Smith, who raised the standards there but unfortunately he has been completely forgotten today, unlike his illustrious contemporary Paul Preuss. Having arrived in Dresden in 1902 at the age of 18 to study, Perry-Smith also became an accomplished rock-climber in the Alps, particularly the Dolomites, as well as a competition skier. He often climbed on these sandstone rocks with his friend Rudolf Fehrmann and together they made numerous first ascents in the local seventh grade, including the *Teufelsturm* in 1906 which in France would correspond to a modern F6a, using equipment which would not allow any lead climbing falls. There were also climbers who developed a rigorous ethic which would survive for decades: they held the modern ecological view that the rock should be preserved as much as possible, climbing in espadrilles (rope soled slippers) and using a minimum of metal supports, from which the tradition of using rope knots jammed in cracks for protection arose.

A hothead driving around in a Bugatti, Perry-Smith sometimes carved his name on the soft sandstone at the summit to show any doubters that he hade made a successful ascent. He returned to America in 1914 on the eve of the First World War and never again set foot on these sandstone spires in the rest of his long life (he died in 1969 at the age of 84). As for Fehrmann, he was the theoretician of the roped party and one of the first to establish the rules of the game of 'their' free rock-climbing, climbing from the bottom up, respecting a minimum space of four metres between points to ensure a maximum of free-climbing and using knots and slings for belaying. He later made an unfortunate political choice, joining the National Socialist party at its inception and dying in 1947 in a prisoner of war camp.

The puruit of harder climbs continued in Dresden. In the 1970s, the great traveller Henry Barber (who will be mentioned again later) went there several times and made some memorable climbs: "*Rost Kante* was opened there in 1927. I attempted to climb it four times, without success. It is a slightly overhanging cliff which I certainly would rate 5.11 (equivalent to F6c) with a first anchor 15 metres from the ground; an absolute horror. We should have more routes like that in America and everywhere in the world."

ABOVE: OSKAR SCHUSTER (1873–1917), SAXONY PIONEER, 1890.
BELOW LEFT: THE AMERICAN OLIVER PERRY-SMITH (1884–1969).
BELOW RIGHT: THE GERMAN RUDOLF FERHMANN (1886–1948).
–
PAGE 23:
ABOVE LEFT: OLIVER PERRY-SMITH SECONDING.
ABOVE CENTRE: AUGUST 1909, AN AID MODE ALREADY CRITICIZED BY THE FREE CLIMBING PURISTS.
ABOVE RIGHT: NOVEMBER 11th, 1913, OLIVER PERRY-SMITH DURING THE FIRST ASCENT OF *SOUTH CRACK* (BLIZRISS, VI+), FALKENSTEIN.
BELOW: ELBSANDSTEINGEBIRGE FROM THE AIR IN 1932, BY WALTER HAHN.

PAGE 24: LEFT: OLIVER PERRY-SMITH, RUDOLF FERHMANN AND A FRIEND STANDING ON THE SUMMIT OF THE BARBARINE NEEDLE, ELBSANDSTEINGEBIRGE EMBLÊME. FIRST ASCENT, SEPTEMBER 19TH, 1905. ABOVE RIGHT: OLIVER PERRY-SMITH DRIVING HIS BUGATTI WITH HIS FRIEND RUDOLF FERHMANN. BELOW RIGHT: OLIVER PERRY-SMITH, 1905.

PAGE 25: OLIVER PERRY-SMITH (CENTRE) AND RUDOLF FERHMANN (RIGHT) STANDING AT THE BOTTOM OF THE SANDSTONE TOWERS.

...AND CLIMBING ON LIMESTONE

The Dolomites in Italy will obviously appear throughout this book. This myriad of limestone towers is more than a natural wonder. With its Alpine winter landscape and its vertical rock faces, it has proved an irresistible challenge to the most daring climbers. Paul Preuss's idol, Georg Winkler was a pioneer there who, at the tender age of 17, made free solo climbs, both ascending and descending (but using a grappling hook) the Torre Winkler, as it is now called, in the Massif des Vajolet. He died in an avalanche on the Weisshorn the following year and the glacier only returned his body half a century later.

The life and career of Hans Dülfer, who died in the First World War in 1915, was even shorter. Nonetheless, with a kind of premonitory urgency, between 1911 and 1914 the German climber made over 50 first ascents, many of them in the Dolomites. While his name has remained famous in France for a style of opposition movements on vertical holds or cracks, or laybacking as it is known in English. He was also the pioneer of the Dülfersitz abseiling method, which uses the friction of the rope wrapped round the body to control descent, as well as being the initiator of numerical rating of grades. It was also in 1914 that the book *Alpinismo acrobatico* by Guido Rey was published, in which he developed these new ideas.

The development of equipment such as the steel karabiner by Otto Herzog naturally enabled greater risks to be taken but, at that time, the lead climber was discouraged from falling as their hemp ropes were not strong enough to guarantee safety.
Tita Piaz, nicknamed the 'Devil of the Dolomites', was Austrian by birth but Italian at heart. At the age of 18, he was the first to climb the Torre Winkler free, without aid and he continued regularly climbing grade 5 routes, always solo and free. Later, an adept of the new 'artificial' techniques such as throwing the rope and the Tyrolean traverse, he was less radical than Winkler or his good friend Preuss. His Alpine career spanned four decades and as a guide he always focused more on safety, of 'surviving rather than shining'. But in 1948 he died in a banal bicycle accident.

During this fertile pre-war period, questions of ethics were already stirring passions, such as the classic but revealing polemic between Piaz and Preuss. Was Paul Preuss really the first free climber? His radical, not to say extremist, convictions led him to push the game to an extreme (rejecting all artificial aids, including pitons). This culminated in his solo ascent of the Campanile Basso in Brenta on 28 July 1911, breaking the barrier of grade 5. While Preuss climbed free, his theory of 'sink or swim' was hard to apply on a large scale.

Another of Preuss's contemporaries was Angelo Dibona. Born in Cortina d'Ampezzo, he became famous for his achievements in his native Dolomites (such as the West Face of Roda di Vael and the North East Face of Cima Grande) and on the more Alpine Massifs des Écrins (first ascents of the South Face of the Meije, renamed

LEFT: THE GERMAN HANS DÜLFER (1892–1915).
CENTRE: THE ITALIAN MOUNTAIN GUIDE TITA PIAZ
(1879–1948).
RIGHT: THE ITALIAN ANGELO DIBONA (1879–1956)
ON THE TRE CIME DI LAVAREDO, ITALY.

Aiguille Dibona in his honour, the Coste Rouge Arête at L'Ailefroide and the North West Face of the Dôme de Neige des Ecrins). Preuss reproached him for his excessive use of pitons but, in fact, Dibona only used 15 in the whole of his career. This anecdote says much about the unbelievable clashes which took place at that time. But in 100 years time, who knows what will be said about present-day climbing?

In passing, it is interesting to note the origin of the term 'varappe' which has long been used by climbers. It was on the small rocky massif of Mont Salève in France that the young people of Geneva set off at the end of the 19th century to explore the Gorge de la Varappe and they took its name when they formed the Cercle de la Varappe, thus themselves becoming specialist rock-climbers known as *varappeurs*. They have included names such as Tricouni, who in 1896 invented the revolutionary nail fastened round the edge of the boot sole and named after him, Michel Vaucher, who climbed the Grandes Jorasses with Walter Bonatti, Loulou Boulaz, the best female mountain climber of the 1930s and Himalayan climbers Roch, Lambert and Dittert, who just failed to reach the summit of Everest in 1952. The *varappeurs* have spread the rock-climbing skills they acquired on this mountain overlooking Geneva to all parts of the world.

PAUL PREUSS
THE LEGENDARY FOUNDER

—

Because all chronologies need a starting point, the name of Paul Preuss is often given as the founding father of free rock-climbing and as the first 'real' climber. This is both true and false, because his ideas were far ahead of their time but, also incredibly rigid, not to say extremist.

Paul Preuss was born in the Austrian mountains in 1886. His background was modest and as a child he was sickly, weakened by polio which left him almost disabled. It was this very disability which made him an assiduous gymnast and a keen walker in the mountains, thus developing the body of an athlete.

He was attracted by the heights around him and soon spent most of his time in the mountains, in both summer and winter. At the end of his short career he had chalked up over a thousand ascents of all kinds, both on rock and otherwise, many of them first ascents and always solo.

He soon stood out for developing what was then a new and extremely radical climbing ethic. He made it a point of honour not to use pitons, then a relatively recent invention, or any other artificial aid. The rope was tolerated but only for safety and, if the climber was unable to climb a route without it, the ascent was not valid. He theorised about the ethics of pure style in several essays which went down in the annals as the 'piton dispute'.
While his contemporaries, such as his friend Tita Piaz, the Devil of the Dolomites, accepted the idea that a climber should always have the physical and mental means to ensure a certain safety margin in relation to the difficulties undertaken, they could not completely reject the use of all 'modern' equipment such as pitons, karabiners and ropes which were all becoming widespread in this first decade of the 20th century. In this respect, he also disagreed with Hans Dülfer who himself advocated a more intensive use of technology.

But Preuss was not just a theorist. He also spent a lot of time training and practising down-climbing. Indeed, he firmly believed that a climber should never start climbing a route which he could not climb down on his own without aid, in other words without rope and without abseiling. These restrictions approached the limits of his system and those who derided him (and they were numerous) invariably highlighted the fact that his concepts would have made him an enemy of modern free climbing which, above all, encourages safety using mechanical aids.

Of all his achievements, the most impressive is still the first solo ascent and down-climb of Campanile Basso (also known as Guglia di Brento) in the Dolomites. By climbing a fifth grade route solo on-sight and then climbing down, there is no doubt that at that time no one else in the world could have done it.

Preuss was also the first professional climber and he was so well-known that in the last years of his short life he lived off the income from the many lectures he gave about his achievements and his theories. He died at the age of 27, appropriately solo, attempting to open a new route on the Mandkogel. On that day his luck ran out.
Being of Jewish origin, his achievements were played down by the fascist regimes of the following decades. But he was rediscovered in the 1970s by Reinhold Messner who wrote a book about him and always saw him as a source of inspiration. His meteoric career and the debates stimulated by the ethics he propounded and applied to his own life can inspire nothing but respect.

LEFT: CAMPANILE BELOWSO SUMMIT PART; THE EAST FACE STANDS ON THE RIGHT, FIRST SOLO CLIMBED AND DOWNCLIMBED BY PREUSS, JULY 28TH, 1911. **ABOVE RIGHT**: PAUL PREUSS WATCHING THE STILL VIRGIN CAMPANILE BELOWSO JUST BEFORE HIS SOLO EFFORT IN 1911. **BELOW RIGHT**: PAUL PREUSS (1886–1913) AND WALTER BING.

AFTER THE FIRST WORLD WAR

Not much happened immediately after the butchery of 1914-1918: the grim reaper had indiscriminately taken his share of the climbers and the task of rebuilding in the countries involved took priority. But with the return of peace and, significantly, with nationalism growing in central Europe, the period between the wars was a remarkable one for climbing. Although at the time there was still no real distinction made between climbers and mountaineers, some showed a clear preference for rock.

In 1921, a new stage in free climbing was reached with the ascent of the *Ha-He Dihedral* in the Karwendel massif by Otto 'Rambo' Herzog and Gustav Haber which, with bivouac stops and a grade VI+, corresponded to a good F6a+ today. In 1911 Herzog had been the first to use karabiners, equipment used by firemen in Munich. As a result it was easier for the climber to attach the rope to the pitons, making it easier to concentrate more on the climb.

Willo Welzenbach was one of the most famous alpinists of this period who collected an impressive list of first ascents on major icy north faces in the Valais, Oberland and Mont Blanc during the 1920s and 1930s. He had had to turn to ice because serious joint problems prevented him indulging his passion for rock-climbing. He died in 1934 at an altitude of over 7,000 metres on the slopes of Nanga Parbat, a climb which started the long love affair of German climbers with the Himalaya. But Welzenbach also went down in the history of climbing in 1925 for proposing a new numerical scale of grades, divided into six levels of difficulty. The barrier of grade 6, the 'limit of human abilities', was symbolically referred to decades later by Reinhold Messner with his book *The Seventh Grade*.

ABOVE: THE GERMAN WILLO WELZENBACH (1899–1934).
BELOW: ILLUSTRATED WELZENBACH GRADING SYSTEM, 1926.

Schwierigkeitsbewertung nach Wilhelm Welzenbach - 1926

1° Grad Leicht

2° Grad Mittelschwer

3° Grad Schwer

4° Grad sehr Schwer

5° Grad überaus Schwierig

6° Grad extrem Schwierig

In the same year of 1925, it was on the immense North West Face of the Civetta in the Dolomites and the faces of the Fleischbank in the Tyrol that the history of the sixth grade was written. Emil Solleder was only 26 years old but he had already had an adventurous life, fighting in the First World War as an adolescent before becoming a gold miner in Alaska for a short time. Now he had decided to devote his life to the mountains as a guide and to tackling the still unclimbed faces of the Dolomites. In 1895 Dimai had already climbed the North West Face of Monte Civetta, a rock wall some seven kilometres wide and 1,200m high. But other climbers discovered a more difficult direct route. By the beginning of August 1925, Solleder had already successfully climbed the North Face of the Furchetta with Fritz Wiessner, mentioned below. A few days later, accompanied by Gustav Lettenbauer, Solleder, he tackled the main face, starting on the most direct route to the main summit, the Civetta Grande, 3,220m, where the wall is highest. A string of difficulties and maximum exposure on a rock face that was still wet and far from perfect, the roped party achieved a feat which resonated for many years. A shooting star, Solleder died six years later, disappearing with a client on La Meije.

Wiessner was the inverted double of Oliver Perry-Smith. Whereas Wiessner was born in Germany and went to the USA, Perry-Smith did the opposite. Born in Dresden at the turn of the century, he was short but physically very talented with an iron will. He continued the work of Perry-Smith and his friends, establishing well-known routes round Dresden and then in the central Alps. In the Wilder Kaiser, his route on the Fleischbank in 1925 has gone down in the history of climbing for its steepness, the Verdon-like grey limestone and his new technique. Today it is still a well-known modern grade F6 route. In 1929 he emigrated to New York. As soon as he set foot in the United States, Wiessner became de facto the best climber in the country, since Europe was significantly ahead at that time. He was a dynamic force in the American climbing community, making several first ascents from the West Coast to the East. On the East Coast in 1935 he went climbing in the Shawangunks which later became the most important climbing centre in the north-east of the continent. In 1939 he was a member of an American expedition attempting to climb K2; its first ascent would have been a major world event but he missed it by 250m. Unlike Solleder, he lived to a ripe old age, still climbing in the Gunks when he was over 80, often following the routes of his youth with the same enthusiasm and sometimes even solo.

ABOVE: THE GERMAN EMIL SOLLEDER (1899–1931).

BELOW: THE AMERICAIN FRITZ WIESSNER (1900–1988).

THE CRAZY 1930s

In the 1930s, the Dolomites continued to be the scene of the most challenging rock-climbing. In view of the equipment available at the time (espadrilles and hemp ropes), the commitment to these 'beyond vertical' rock faces was exceptional, as Georges Livanos famously put it. This was truly a new golden age, that of grade six, real and sustained, its importance reflected both in the degree of technical difficulty and the level of commitment. The beauty of movement, economy of aid (in other words, using the minimum number of pitons) and climbing as free much as possible were the essential characteristics for the leading climbers of the time.

Unlike these purely aesthetic adventurers, Domenico Rudatis was one of the first people to associate the word 'sport' with climbing and to insist that the maximum difficulty must be combined with appropriate safety precautions: 'Safety measures which do not guarantee to preserve life but which sometimes save it must be the norm for all climbers: to refuse them would be absurd'.

Italians still remember and respect their climbing countrymen and with good reason. In the 40 years from the 1930s, no one equalled their audacity, especially taking into account the equipment of the period. It was no longer just a matter of reaching summits or climbing rock faces but more a matter of tackling the steepest and most aesthetic routes which it would have been impossible to think of doing a few years earlier. Some unforgettable names of the time are those of Soldà, Carlesso, Vinatzer, Detassis, Gervasutti and Comici. Gino Soldà was a tall young man with brown hair whose photographs bear an uncanny resemblance to the actor Vittorio Gassman. The personification of elegance, Soldà was born in the Dolomites. He was also an

LEFT: THE ITALIAN GINO SOLDÀ, (1907–1989).

RIGHT: THE ITALIAN MOUNTAIN GUIDE GIUSTO GERVASUTTI (1909–1946).

—

PAGE 33:

ABOVE: DOLOMITES GRADE 6, *FRANCHESCHI ROUTE*, TORRE GRANDE D'AVERAU, 1930s.

BELOW: THE ITALIAN RAFFAELE CARLESSO, (1908-2000).

excellent skier and took part in the 1932 Olympic Games at Lake Placid. Having obtained his diploma as a mountain guide, he climbed many existing well-established routes. Then, in 1936, he made the first ascent of the South West Face of Marmolada di Penia, followed by the first ascent of the North Face of Sassolungo, the clean, austere lines of his routes still inspiring respect. At the age of nearly 50, he took part in the successful national expedition that climbed K2 in 1954.

Even more athletic and sporty, Raffaele Carlesso was neither a professional, nor a guide, nor a local. He had quickly realised the importance of training and of setting oneself defined objectives. His times were remarkable and his incredible knowledge of each route enabled him to accomplish masterpieces such the South Face of the Torre Trieste (Cibetta, 1934) and the North West Face of the Torre di Valgrande. He never stopped climbing and remained active for over six decades. He was nearly 60 when he climbed the direct Brandler-Hasse route on the Tre Cime, the Comici at almost 70 and he was still climbing at the age of 80.

Batista Vinatzer's list of achievements may be less long but experts such as Messner see him as one of the first explorers of the upper levels of the sixth grade. Also an advocate of strong commitment associated with a minimal use of fixed points, he applied these principles to milestones such as the North Face of the Stevia ridge (1933) and the South Face of Marmolada (Vinatzer route, 1936).
As for Bruno Detassis, he was the local boy of the group. Born in Trento in 1910, he is widely remembered as the ever-present guardian of the Brentei refuge, famous for his enormous, legendary beard. It was in the Brenta Dolomites that he revealed his amazing skills as a climber, opening up celebrated routes such as the North East Face of Brenta Alta (1934) and the Via delle Guide on the Crozzon di Brenta (1935). After more than 200 first ascents, he continued to be active among the peaks he loved until the end of his long life in 2008.

Giusto Gervasutti, 'Il Fortissimo', is best known for his incredible Alpine achievements in the massifs of Mont Blanc and Les Écrins, which were to a large extent the result of the technical climbing skills he acquired in his youth on the limestone rocks of Sass Maor and Civetta. His 1942 route on the East Face of the Grandes Jorasses, achieved four years before his fatal accident, probably include some of the hardest high-altitude free rock-climbing of that period, in a particularly remote and austere location.

Today it is hard to recognise the true extent of these achievements because the climbs of these pioneers were later made less challenging by the excessive use of pitons from the 1950s onwards. Their exploits were forerunners of the trend of the 1990s for opening 8th-grade routes from the bottom up involving strong commitment. The major event of this period was undoubtedly the solo ascent of the Comici route on the Cima Grande in 1937 by Emilio Comici himself. In doing so, 'he left all his fellow climbers standing'. He had mastered his art and disregarded the exposure as few are capable of doing even 80 years later.

EMILIO COMICI
PORTRAIT OF THE ARTIST AS A CLIMBER

—

The summer of 1940 was coming to an end in the delightful little valley of Selva di Val Gardena in the Dolomites. At the bottom, stretched out among the pines as if asleep in the grass, was the body of Emilio Comici, who had died at the age of 39. A few moments earlier he had been helping a young girl discover rock-climbing; he had tied three old abseiling cords together to make a rope but it could not take his weight when he hung from it and he fell from a height of 50 metres.

His was a tragic, dramatic death, out of character with the modesty and integrity of someone who was probably the greatest climber in history. Such a superlative is often a cliché but it is completely justified for a man who, having discovered mountaineering late in life, was the first climber to add an aesthetic dimension to rock-climbing with his concern for harmonious movements.

Emilio Comici was born in 1901, not in the mountains but in Trieste on the Adriatic coast. At first he followed his intellectual interests but in the course of his short life he transferred his enthusiasm for music and poetry to rock-climbing, giving it an artistic dimension and finding inspiration for his climbing body language in ballet. He was 24 when he discovered the mountains and the possibility of transferring his athletic skills to rock-climbing. Leaving behind his earlier passion, potholing (he set a world depth record in 1926), he took advantage of being in the Dolomites to develop his new interest. His progress was meteoric and in 1929 he opened the first Italian sixth grade route, which at the time officially defined the limit of human abilities.

In two epic days in May 1931, he made the first ascent of the austere and dangerous 1,200m North Face of the Civetta, another sixth grade route which was first repeated by Kasparek and Cassin. At that time Comici had left his job and became a guide at Misurina but was soon rejected by the 'traditional' guides who thought him too unconventional. At the time he had already thought of how to build a training rock specially for climbing, which he called the 'Rocodrome'. Looking at the almost humorous drawing he drew, it is a remarkable vision of what the rock-climbing walls of today would look like.

In August 1933, accompanied by the Dimai brothers, he joined the circle of the famous with an impressive first ascent of the North Face of the Cima Grande di Lavaredo at the heart of the famous Tre Cime. This legendary route, which still inspires respect today, clearly reflected Comici's ethical and aesthetic concerns. It was not the summit or the first ascent which mattered most but the means used (a minimum of pitons for direct aid) to achieve it and, in particular, the line taken which had to be as ideal and direct as 'a drop of water falling from the summit'.

Four years later, in 1937, he returned to this wall on 'his' route but this time on his own. Three and a half hours and 500m later he reached the summit. What can be said about this extraordinary exploit 70 years later? It was decades ahead of its time; a performance reminiscent of his mentor Paul Preuss, of Hermann Buhl on Nanga Parbat, of Reinhold Messner who in 1968 completed the first solo and fourth ascent of the Droites North Face and of Claudio Barbier and his subsequent ascent of the Tre Cime (see later in this book). These were all tributes to Comici, who was nicknamed the 'Angel of the Dolomites'. His mental and technical break with what was then the normal practice was so great that few people realised its importance at the time.

EMILIO COMICI FREE-CLIMBING A GRADE 6, ALREADY WITH SOFT CLIMBING SHOES AND THE GESTURE AND A MORPHOTYPE OF TODAY.

Comici was also the first to launch the idea of the solo enchainment. In the same year, 1937, at Campanile Basso, made famous by the first solo ascent by Paul Preuss, he rushed up the 350m of the *Fehrman* in one hour 15 minutes, still a remarkable time today. Then he linked with the *Preuss* route in half an hour, initiating a new direct finish then descending by the same route in a solo down-climb.

There are awe-inspiring photographs of the 1930s showing Comici pushing the limits of free climbing without a harness, equipped only with steel pitons, espadrilles and a hemp rope round his waist. These photographs appear in the remarkable illustrated biography of him written by his friend and climbing companion Severino Casara[1]. The most striking aspect of these period photographs is their timelessness, the gestures, expressions and muscles being exactly the same as those of today.

Comici used very little belaying and a minimum of aids while developing all the usual movements of the modern rock climber, even to the point of practising deliberate falls. This was at a time when the credo of all good climbers was first and foremost not to fall, which further set him apart in the eyes of traditionalists.
Small and light, he had the body of a modern climber. He was charismatic and avant-garde as climbers like Chris Sharma and Adam Ondra are today and at their age today, Comici would undoubtedly be climbing grade F8c and beyond.

Not much attracted by the great Alpine walls, he did not take part in the competition to conquer the north faces of the Matterhorn, the Grandes Jorasses or the Eiger, which is a pity. On the other hand, he discovered new exotic climbs on his travels in Egypt, Spain, Croatia and Greece.

Comici became a legend and there is no doubt that dying young played a part in this. Nothing impresses people more than a shooting star. The benefit of not ageing leaves the powerful image of a youthful climber in people's minds. In just a few years, little more than a decade, Comici carried out exploits as if he knew his days were numbered. Today, more than ever, his star shines brightly, inspiring everyone to add a touch of elegance to the statistics of his achievements.

PAGE 36: COMICI TAKING A FALL DURING A TRAINING SESSION WITH HEMP ROPES!

PAGE 37: EMILIO COMICI (1901–1940).

[1] *L'Arte di arrimpicare di Emilio Comici* by Severino Casara. Ed. Hoepli, 1947

Finally, it is impossible to speak of Comici without mentioning his great 'rival', the enduring Riccardo Cassin. Was he the greatest Italian mountaineer of the 20th century? His list of achievements and his long life should entitle him to this honour but that is without taking into account Walter Bonatti and Reinhold Messner (Italian by birth, although culturally German). Italy is an incredible country which has probably given us the three 'greatest' mountaineers as well as someone of Comici's calibre. Riccardo Cassin was the conqueror of North East Face of the Piz Badile, the Walker Spur on the Grandes Jorasses, Gasherbrum IV and his eponymous route on Mount McKinley, as well as being the creator of a famous equipment brand of the same name but, first and foremost, he was an exceptional man of the Dolomites. His biography by Georges Livanos is entitled *Cassin, il était une fois le sixième degré* (Cassin: Once upon a time there was the sixth grade) and naturally its climax is the first ascent of the North Face of the Cima Ovest on the Tre Cime in 1935.

After Comici's success on the Cima Grande in 1933, the Cima Ovest was left as the 'final problem' and the one whose conquest was most sought after. As Livanos points out, the wall had already repelled over 20 attempts: 'Four years after the conquest of the North Face of the Cima Grande, the Ovest still remained a utopian dream and, in 1935, after relentless assaults by the best climbers, it still remained the perfect symbol of the unassailable face'. The story of the ascent of the Ovest, told by the Livanos 'Le Grec' in his delightful Marseillais language, remains a monument of Alpine literature.

Big names such as Carlesso, Dimai and Comici had effectively made it their goal but the problem of the great traverse across the middle of the face remained insoluble. It is important to remember the enormous spirit of competition which existed at the time. When Cassin and his companions Ratti and Rossi appeared on the scene, a German roped party was already about to start off, having set up camp on the scree overnight. Being both cunning and quiet, the Italians managed to get in front of them on the rock face. The Bavarians tried to overtake them by going through an impasse. Cassin took things in hand and attacked the famous traverse, soon reaching the ultimate point where Comici had given up. According to Livanos it took him seven long hours to get across the key pitch. Admittedly, it was not free but it was an impressive achievement in view of the equipment available at the time: etriers, the rope tied round the waist which in the end threatened to cut the body in half and espadrilles. This was followed by a horrible night in a bivouac hanging from the rock face in a terrifying thunderstorm. Cunningly, Ratti pulled behind him a rope 200 metres long which, overhangs permitting, ended at the foot of the rock face. This enabled the third member of the team, Rossi (who had come down) to supply them with food and drink for a second bivouac before tackling the exit cracks. Sportingly, the Germans went up via aa different route to support them as they reached the summit. Back in Lecco, where they had come from, the three 'spiders' were hailed as heroes and made the headlines in the papers. The legend was taking shape.

Cassin survived his idol Comici by nearly 70 years. He died peacefully in his bed in 2009 at the age of 100.

THE ITALIAN MAESTRI OF THE 1930s, RICCARDO CASSIN (LEFT), EMILIO COMICI (CENTRE) AND CASSIN'S PARTNER, MARIO DELL'ORO AKA BOGA (RIGHT).
–

PAGE 39:
LEFT: THE ITALIAN RICCARDO CASSIN (1909–2009) ON HIS BELOVED GRIGNA.
ABOVE RIGHT: THE TYROLEAN BATISTA VINATZER, (1912–1993).
BELOW RIGHT: THE ITALIAN BRUNO DETASSIS (1908–2008).

MAGIC MUSHROOMS ROUND PARIS

At the same time, the Frenchman, Pierre Allain became a precursor with his first ascent of the North Face of the Aiguille de Dru during which, wearing just espadrilles, he climbed the most difficult free pitch in the Mont Blanc massif at that time, the Fissure Allain. Far from being a native of the mountains, Allain was born in Paris and it was on the small boulders in the forest of Fontainebleau that he developed his remarkable techniques. These mushroom shaped lumps of rock were a long way from snow-covered summits or tall vertical rock faces but, *Bleau*, as the rocks at Fontainebleau are known, had very early on generated a very active and prolific rock-climbing community. There is no doubt that its location, close to one of the major European capitals, with easy access by train and a temperate climate contributed to its popularity.

From the last quarter of the 19th century, marked by the creation of the Club Alpin Français (admittedly a conservative organisation but also a unifying one), to the beginning of the First World War, the climbing community was brimming over with energy and Parisian mountaineers in particular began the realise the training potential of these rocks which are up to 15m high in some places.

In 1910 the *Groupe des Rochassiers* was founded: a handful of visionaries who planned to launch themselves into the systematic exploration of new areas, usually starting from the railway station of Bois Le Roi in Paris. It would be reasonable to declare this station a historic monument of rock-climbing, since countless generations of climbers have discovered *Bleau* and rock-climbing through it. In my case it was in the 1970s and the memory of these trains are still very vivid being packed as they were in both directions, while some travellers hid under piles of rucksacks to avoid paying for tickets.

Wehrli, Mignot, Prestat and then the De Lépiney brothers were the first 'names' to emerge. The ascent of the legendary Prestat Fissure by Jacques de Lépiney in 1914 introduced the fourth grade. The use of espadrilles rather than the traditional studded boots was considered an intellectual revolution at the time. These beach shoes were also worn by other pioneers such as Comici and Cassin.

These were the very same people – at least those who survived the Great War – who excelled both on high rock faces and on the small *Bleau* rocks and they also founded the Groupe de Haute Montagne and the Groupe de Bleau in 1924. This period between the wars was a golden age.
The concept of the group is an interesting notion in sport. Climbing is an activity which is essentially individual but it is often carried out roped to another person or sometimes to several. This is particularly true when bouldering: lining up, working on movements, emulation, everything contributes to improving one's performance and being motivated by one's friends. This is also where people find it easy to establish social links because all levels can co-exist.

ABOVE: PIERRE ALLAIN (CLIMBING) AND RAYMOND LEININGER, FONTAINEBLEAU, 1930s.
BELOW: A FAMILY DAY IN FONTAINEBLEAU, 1930s.
—
PAGE 41:
PIERRE ALLAIN, TRYING HIS NEW HOMEMADE PA RUBBER-SOLED SHOES.

ADVERT FOR THE PA CLIMBING SHOES, 1960s.

—

PAGE 42:

ABOVE AND BELOW RIGHT: PIERRE ALLAIN JUMPING

BETWEEN BOULDERS AT FONTAINEBLEAU, 1930s.

BELOW LEFT: PIERRE ALLAIN (1904-2000).

Not just anyone can join the Groupe de Bleau; people must be nominated, then officially elected. Members include names which would become 'greats' in the rock-climbing world: Bobi Arsandaux, Marcel Ichac (who would become a famous filmmaker), the Leininger brothers, Pierre Chevalier, Jacques Boell and many others. Several of these climbers would take part in the first great official French Himalayan expedition to Hidden Peak (Karakoram 1936). This clearly showed the influence of this gang of 'bleausards'; heralds of rock-climbing and the mountains as a way of life. Being amateurs who were more than enlightened, 'shining lights of rock-climbing' or 'Convicts of the Cuvier Academic Club', they were always performing wherever they went, never using local guides, which was quite unusual in those days. They were really the first to 'work' on moves until successful, in the sporting sense as understood today.

Pierre Allain joined the group at the beginning of the 1930s. A natural performer, having discovered the Fontainebleau sandstone where he set the first sixth grade with the famous Allain Angle. He also applied his amazing technical skills to the finest Alpine faces. The South Face of La Meije in 1934 and the North Face of the Drus the following year, still in espadrilles, are perfect examples. He even attempted to overcome the 'last big problem' of the Alps, the Walker Spur on the Grandes Jorasses before being beaten to it by Cassin and his colleagues. After the war he was the third man to climb it, accompanied by a several others who would make a name for themselves in the 1950s. In addition to his list of boulders and competitions, Pierre Allain, the leader of the Groupe de Bleau, was also an incredible visionary as far as equipment was concerned: he devised rubber-soled boots (known as PAs, precursors of the legendary EB rock-climbing boots), 'light' karabiners made of alloy, descendeurs for abseiling and natural down for sleeping bags and high altitude clothing. All these innovations were first launched as prototypes or 'limited editions' for a select few but their democratisation literally revolutionised mountaineering in the following decades. Only Yvon Chouinard in California would be both a rock-climber and an equally prolific manufacturer.

Those inspired by reading Pierre Allain's 'bible', *Alpinisme et compétition* over and over included Messner as well as Berhault, Edlinger, Sharma and Ondra.

Although the Second World War temporarily halted all this activity and sounded the death knell of the Groupe de Bleau, this first Fontainebleau 'golden age' would become a pattern for the future. In the Forest of Fontainebleau, the level of bouldering continued to rise as nowhere else in the world. But paradoxically, the French have distinguished themselves more on the high mountains of the five continents (including the unforgettable Annapurna, the first ascent of an 8,000m peak), than on rock faces. Obscured by the proliferation of artificial rock-climbing, they were soon overtaken by the free-climbing spirit which had arrived from California and Britain.

Like a sombre parenthesis, the Second World War which spread to all the continents made these pleasurable climbing activities seem a frivolous occupation until with peace they became an indispensable means of enjoying life once more.

02

THE
BIRTH
OF A
SPORT

WHILE THE DECADE OF THE 1950s

WAS HUGELY SUCCESSFUL FOR MOUNTAINEERS, ESPECIALLY IN THE HIMALAYA WITH THE SYSTEMATIC CONQUEST OF THE HIGHEST PEAKS IN THE WORLD, THE RESULTS FOR FREE-CLIMBING WERE MORE MIXED. ADMITTEDLY, IMPRESSIVE ROCK FACES WERE CONQUERED, FROM THE DOLOMITES TO EL CAPITAN BUT, WITHOUT ANY RESTRICTIONS ON AID-CLIMBING, ITS PRACTICE WAS AT ITS PEAK. WITH THE MASSIVE USE OF AID, ETRIERS, FIXED-ROPES, HAMMERS, BOLTS AND PITONS OF ALL KINDS, CLIMBERS DRILLED, PEGGED, HAMMERED AND HAULED THEMSELVES UP WITH THE SOLE OBJECTIVE OF SECURING A FIRST ASCENT. AT THE SAME TIME, THESE EXCESSES AND THE REJECTION OF WHAT THE ENGLISH CALL *FAIR PLAY* EVENTUALLY BROUGHT ABOUT AN ETHICAL AWARENESS BUT THIS IN TURN LED TO THE MODERN CONCEPT OF FREE-CLIMBING.

PAGE 44:

DURING A 'BACHAR DAY' AT JOSHUA TREE, JOHN BACHAR SOLOING *THE MOLAR*, 5.11B.

—

PAGE 46:

EL CAPITAN, HEART OF THE YOSEMITE VALLEY.

ONCE UPON A TIME IN THE 'VALLEY'

Westerners have been exploring the Yosemite Valley since the 19th century and from the 1930s, pioneers made various assaults on the enormous rock faces flanking it but, as noted earlier, the level of activity, the number of participants and the technical level of American climbers at that time was much inferior to the situation in Europe.

From 1945, the development of this world-famous rock-climbing Mecca grew exponentially and a whole book would not be enough to cover the subject in detail. A large part of this story has already been beautifully told in one of the best rock-climbing book ever written, *Camp 4* by Steve Roper, who is a well-known climber and an informed observer.

One notable pioneer was John Salathé. Born in Switzerland in 1899, he emigrated first to Canada, then to the United States where he led a traditional sedentary life. Then, at the age of 46, he started rock-climbing, encouraged by the spiritual 'visions' he had had. Soon, he specialised in the high rock faces that were still unclimbed because they required a massive use of artificial aid. Salathé had been trained as a blacksmith and he soon realised that the pitons imported from Europe were too soft for Yosemite granite. He therefore developed and manufactured his own designs using chrome-vanadium steel, which became known as the 'Lost Arrows'. Legend has it that these first pitons were made from a Model A Ford axle which were indeed made of chrome vanadium. Yvon Chouinard then took them over but by now using chrome molybdenum and marketed them on a large scale (later, Chouinard also invented other essential accessoriessuch as RURPs; micro pegs for micro-cracks, originally made from saw blades).

Implementing bivouacs on rock faces, pitons and hand-drilled bolts, with this massive reliance on artificial techniques and these new approaches, it was Salathé who made the first ground-up ascent of the *Lost Arrow Spire*, the impressive detached pillar next to the Upper Yosemite Falls and the first ascents of the South West Face of Half Dome (1946) and the North Face of Sentinel Rock. The celebrated *Steck-Salathé*

MENTOR AND DISCIPLE: JOHN SALATHÉ (1899–1993) AND YVON CHOUINARD IN YOSEMITE DURING THE 1950s.

route up the Sentinel is one of the most famous in America and it was the scene of one of the first demonstrations of speed climbing in 1961 by Royal Robbins and Tom Frost when, roped together but climbing at the same time, they completed it in three hours 30 minutes. Robbins had already achieved the second ascent of this route in 1953, when just 18 years old. As for Salathé himself, the rest of his life was eccentric. Having abandoned his family and become increasingly interested in mysticism, he first returned to Europe for a few years and then returned to the US where he drove around the country on his own in a VW Combi during the 1960s and 1970s. It was a marginal way of life but a healthy one, because he was well into his 90s when he died in 1992.

The 1950s saw first ascents of the *Regular North West Face* of Half Dome, then *The Nose* on El Capitan which was besieged by Warren Harding. Disappointed because he had lost Half Dome to Robbins, in spite of his own attempts, Harding set his sights on the impressive prow of El Capitan. Fond of playing jokes, famous for his drinking and looking like a craggy adventurer, Harding was the complete opposite of the smooth, well-mannered Robbins for whom the end never justified the means. Nevertheless, his ambition to do better gave him the strength to persevere, even if his organisational set-up looked a bit like a construction site. In contrast to the advanced single push style used by Robbins, Harding and his team followed a Himalayan technique, setting up camps on the rock face and using countless pitons and fixed ropes, anything needed to make headway. At the end of autumn 1958, more than 18 months after he had started and after 47 days of 'working' rather than rock-climbing, the first ascent was completed. Throughout his life Harding had always burned the candle at both ends, ending up poor and weakened by alcohol when he died in 2002, while Robbins flourishes still after a successful career in the outdoor industry.

In the early 1960s a new generation of Californians emerged, born just before the war and inspired by Kerouac and the Beat Generation. As Steve Roper remarked in his introduction: More than anything, we loved the open air life and the challenges it offered. For many of us in the 1960s, the world (particularly our country) seemed to have lost its way. Perhaps it was to avoid taking our place in society that we remained glued to our rocks. We, the rats in the Valley, had mostly been rejected by the big universities which anyway led nowhere very fast. Camp 4 was divided between the intellectuals and a similar number of pseudo-intellectuals. Sometimes perhaps a little boastful, we were simple people, kind and pure. Some could undoubtedly be considered neurotic and we were all marginals'. Yvon Chouinard, long before founding Patagonia and Black Diamond and becoming the successful businessman he is today, confirms this: 'We lived on the fringes of society. America was moving in the wrong direction and we did not want to be part of it'.

This meant that it was the now legendary Camp 4 which was the actual and symbolic epicentre of this generation (and the following ones). Situated reasonably close to the necessary facilities and the main rock faces, pleasantly shaded and surrounded by boulders (including *Midnight Lightning*), the group could live under canvas throughout the summer season.

The authorities of the National Park have not always been kind towards the climbers, although they are a 'special' set of people who have contributed to its worldwide fame. Some 15 years ago there was even talk of demolishing Camp 4 and replacing it with a residence for employees of the Park. Eventually, thanks to the efforts of figures such as Tom Frost, Camp 4 was placed in the National Register of Historic Places in recognition of its role in the development of rock-climbing in America and it is still very active. Today, it is almost a miracle to find a place in Camp 4, even for a short time.

CHUCK PRATT (1939–2000) AT VERNAL FALL, YOSE-
MITE, 1968.

—

PAGE 49:

ABOVE: CHUCK PRATT AND YVON CHOUINARD IN
ACTION, 1964.

BELOW LEFT: WARREN HARDING (1924–2002) ON HIS
WALL OF *WALL OF EARLY MORNING LIGHT*, EL CAPITAN,
1970.

ROYAL ROBBINS
THE UNCROWNED KING OF YOSEMITE

In the post-war history of Yosemite, the name of Royal Robbins is undoubtedly the first which comes to mind. Before being known internationally for his brand of outdoor clothes (similar to the commercial success of his friend Yvon Chouinard), Robbins, who started climbing at a young very age, was the most daring and talented climber of big walls of his generation.

In 1957, at the age of just 22, he was the leader of the first ascent of the *North West Face* on Half Dome. The cornerstone of North American rock-climbing, this was the first climb to be rated VI on the American grading system, reflecting not only its technical difficulty but also its overall length and commitment. Today, it is still a must for any accomplished visitor to Yosemite. Very soon and in contrast to Warren Harding with his siege of *The Nose*, the Californians became the champion of cleaner, more uncluttered free climbing, using fixed pitons as little as possible and with greater commitment.

The 1960s were Robbins's most glorious decade. In 1961 on the big walls of El Capitan, after a first repeat of *The Nose* in nine days, accompanied by Tom Frost and Chuck Pratt, he climbed *Salathé Wall*, named as a tribute to John Salathé the great pioneer on these cliff faces. *Salathé Wall*, 900m long finishing with the renowned overhanging headwall (climbed free much later in 1988 by Todd Skinner and Paul Piana) was then the most difficult route in the world. In 1964, Robbins, again on El Capitan with the same team (plus Chouinard), the difficulty rating rose a further notch with their ascent of *North America Wall*.

At the same time, Robbins, a mountaineer as well as a rock climber, now focused on the Alps, especially on Chamonix which was particularly popular at that time. In 1962, he made the first ascent of the symbolic steep granite West Face of le Petite Dru by the *American Direct* route accompanied by Gary Hemming, the 'beatnik of the mountains' and future conqueror of the South Face of the Fou. It was an ascent which revealed the technical superiority of the Americans over the Europeans. Three years later, Robbins rammed the point home and climbed the same face again by a different line, called the *Directissime*, (a similar name to his previous route). This time, his climbing companion was fellow American John Harlin who was killed a few months later attempting a winter direct route on the North Face of the Eiger. Back in the Yosemite, he returned to his original technique after using artificial ones in Europe. Robbins increasingly advocated the use of nuts which he used on the first ascent of the well-named *Nutcracker*, a classic route, without using any pitons even at the belays.

This philosophy reached its peak in 1971 with the controversy of the *Wall of Early Morning Light*. The previous year, as if in a kind of trance, Warren Harding had spent almost a month on this steepest and still unclimbed part of El Cap. Yard by yard, using hundreds of bolts, he advanced to the summit, refusing the offer of helicopter assistance. Scandalised, Robbins repeated the route using these bolts, then breaking them after him. But faced with difficulties he had underestimated, he soon gave up and Harding went up in his estimation.

As a kind of vertical testament, Robbins's book *Advanced Rockcraft*, published in the early 1970s, presented his ideas and his philosophy of rock climbing which were, in fact, very close to Messner's in *The 7th Grade*: the preservation of the rock face and the encouragement of ideas of adventure and creativity in the act of climbing, respecting clean-climbing ethics. As an alter-ego of John Gill for bouldering, today, Robbins is recognised as a rock-climbing icon by a whole American generation.

PAGE 50: ROYAL ROBBINS LEADING THE FINAL PITCH OF *HORN*, SHIPROCK, NEW MEXICO, 1964. PAGE 51: ROYAL ROBBINS AFTER THE FIRST ASCENT OF TIS-SA-ACK, HALF DOME, YOSEMITE, 1969.

Although, Royal Robbins was the best known practitioner of free climbing (see box) he was not the only advocate. Another was one his friends, Chuck Pratt, one of the greatest adventurers who accompanied him on the second ascent of *The Nose* in seven days ('our greatest adventure') and the first ascent of the *Salathé Wall*. Quiet, solitary and with a massive build, he hated all publicity surrounding his name, preferring action to words. His companions remember him as one of the first climbers to be interested in style. He seemed to be fascinated by Aleister Crowley, mentioned earlier, often quoting his phrase 'Every intentional act is a magical act'.

Even less well known is the name of Frank Sacherer. More so than Robbins, he was obsessed by clean, free climbing. Very active between 1961 and 1965, according to Chouinard: "He was always climbing on the verge of falling and rarely stopped to put protection in." Accompanied by the young Jim Bridwell, (before he became known as *The Bird*), he was the first to try climbing *The Nose* in one day and/or free. Their attempt came to a sudden end after a fall but their determination had already been eroded. Sacherer quickly freed many great routes free, such as the *Direct North Face* and *North Spur* of Middle Cathedral Rock as well as the *North East Spur* of Higher Cathedral. He was a distinguished scientist and emigrated to Switzerland in 1969 to work at CERN where he became a famous theoretician on accelerated particle physics. A passionate climber in the Alps, he died in 1978 when caught up in a storm in the descent of Le Linceul ('The Shroud') on the Grandes Jorasses. His ashes rest in Chamonix.

PAGE 52: YOSEMITE VALLEY, EL CAPITAN ON THE LEFT AND HALF DOME BEHIND CENTRE.

PAGE 53: FRANK SACHERER (1940–1978) IN 1965.

MEANWHILE,
ON A SMALL ISLAND...

The British, living up to their legendary originality, also invented a rating scale with two parts which is anything but clear and simple, however it is perfectly adapted to their philosophy of boldness, systematically associated with technical difficulty (see appendix). It is hard to compare it to other scales because its progression is intentionally very close towards the top and a similar rating can reflect varying difficulties.

In *Unjustifiable Risk?*, a history of British climbing and mountaineering, Simon Thompson gave a clear summary of the social evolution which has also taken place in other Western countries: 'Before the First World War and even in the years between the wars, most top level climbers were middle-class if not upper-class, for whom climbing was a pleasant pastime but little more. After 1945, this tradition of pure amateurism declined. Greater specialisation has made the world of climbing less varied and perhaps in some ways less interesting but there is no doubt that it has contributed to raising its technical level. One of the most ironic aspects of the emergence of working class people in the world of climbing is that as top climbers, many of them became professionals and worked less at conventional jobs than the more prosperous classes whom they succeeded.'

In the early 1950s, the most famous climber was undoubtedly the young Joe Brown, a trained plumber. Bold and visionary, especially in relation to climbing cracks of variable widths, he was also one of those pioneers using nuts or chocks, wedge-shaped metal pieces with wire or rope attached which enabled belaying in cracks instead of using pitons. This resulted in a faster, cleaner kind of climbing. From the Peak District to Wales, Joe Brown made some immortal classic climbs such as *Right Eliminate*, *Cemetery Gates* (E1 5b, 1951) and *Cenotaph Corner* (E1 5b, 1952).

He often climbed in a roped party with Don Whillans, three years younger than him. More solid and stockier, Whillans also expanded the range of difficulties on gritstone for example, in 1958 with his first ascent of *Goliath* (Burbage South, E4 6a, the equivalent of a F6c).

Nicknamed 'The Baron', Joe Brown was, like Royal Robbins on the other side of the Atlantic, a methodical, reserved leader who had a very long career, making more than 600 first ascents over five decades. Whillans, on the other hand, known as 'The Villain' (the title of his biography), was famous for his exuberance, like many climbers enjoying a drink in the pub after a hard day's climbing. He died in 1985. In many ways he is reminiscent of Warren Harding and the opposite of his contemporary Royal Robbins.

In 1962, Pete Crew, a brilliant climber of 20 years old, made a big impression by being the first to climb *Great Wall* (E4 6a) on Cloggy in Snowdonia; a climb on which Joe Brown himself had given up on two attempts, restricted by his decision to use no more than two pitons per pitch. In the 1960s, a new generation was taking over, discovering

LEFT: DON WHILLANS (1933–1985), 'THE VILLAIN'.

RIGHT: PETER CREW.

—

PAGE 54:

ABOVE: JOE BROWN.

BELOW: JOE BROWN DURING THE 60S AT CLOGWYN DU'R ARDDU.

new places to climb, notably on the pleasant English, Scottish and Welsh coasts. For example Gogarth on Holyhead Mountain on the island of Anglesey, a huge headland overlooking the Irish Sea, was explored by Martin Boysen and Baz Ingle in 1964. Just traversing under the crag above the sea is an adventure in its own right, surrounded by seagulls and seals. Boysen was probably the most gifted climber of that period, setting new standards in the Lake District and Wales with ascents such as *Nexus* (E2 5b, on Dinas Mot, 1963), *The Medlar* (E4 6a, 1964), *The Skull* (E4 6a, 1966) and *Capital Punishment* (E4 5c, on Ogwen's Suicide Wall, 1971).

ABOVE LEFT: GOGARTH, NORTH WALES.

BELOW LEFT: MARTIN BOYSEN.

RIGHT: *A DREAM OF WHITE HORSES*, GOGARTH, 1968.

The cliffs of Gogarth experienced a golden age in the late 1960s with gems such as *Citadel* (E5 6b) by Jack Street/Geoff Birtles and *A Dream of White Horses* 1968, HVS 5a, by Ed Drummond and Dave Pearce. In 1979, Drummond climbed Nelson's Column in London as a protest against apartheid in South Africa and in 1971, still at Gogarth, Alan Rouse raised the bar climbing *Positron* (E5 6a), today's equivalent to a 5.11d or a F7a grade: 'The final pitch is extremely impressive, requiring total commitment after the crux move', to quote the description in the 1977 Gogarth guidebook. Arriving in one piece at the top of each of these pitches was an adventure in itself and this achievement was followed by free-climbing and even solo first ascents.

What all these legendary British climbers from the 1950s to the 1970s had in common was that they were better than anyone else at being able to transfer the technical skills acquired on their 'little' lumps of rock and ice onto the highest mountains of the world. For instance, in 1955 Joe Brown was the first to climb the 8,586m Kangchenjunga, the third highest summit on earth and the following year he climbed the challenging Muztagh Tower in the Karakoram range. From the Central Pillar of the Frêney (Mont Blanc, 1961) to the South Face of Annapurna (1970), the likes of Chris Bonington, Whillans (with his illustrious companions Dougal Haston and Doug Scott) were among the great climbers of the day. Whillans also designed the eponymous sit-harness used by many young free climbers in the 1980s and still in use today. Martin Boysen took part in the great climbing expeditions of the time, including Trango Tower and the South West Face of Everest (1975). As for Alan Rouse, an outstanding and determined mountaineer, he died in the tragic summer of 1986 on the slopes of K2, the second highest mountain of the world, having been the first British mountaineer to reach its summit.

In the rest of Europe, except perhaps in the new German Democratic Republic, a country about which there is less information for obvious reasons, climbing mostly took place with artificial aid though some maestros made ascents with dubious protection. Georges Livanos, known as 'Le Grec', is well-known both for his climbing exploits and his inimitable literary style: his book *Au-delà de la verticale* is a classic and he has set records from the Dolomites to the Calanques of Marseilles. His masterpiece remains his 1951 route on the Su Alto peak, at the heart of the enormous North West Face of the Civetta in the Dolomites.

ABOVE: ALAN ROUSE (1951–1986).
BELOW: SONIA AND GEORGES LIVANOS (1923–2004).

CLAUDIO BARBIER
A DAY TO GO DOWN IN HISTORY

Like Gary Hemming, Claudio Barbier was a completely individual marginal character. Born in 1938, in the 1960s this Belgian climber originated the idea of painting the pitons which he did not use yellow ('jaunissement'). He did this on the Belgian rock faces in Freyr to identify the pitons which were not needed as a rest or as an aid, thus highlighting the new possibilities of free-er, more sporty climbing. It was on the same banks of the river Meuse, in Yvoir, that he died in 1977, in a banal accident while clearing vegetation off a new route.

His real fame developed far from his native country, on the vertiginous rock faces of the Dolomites. Not a particularly talented climber when he started, he soon developed a foolproof technique through hard training and repeated falls, excelling in crimping while wearing rigid mountaineering boots. He was passionate about climbing and devoted himself completely to this activity. He lived by doing odd jobs, then by dealing in mountaineering books (he was knowledgeable bibliophile and obsessive about condition), as well as receiving some financial help from his family. While this marginal life style was common in the Yosemite Valley, it was much rarer and less understood in Europe at that time.

From the end of spring until the beginning of autumn, the period of the university vacation, he would move to the Dolomites, making climbs from the Tre Cime to the Civetta, frequently on his own and always in record times. Commanding the respect of the Italians in spite of his northern European origins, they elevated him the rank of 'Maestro' and so 'Claude' became 'Claudio'. He flourished throughout the 1960s, his impressive statistics numbering hundreds of ascents.

In the course of just one glorious sunny day towards the end of the summer, his name became a legend. It started with a disappointment, a cancelled plan for a new route on the Cima Grande had put him in a bad mood, a state of mind which sometimes encourages the taking of mad risks. On 24 August 1961, he left the Locatelli refuge and turned the terrifying north faces of the Tre Cime di Lavaredo into his own exclusive playground. First he climbed the Cassin of the Cima Ovest, then the Comici of the Cima Grande. Not content with climbing these two formidable monuments of pre-war transalpine mountaineering, he continued along the Preuss to the Cima Piccolissima, along the Dülfer to the Punta di Frida and finally along the Innerkofler route to the Cima Piccola. With almost 2,000m of climbing in less than nine hours, a crazy solo cavalcade albeit not always free-climbing, he attracted tremendous admiration as well as some incomprehension from the rest of the climbing and mountaineering community throughout the world.

Thus, some 20 years ahead of its time, he had invented the modern concept of 'enchaînment' or multi-route climbing which Berhault, Boivin, Profit, Escoffier and others took up later.

In Italy, the top climber was Cesare Maestri. Aware of the need for daily physical exercise, legend has it that the *Spider of the Dolomites* would even do press-ups while making love. He made some magnificent solo climbs in the tradition of Preuss and Comici but his life changed in 1959 when he tackled Cerro Torre in Patagonia, the 'hardest mountain in the world', by a route which is still unclimbed to this day. His claim to have reached the summit, combined with the disappearance of his roped climbing companion Toni Egger during their descent, is one of the great mountaineering mysteries of the 20th century, comparable to Mallory and Irvine's equally mysterious disappearance on the slopes of Everest. It is a mystery which turns out to have been pure deception; a police-like investigation lasting over 50 years appeared to have come to an end when the best experts in the field, such as the Argentinian Rolando Garibotti, openly accused Maestri of having lied since, at the time, it would have been impossible to reach the summit by the route described. Meanwhile, to silence his critics, Maestri returned to Cerro Torre in 1970 and by a different route to the 1959 one and armed with a petrol-driven compressor he drilled hundreds of holes for bolts and created an artificial route in order to reach, not the summit itself but

LEFT: ROBERT PARAGOT CLIMBING *STALINGRAD*, ONE OF THE FIRST FB 6TH GRADE CLIMBS IN FONTAINEBLEAU.
RIGHT: CESARE MAESTRI SOLOING DURING THE 1950s.
–

PAGE 61:
IL MAESTRO OF THE 1950s, CESARE MAESTRI.

the shoulder beneath the summit ice mushroom. Consequently the actual first ascent was not made until 1974 by Casimiro Ferrari, who climbed another, more icy face. Many years later, as we shall see, the famous compressor was again at the centre of an ethical battle.

The 1960s will be remembered for several isolated exploits involving personalities with exceptional abilities. In August 1961 Claudio Barbier climbed the five north faces of the Tre Cime di Lavaredo in the space of 15 hours. Barbier was also a brilliant precursor on rock; the father of 'jaunissement' In France, at the beginning of free climbing, starting around 1975, we were inspired by Barbier. We used to say 'jaunissement' (yellowing) as explained below.

Another legend is Reinhold Messner who was also prominent in the Dolomites for his impressive solo ascents: the North East Face of Punta Tissi, the direct North Ridge of Sassolungo, the direct South Face of the Marmolada, the North Face of the Furchetta and the *Philip-Flamm* dihedral of the Civetta. In 1968, with his brother Günther, he opened the *Mittelpfeiler* on the Heiligkreuzkofel in the Dolomites. He pushed free-climbing forward with a compulsory passage of F6c which was not repeated until 1979. It was undoubtedly the first route of this level in the Alps.

In all this, the key word is commitment and the setting is always Alpine. Messner, who in his great 'Dolomite' years was always at the forefront of rock-climbing, never ceased to emphasise the importance of the concepts of commitment and adventure. For him, rock faces are and always will be training schools.

Elsewhere, it was in the field of bouldering that a few mavericks distinguished themselves. In Europe, Fontainebleau established itself as the definitive laboratory of the ultimate movement. This was where, in 1947, the concept of circuits was developed, with the difficulty graded by colours. At the same time, the first really supple climbing shoes with rubber soles were developed, a French innovation subsequently adopted by climbers throughout the world. Meanwhile, Robert Paragot raised the level further when at Bas-Cuvier he climbed *Le Joker* (f6c/f7a, that is, V5), followed by Michel Libert who with his ascent of *L'Abattoir* was the first to exceed the seventh bouldering grade in the early 1960s. Also taking advantage of the nearby rock faces of Le Saussois, these Parisian climbers had the ideal training conditions to prepare themselves to tackle and defeat the 'last problem of the Alps', the West Face of Le Petite Dru (1952) and more distant ones such as the South Face of Aconcagua (1953) and Muztagh Tower in the Karakoram range (1957).

Across the Atlantic, almost completely anonymously, a mathematician had developed a passion for the dynamics of the movements in rock-climbing and the development of pure strength. Applying his scientific approach to the subject, he developed a special training programme and specific equipment which enabled him to reach a level which was far superior to that of the Fontainebleau masters. Thus was born the legend of John Gill, which led to the first V8 and V9 climbs from 1957 onwards.

REINHOLD MESSNER
FIRST A CLIMBER, THEN A MOUNTAINEER

Reinhold Messner is known above all as the greatest living Himalayan climber, the first to have climbed the 14 'eight-thousanders' and the first to climb Everest solo and without oxygen. Even before that, he was probably the best mountaineer in the world. In 1969 he had made the fourth ascent and first solo climb of Les Droites, armed with an ice dagger in the style of *Basic Instinct*, in the incredible time of eight hours and, in 1975, he climbed the North Face of the Eiger in barely 10 hours with Peter Habeler, his climbing companion at the time. This was when Walter Bonatti described him as 'the ultimate hope of great mountaineering' .

Less well-known is his 'climbing' period of the 1960s. While the Americans were in the vanguard both in bouldering and on big walls, it was Messner who, following in the footsteps of the whimsical, brilliant Belgian Claudio Barbier, rationalised and theorised modern climbing on the European side of the Atlantic.

He was introduced to mountaineering by his father at a very young age, in the early 1950s. He often climbed in a roped party with his brother Günther until his tragic accident on Nanga Parbat when Günther disappeared during the descent (after 35 years, his body was finally found and formally identified by DNA tests).

Having enrolled at the University of Padua (where he later briefly taught mathematics), he forced himself to run up steep slopes every morning, pull up on any ledges he could find and to make solo climbs on nearby rocks. By the time he was 20, his list of climbs was extremely impressive, especially in the Dolomites. His heroes were climbers such as Mummery, Paul Preuss, Comici and Bonatti. They all had one thing in common, apart from their 'vertical genius': each one was a maverick in his day, visionaries who knew that limits were there to be exceeded.

Although Italian by birth, in his heart he is first and foremost Tyrolean and German. It was in his native Dolomites that he focused on such notions as competition, professionalism, the necessary social recognition of performance and the development of new training methods. At that time, the sixth grade still represented 'the limit of human possibilities'. But Messner could already see an additional grade on the horizon, the need to 'raise the level of difficulties' and it was in his famous book *The Seventh Grade* that all these ideas matured.

A passionate combination of thoughts on the development of the discipline and descriptions of climbs, this book had an overwhelming impact on climbers and mountaineers throughout the world because the concepts developed in it were based on actual performances in the field which no one could refute or even equal at the time.

Among the other things he describes is his training on an 80m-long traverse off the ground which would repeat over six times before collapsing – the equivalent of climbing almost 500 metres. Not many people were doing this sort of thing in the mid-1960s. What followed were repeat climbs and first ascents galore, bold solos and an already intransigent ethic of free-climbing: 'In first ascents, I also gave up pitons as well as all artificial traction. When I am unable to continue without such aids, I am already prepared to give up, to leave the problem open.'

The only negative effect of this strict ethic was his absolute refusal to use aids such as bolts, which at the time were a legitimate response to the overindulgence in 'straight lines' at any price of the 'artificial' era. But in the end this turned out to limit his progress as increasingly difficult free climbs, particularly on limestone, cannot be achieved without bolts. Messner did not really invent a new kind of free-climbing but he definitely created a new kind of sport mountaineering, based on the concepts of commitment and adventure.

In 1968, again accompanied by his brother, he opened the *Mittelpfeiler* on the Heiligkreuzkofel. It is hard to recall but this was a climbing milestone: the route includes a compulsory passage of a present-day F6c which was only repeated in 1979. The summer of 1969, when he was 25 years old, will remain known for his great solo Alpine exploits, just as a decade later the summer of 1979 would be marked by Patrick Bérault's achievements. Messner conquered the North Face of Les Droites but he also made great solo climbs in the Dolomites on iconic routes: the 1,000m high *Philipp-Flamm* on the North West face of the Civetta, the North Face of the Sassolungo and also the opening of the direct exit of the *Vinatzer* route on the South Face of Marmolada which can still make modern climbers nervous today and which, in his opinion, represented the apogee of his career as a pure 'rock climber'.

Paradoxically it was this dazzling talent which was going to keep him away, almost forever, from rock faces and his beloved Dolomites. His growing reputation earned him an invitation from the fearsome Dr Herrligkoffer to join the expedition on the 4,500m high Rupal Face of Nanga Parbat, the tallest mountain face in the world. There he lost his brother, after which his slow psychological rebirth and the serious frostbite he suffered guided the rest of his career almost exclusively towards the highest peaks in the world. He now focused on the 'death zone' and detached himself from the boom in rock-climbing as a self-contained activity.

Today, a patriarch and a guru for the next generations, it is more than likely that from the top of the ramparts of his castle in his native Tyrol, he continues to watch with a disapproving eye the performances of modern 'gymnasts' wrestling with the ninth grade using the bolts which were he abhorred in the past. Whether he likes it or not, in a way he has had a lot to do with it.

PAGE 62: REINHOLD MESSNER. PAGE 63: REINHOLD MESSNER IN THE DOLOMITES, 1960s.

JOHN GILL
AT THE ROOTS OF THE MOVEMENT

———

John Gill is another character who occupies a remarkable place in the story of climbing, having revolutionised the sport in several ways. The use of chalk, the defined lunge as a style form, the development of specific training, climbing boulders not repeated for over 20 years, all this and many other things are due to the 'Master of Rock', as he was described in the title of the book written about him by Pat Ament.

A high-flying scientist, John Gill is also known for his mathematical research into subjects as indefinite as the analytical theory of fractions. His dynamic approach to vertical movement is also the result of methodical thought.

In the 1950s, he applied his gymnastic skills to climbing. Instead of trying to climb ever higher or more mountainous faces, he was the first to translate rock-climbing movements into straightforward gymnastics on a vertical or sloping plane. Long before the young athletes of today, he complemented his rope-climbing skills (his speciality in gymnastics) with more specific exercises: several swift one-arm pull-ups on narrow ledges, the iron cross and, last but not least, his famous one-arm front lever, a challenge for many aspiring climbers.

He introduced the use of chalk, used in gymnastics competitions, to reduce sweat and improve the skin's grip on holds. Today, its success is evident, as are the visual consequences of using chalk in every part of the world where climbing takes place.

But it is in the spirit of a Gill threw, not desperate before the fall and lack of strength but rather a harmonious and rapid movement to the next shot. Instead of using pure static strength, acceleration control allows a saving of resources and increased performance. But his most important contribution was 'controlled dynamics'. In Gill's mind a climbing movement should be like a harmonious movement to reach the next hold. Rather than using pure static force, a controlled accleration allows a saving of resources and gives increased performance. Years later, Wolfgang Güllich and his campus board were inspired by this style of training.

As in gymnastics, there is also an aesthetic consideration, the search for the perfect movement, which according to Gill's criteria should be as fluid as possible. The title of his magazine article *The Art of Bouldering* sums it up perfectly. He was not immediately recognised by the world at large, nor was he interested in media coverage, unlike the pioneers of the big walls in the Yosemite during the same period but, nevertheless, it is thanks to him that bouldering became an independent activity in its own right. At the end of the 1950s he reached the upper part of the seventh grade with problems which today are still rated V8 and V9 on the modern American scale. The *Thimble* on the Needles of South Dakota is a highball boulder of 10 metres, which was already graded 5.12 when he climbed it unroped in 1961. In other words, he was a visionary, 20 years ahead of his time.

Much later, still an athlete at the age of nearly 60, with rippling muscles, barely a trace of salt-and-pepper in his beard, he was always on the go, still interested in new things and the opening of new routes, whether bouldering or as a 'solo option'. Clearly for this man, whose era preceded that of sponsors, whether or not he was famous has never been an issue.

Today, at the age of nearly 80, he has almost Buddhist views with a Zen tendency, based on the inevitable impermanence of achievements and the vanity of the appreciation of difficulties, the quasi-mystical quest for a 'kinaesthetic awareness' or an awareness of movement. So, the guru of the one-arm front lever and the one-finger pull-up was (and still is) first and foremost a 'spiritual' climber. For him, of whom the body is merely the vessel enabling the climber to travel in pursuit of an inner satisfaction, subordinate to access to a 'new form of reality' which itself is determined by the 'gracefulness of movements and their precision'.

ABOVE: SO MANY CLIMBERS DREAMED LOOKING THIS IMAGE: JOHN GILL PERFORMING HIS LEGENDARY ONE ARM FRONT LEVER. BELOW LEFT: JOHN GILL ON *FLYING BUTTRESS*, NEEDLES, SOUTH DAKOTA, 1964. BELOW CENTRE: JOHN GILL IN THE SHADES MOUNTAIN, ALABAMA, 1963. BELOW RIGHT: JOHN GILL ON *HIDDEN OVERHANG*, DIXON SPRINGS, ILLINOIS, 1965.

THE EMERGENCE OF FRANCE

Let us now look at rock-climbing in France.

'Free climbing' has been around for a long time but the term did not always have the meaning it does today. In the past, it meant climbing 'free' between each peg. So, everything was allowed: tight rope, using karabiners as handholds and pitons as footholds. On a run-out, between pegs, the grade could be as high as our current F6b on the hardest routes.

But there was no real notion of continuity. The grade of the route was determined either by the difficulty of the moves or by the exposure or the extent of the run-out between runners. Sometimes climbers wanted to miss out a peg altogether. Longer, more exposed run-outs could be made by removing pegs as, for instance, in 1967 when Jean-Claude Droyer climbed the *Super-Échelle* route in Le Saussois in this way.

Sometimes, a committing run-out was made longer but, in climbing terms, falling was not an option and was considered a mistake. In those days rigid Vibram shoes or semi-rigid (Terray-Saussois style) boots were the most popular.

The rating of difficulties was still based on the classic Welzenbach system divided into six grades; the sixth being considered 'the limit of human possibilities'. Therefore, the top grade was 6 and no one seriously considered having a seventh. At Fontainebleau, where that problem might reach such a level, it was decided to keep the sixth grade while adding to it: VIa, b, c, d, e, f and so on.

On the local Paris rocks of Fontainebleau, the mountain spirit was pushed slightly into the background as the equipment of the routes was improved. Thus, in 1961, at Surgy, at the instigation of Guy Richard, all equipment was revised and a large number of pitons were secured to the rock face with cement. Similarly at Le Saussois fixed equipment became the rule; at Saffres even a power drill was used because the crag there was used a lot for training and safety was paramount.

But on larger-scale crags or at higher altitudes, the mountain spirit survived and climbing remained first and foremost an adventure. There was, for instance, the new routes being done in the Verdon Gorge which were systematically climbed 'ground up', often with plenty of aid. Nuts were not yet widespread but they were beginning to appear. In 1974 in *La Montagne,* the magazine of the Club Alpin Francais, Patrick Cordier highlighted the problem of damage caused to the rock by the repeated knocking in and removal of pitons and pointed out the ecological benefits of nuts instead.

What are the most famous crags in France? In the north, the premier cliff is undoubtedly Le Saussois on the banks of the Yonne in Burgundy. After WW1, these

JEAN-CLAUDE DROYER.

—

PAGE 67:

ABOVE: A CLIMBER ON *LA SUPER ECHELLE*, 7A, LE SAUSSOIS.

BELOW: CLOSE TO THE YONNE RIVER, THE BURGUNDIAN CRAGS OF LE SAUSSOIS.

limestone crags, discovered in the late 1930s by Maurice Martin, became a favourite a haunt for Parisian mountaineers such as Couzy, Desmaison, Paragot and Bérardini and they soon became internationally famous. The legends associated with Le Saussois are countless. For instance, there was Gary Hemming in the late 1960s who attempted to climb the *Super-Échelle* free but got no further than the first pitch of the route. In 1975, the toughest routes were *La Mantra*, an overhang above the *Échelle* with two pitons and above all the *Président* and *L'Ange*. As for *L'Ange*, the old 'artificial' route using anchors was 'recreated' in 1972 by Jean Fréhel and Patrick Cordier and it is the test piece for those who claim to be strong. The climbers at the time included Bernard Mellet, Jean Fréhel, Jean-Claude Droyer and Patrick Cordier. Still in Burgundy, Surgy, Saffres and Cormot are worthy complements to Le Saussois.

DEEP GORGES

At the heart of the Alpes de Haute-Provence, the cliffs of the Verdon Gorge are beautiful to look at but they also command respect because of their height of up to 300m and their isolation. Discovered by climbers in 1966, the first routes were the obvious ones, the great cracks of the Escalès cliff: *La Demande* in 1968, the *Éperon Sublime* and *Luna-Bong* in 1970. Guy Héran, François Guillot and Joël Coqueugniot were soon joined by Bernard Gorgeon and his friends: Jacques Nosley, Jacques Keller and the guide Pepsi.

A native of Marseilles, François Guillot was the most talented. He learned his skills in the nearby Calanques, that 'sea and mountain' paradise which earlier on had produced legends such as Gaston Rébuffat and Georges Livanos. In the post-war years, this enormous white limestone massif rising from the Mediterranean became the most active climbing centre in the South of France. There, climbers experimented on the vertical rock and all the techniques which subsequently were so successful in the Verdon. In the Calanques or in Chamonix (the first repeat of the *Directe américaine aux Drus*), Guillot and his companions tackled the most difficult itineraries in record times and matched in free-climbing the level achieved by Messner in the Dolomites at the same time. Guillot's career has been long and varied and included the rescue of German climbers in the Drus in 1966 plus expeditions to the West Pillar of Makalu in Nepal and FitzRoy in Patagonia) and today he is still an active and accomplished modern free climber.

In the early 1970s climbers were attracted by the big aid-climbing walls such as the *Paroi Rouge*, the *Mousson*, the *Castapiagne Rouge*. The legend of the Verdon was born: stark shapes and perfect verticality, everything contributed to the international reputation of the gorge. At first it was the terrifying cracks which made the headlines

CLAUDE CASSIN AND FRANÇOIS GUILLOT, VERDON, 1968.

—

PAGE 69:

ABOVE LEFT: FRANÇOIS GUILLOT.

CENTRE LEFT: CHRISTIAN GUYOMAR (1948–2011), FREE-CLIMBING ON LES DEUX AIGUILLES, ONLY PROTECTED WITH SKYHOOKS.

ABOVE LEFT: RON FAWCETT FREEING *LE TRIOMPHE D'ÉROS, MOUNTAIN* COVER, 1978.

RIGHT: L'ESCALÈS, CROWN OF THE VERDON GORGES.

61
MOUNTAIN
55p / $1.60

but soon a new generation of face routes developed. The tall grey pillars were appealing but their density was discouraging. However, little by little drops of water had formed grooves in the vast limestone walls and these could be climbed.

First it was the *Triomphe d'Éros*, climbed by Jean-Claude Droyer in 1974, which only touched on the problem, followed two years later by the climbs of *Nécronomicon* and *Pichenibule* by Jacques 'Pschitt' Perrier, who still today is one of the most passionate climbers around.

In the Verdon, climbing was serious but still not free in style. Then, a significant change took place during in autumn 1977 with both British and French participants. The duo Pete Livesey and Ron Fawcett stood out among the English climbers. Although he discovered rock climbing rather late in life, Livesey, aged 35 and the older of the two, was already a globetrotter. A regular in the Yosemite Valley and a slightly provocative character, he found the Verdon pleasanter and more authentic, as well as being suited to natural runners. As for Fawcett, he had the energy of youth and was soon to take the leadership of the new wave of British climbers.

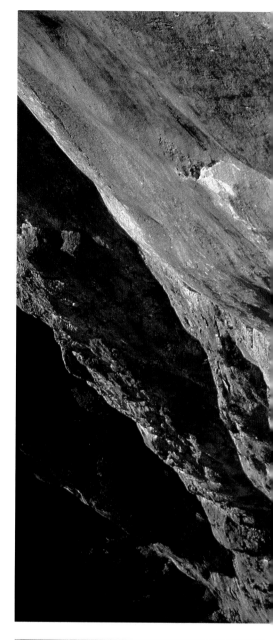

In the course of just a few days, the two men made first free ascents *Pichenibule* (without the bulge), *Nécronomicon*, *Luna Bong*, *Roumagaou*, *Solanuts* and *Triomphe d'Éros*: the manifesto of routes of their friend Droyer. Now nudging the modern seventh grade in the Verdon, the achievements of the British spoke for themselves and made the locals aware of the vastness of these cliffs. Now performance was not only associated with opening new routes but also with the pure style in which they could be climbed free. Because of its vastness, the Verdon is undoubtedly where French climbing social and cultural climbing codes of practice have been most lastingly laid down. In a way, the Verdon is the Yosemite of France. Its history has been magnificently and comprehensively told by Bernard Vaucher in his book *Les Fous du Verdon (The Madmen of Verdon)*.

Not far from there, near Aix-en-Provence on the Montagne Sainte-Victoire immortalised by Cézanne, is the crag of Les Deux Aiguilles where free-climbing was the most advanced in France at the time. Above all, this was due to the impetus of one man, Christian Guyomar. Discovered in 1967, the wall of Les Deux Aiguilles is a climb on very compact limestone slabs with small holds. In 1973 Christian and Martine Guyomar and Christian Hautcoeur began opening a series of important routes: *Tamanrasset*, *Médius*, then the *Pagode*, *L'Ovni* and the *Super-Médius*, followed by the *Barnett* in 1974 and the *Lévitation* in 1976. Grade seven was beginning to be mentioned and the area of Les Deux Aiguilles would be the first in France to include this rating.

Although he did not strictly create new routes in the tradition of free climbing, Guyomar was much more than somebody who pulled on pegs. Routes such as the *Lévitation*, the *Médius* and the *Hyper Médius* included pitches on a level of difficulty previously unknown at the time. Climbing almost every day, he opened routes systematically from the bottom in similar style to how it was done in Dresden. He refused to use bolts and his routes were often extremely bold. On *L'Ovni, the key passage was protected by a*

PAGE 70 BELOW:

LAURENT JACOB BELAYED BY DAVID CHAMBRE ON *GRAVITY'S RAINBOW*, F7C, A ROUTE FROM THE 1980s AND A PHOTO THAT CAPTURES THE MAGICAL ATMOS-PHERE OF VERDON.

—

PAGE 70 BELOW:

CHRISTIAN GUYOMAR IN THE CENTRE AND STÉPHANE TROUSSIER ON HIS RIGHT.

tiny Bashee, a small lump of lead with a wire loop attached which was hammered/moulded into an irregularity in the rock. It eventually exploded a few years later after stopping numerous falls. In order to make up for this lack of protection, Guyomar introduced the use of skyhooks, even taking deliberate falls, using them at a time when everyone else refused to fall intentionally on even the best pitons. Relatively isolated, Christian Guyomar was undoubtedly a precursor, in the same way as Jean-Claude Droyer but he was less provocative, letting his achievements speak on his behalf. But, elsewhere and more generally in Western Europe, free climbing, as it is understood today, did not become established. Falling off was still considered a mistake, something to be avoideduy at all costs. Rock faces were first and foremost schools for learning safety and speed.

BRITAIN IS BACK

In 1975, the vision and raison d'être of European climbing were still first and foremost 'genetically' Alpine. In Italy, Gian-Piero Motti and his friends Allessandro Gogna, Ugo Manera and Gian-Carlo Grassi founded the *Nuovo Mattino* movement, based on a libertarian approach to the mountains and climbing where, inspired by the new itineraries of the Val d'Orco, the difficulty had to stem from the mountain and not from the climber: 'A serene acceptance of one's limits, in a spirit of enjoyment, while deriving the maximum pleasure, as you would in a game, from an activity which for a long time was notable for the denial of this pleasure in favour of suffering.'

In some parts of the world, some quite close to France, things have changed and mentalities have evolved considerably. In Britain, free climbing has been carried out for many years. The British cliffs may not be the most beautiful in the world but they have a unique atmosphere. Sometimes over only a few metres, as if by magic, amazing sensations

TRAD CLIMBING IN CORNWALL, LUNDY ISLAND.

LEFT: TOM PROCTOR (1947–2001).

CENTRE AND RIGHT: PETER LIVESEY (1943–1998).

of adventure and involvement can be experienced, worthy of the great Alpine rock faces. The changeable climate often accentuates the dramatic nature of this atmosphere.

In 1975, the tradition of climbing completely free was already well-established. The most active zones were clearly defined: Cornwall, Wales and, in particular, the area around Sheffield on the limestone and gritstone of the Peak District. The British ethic was clear; the climber systematically tackled the route from the bottom and when he fell, he immediately climbed back down to the bottom, leaving his rope clipped to a karabiner for the next attempt. This started to change in the late 60s. Tom Proctor was an icon of British climbing based around Stoney Middleton where his first ascent of *Our Father* with Geoff Birtles in 1968 heralded a new approach to limestone climbing. It was bold, steep, dangerous and currently graded E4 6b, 5a. Climbers travelled from far and wide to attempt it with most failing in the early days and it was regarded as being the hardest climb in the UK for some time and probably one of the first 7th French grade in History, definitely way ahead of its time. *Our Father* was an early example of pre-inspection by abseil. Proctor, quiet by nature but 'the strongest man in the world' continued to dominate the Peak District limestone scene throughout the 70s plus other first ascents elsewhere such as *Deygo* at Gogarth. By the early 70s, one of the most active climbers was Pete Livesey (mentioned earlier) who was well ahead of climbers like Ed Drummond, Tom Proctor, Geoff Birtles and the young Ron Fawcett, then only 19 years old. In 1974 Livesey conquered the legendary *Right Wall* (E5 6a) of Dinas Cromlech. His ethics were fairly vague: no top-roping or working the moves but abseiling to check the holds and nut placements. Nuts! These were already the subject of a cult, being attributed many qualities: safety and unobtrusiveness, not to mention the ability to increase commitment.

RON FAWCETT.

—

PAGE 74:

LEFT: JOHN ALLEN, RISING STAR OF THE BRIT SCENE
OF THE 1970s.

RIGHT: RON FAWCETT IN *L'ORLA*, E1 5B, CURBAR EDGE,
PEAK DISTRICT.

Livesey was already talking about the importance of winter training on indoor climbing walls, highly developed in British gyms where climbing without a rope, as in bouldering, enabling the climber to work on specific moves while the level of difficulty gets harder at the same time. He also knew where he stood in relation to Alpine climbing: 'We have been accused by the Continentals of being decadent in climbing because we climb without rucksacks and climbing boots. They believed that our approach to climbing should be seen as merely training for mountaineering. They were indignant when we replied that our way of climbing embodied the basic qualities of mountaineering.' This declaration was made in May 1976 during an international meeting organised by the British Mountaineering Council, when it became quite obvious that the British delegation which included Livesey, Fawcett, Proctor and Littlejohn were bitterly opposed to any kind of organised competition in rock-climbing, in response to the Russian delegation's suggestion of an international climbing competition. John Allen was another English climber at the time who would also become a legendary figure. His climbing career was short-lived but dazzling. Together with Steve Bancroft, he opened or free-climbed several of the major routes in the Peak District such as *Profit of Doom*, *Old Friends* and *London Wall* and in Wales, he freed *Great Wall*, some of these routes reaching the French grade 7a/b, with considerable seriousness as well.

The first free ascent of *Great Wall* highlighted the great debate over the use of chalk, which divided the British climbing community. The fact that John Allen had used chalk, seen by some as a pollutant, made the headlines of the legendary and now defunct *Mountain* magazine in July 1975. For *Mountain*, chalk 'was a convenience which had become popular over two particularly hot summers and which must, at the very least, be considered contrary to climbing ethics'. On the other hand *Crags*, the first magazine devoted exclusively to rock-climbing, encouraged its use and was supported by Fawcett ('Using chalk is better than going over a route again with aids or cluttering it with useless nuts') and Livesey ('Chalk is like EB climbing shoes, it makes rock-climbing moves more elegant, more dynamic and more accomplished'). When Ed Hart climbed the *Great Wall* again without chalk, he commented that 'this climb has restored the route to its original pure state'. With the benefit of hindsight, these words sound rather ironic. The 'Clean Hand Gang' finally lost the battle and it became the norm to climb with chalk on British routes spreading, as it did, throughout the world.

Among the young generation, Ron Fawcett was the climber who made the strongest and longest-lasting impression thanks to his complete devotion to his passion and his status as Britain's first rock athlete. Indeed, his autobiography is called *Ron Fawcett: Rock Athlete*. His ascents of *Lord of the Flies* (E6 6a, Dinas Cromlech, 1980), *Strawberries* (E6 6b, Tremadog, 1980) and *Master's Edge* (E7 6b, Millstone, Peak District, 1983) are still seen as milestones in the United Kingdom. But, at the time, being a professional climber was synonymous with living frugally. I remember going to Derbyshire with Jean-Claud Droyer where Fawcett and his wife welcomed us warmly to their little cottage, hidden on the moors. Life was spartan and stomachs were empty. At the end of our stay we invited them to a local restaurant to thank them and taking advantage of this golden opportunity, they wolfed down everything as if it was the end of 40-day fast.

ONCE UPON A TIME IN THE EAST

At the same time, on the other side of the Iron Curtain on the banks of the Elbe, things were as they had been for decades. On the cliffs there, sometimes 100m high, people have been climbing for generations, on the walls, ridges and cracks where the sandstone holds are mildly reassuring.

These were the years when local Generals would walk around with rows of medals on their lapels, when this part of Germany was the German Democratic Republic and effectively a satellite Soviet state. But climbing in the Elbe Sandstone Mountains was much older than Communism.

In the 1950s the threshold of the current F6c grade was crossed; apart from Yosemite, these mountains were the only place in the world where such a level of difficulty existed. At that time, it was in Dresden that the greatest concentration of free climbers of all levels was to be found.

Defying the difficulties of the journey (in particular, at the border where all Western currency had to be turned into local currency which could not be exchanged back later), the first Western climbers appeared in the 1970s and the early 1980s. They included the American Henry Barber, Germans Kurt Albert and Wolfgang Güllich and last but not least the Frenchman Jean-Claude Droyer. They were all very impressed by the level of boldness and fascinated by the purity of the Saxon climbing ethics. Gradually, through the influence of Western magazines, the area became better known. It was indeed from the Saxon tradition, which seems so rigid today, that modern climbing as it is now practiced is derived, even on the most sophisticated artificial boulders.

More than the originality of the rock, what makes the pillars of Dresden so special are the rules which apply to climbing them. From the very start, style and method were seen as more important than the mere objective of reaching the top at all costs. Standards were therefore set and they were sufficiently accepted by the whole climbing community for them still to be applied today.

Thus a minimum 'regulation' distance (generally four metres) was stipulated between each runner, those being the 'ring', a metal spike up to 30cm long, (still made using traditional methods and the ancestor of the resin-fixed bolts of today) which must still be placed on the lead using a hand drill and hammer. These rings bolts may only be used as runners and a route cannot have more than a limited number of points. If these rules are not respected, the route is not recognised by climbers or by the 'official' authorities, so the route may be stripped of the bolts. This clearly reflects the strength of the Communist ideology which has infiltrated a sport which for the rest of the world has always been a symbol of freedom.

In order to preserve these fragile rocks, metal nuts of every kind are forbidden, even Friends. Instead, knots on slings jammed in the cracks are commonly used and they appear to be just as effective and, for blanker faces, (lunules) threaded slings

PAGE 76/77 ABOVE:

THE FAMOUS SANDSTONE TOWERS OF ELBSANDSTEINGE-BIRGE.

—

PAGE 76 BELOW:

BERND ARNOLD.

—

PAGE 77 BELOW:

BERND ARNOLD BAREFOOT.

through drilled holes are used. As for chalk, it too is forbidden but sawdust replaces it very well and specially adapted slippers are worn instead of shoes. Some climbers, such as Bernd Arnold, prefer climbing barefoot in order to use their toes to take advantage of the holes. He would wear no harness, just an ordinary rope of questionable origin around his waist. Nevertheless, in an interview in 1982 by Droyer, Arnold conceded that in view of the height of the potential falls, 'good quality Western ropes are advisable all the same'.

Since the reunification, little has been heard of the Elbe sandstone and a new generation of climbers there. It seems that on the towers themselves, ethics have changed little, thus preventing any development towards higher levels of difficulty. Instead of rebelling, young climbers have preferred to perpetuate the existing traditions, or go and climb elsewhere. The crags have no overhangs and the place with its rock faces rests in a time that has passed.

Although all the administrative obstacles have gone and Dresden is easily reached by motorway, for 'modern' climbers, Europe's Eastern frontier still seems to stop at the Frankenjura. It must be said the rocks there involve precarious, technical climbing with rather unimpressive ratings. In other words, it is challenging enough to be frightening but the reward for success at only F7b is not very impressive.

In 1998, an article appeared in the magazine *Grimper* devoted to the Czech Republic, also on the banks of the Elbe and with the same climbing ethics but on the other side of the border. There the indefatigable traveller Jean-Minh Trinh-Thieu noticed a cautious evolution on the part of the Czech elite towards a few routes equipped 'Western style', finally making the leap to our eighth grade. Nevertheless, this minirevolution does not yet seem to have spread to the former East Germany and perhaps that is the most interesting aspect. In spite of the social and political developments which have taken place, the strict climbing rules which prevail seem to resist all changes.

All the same, it is remarkable that Dresden remains the only region which has not been affected by 'Western imperialism', continuing against all odds to climb 'differently'. Jean-Minh finished his article with the promise of the 'next report in a few years' time.' But since then, nothing new has appeared.

THE TWO SIDES OF THE IRON CURTAIN
BERND ARNOLD AND HENRY BARBER

Born in 1947, Bernd Arnold symbolises more than anyone the spirit of the Elbe. Never has the balance between a man and his climbing area been so perfect as in the case of him and the Elbe Sandstone Mountains.

Enjoying a quiet family life and working close by, the East German started climbing at a very young age, in the early 1960s. Once an adult, he tried to have the excessively rigid rules evolve so as to set new standards.
Leaving cracks behind, throughout the 1970s he concentrated on rock faces and ridges, which naturally implied much more delicate belays. In 1970, with the route *Ziebziger Weg* he was the first to inaugurate the local ninth grade (a rating scale inspired by that of the UIAA), which corresponds roughly to the French seventh grade.

For two decades, all the most important routes were the work of this barefooted man. *Feuerwand*, *Wand der abendröte*, *Superlativ*, *Tausendmarkwand*, each of which would stand out in its time, each of which involved lengthy preparation; studying the holds and possible positions for the runners, attempts, down-climbing, falls, everything until a final ascent was made.

Arnold and his friends organised themselves as a team to bring each project to a successful conclusion. They kept their distance from the Communist authorities and looked down on the speed competitions which were then being organised in the Soviet Union. Although the ascents and unofficial titles were ratified by the Ministry of Sport, the climbers in Arnold's gang remained in their corner and were left in peace.
The end of Bernd Arnold's golden age coincided roughly with the fall of the Berlin Wall. Taking advantage of access to the West, he was able to escape from his 'gilded cage' and discover greater challenges. He climbed the great rock faces of Trango Tower in the Karakoram range of the Himalaya along with Güllich and Kurt Albert and then, *Royal Flush* on Mount Fitz Roy in Patagonia.

PAGE 78: BERND ARNOLD IN 1957, AGED 10 AND ALREADY AT HOME. PAGE 79: STILL BAREFOOT, BERND ARNOLD SUCCEEDED TO COMBINE THE EAST GERMAN RIGOR TO THE WESTERN FREE CLIMBING SPIRIT.

Henry Barber was one of the first Westerners to visit East Germany, in 1976, together with Steve Wunsch and the veteran Fritz Wiessner, who was returning to the scene of his first climbs. Barber was undeniably one of the most outstanding figures on the American scene and to some extent he was Arnold's spiritual and ethical alter ego on the west side of the Atlantic. While he was clearly impressed by the difficulties already overcome in Dresden, this was reciprocal, the local Germans had never seen such a bold climber.

Also keen on steep ice-climbing, in 1978 Barber was involved in a bad accident on Kilimanjaro and gradually faded from the top level which was becoming more and more involved with sport and technology. Barber has always been attached to a culture of austerity: climbing solo or with the minimum of equipment and protection. Interviewed in 2007, he declared that 'of all my travels, the place which has inspired me most is undoubtedly Dresden. Back in the United States, I still continue climbing with bare feet, it is more efficient and sensual, one feels better, even when soloing.'

One of the most influential figures in the United States was undoubtedly Henry Barber; 'Hot Henry', whose golfer's cap and penchant for beer became legendary. He cut his teeth on the American East Coast, at the Shawangunks where he benefited from Stannard's experience. In 1973, then aged 20, he arrived in Yosemite and made a dramatic start by successfully free climbing *Butterballs* (5.11/5.11+), which as a result became the hardest free route in the valley. He then soloed the *Steck Salathe* on the Sentinel at great speed: 'I did it because one of my best friends, Roger Parke, was killed there last year. We were very close and I wanted to go there to pay him homage. Not finding anyone to accompany me, I decided to do it solo. It usually takes at least a full day for a roped party of two while I did in two and three-quarter hours.'

Barber is a true monument in the history of free climbing, criss-crossing the world from crag to crag, often playing a leading role in the evolution of standards. His observations about the early 1970s is particularly interesting. On his first trip to England, he was interviewed by *Mountain* magazine (no. 34, May 1974). In it he stressed the great impact of the use of nuts. In his opinion their popularisation by 'prophets' such as Chouinard and Stannard had completely revolutionised the world of American climbing. Barber already came across as a professional free-climber. In the previous two years, he had been climbing five or six days a week, tackling several routes day and spending a long time (up to eight days) on the more difficult ones. For him, working on a route was the same as a gym session. All the foundations of sport climbing had already been laid. His climbing ethic was also very strict: maximum use of nuts for runners and above all the refusal to use any aid: 'Ethically it is a bad thing.'

AMERICAN INSPIRATION

But for the moment, the leading country in the field of free climbing is still undoubtedly the United States. Since 1965, free climbers have made their mark on both the West and East coasts, thus breaking the trend of aid-climbing. In Yosemite, Royal Robbins, Layton Kor, Yvon Chouinard and above all Frank Sacherer have already been mentioned. Sacherer, from the start, developed a very strict ethic, completely rejecting aid-climbing and concentrating exclusively on free climbing. In Colorado, the pioneers were Pat Ament and Roger Briggs who in 1966 crossed the 5.11 barrier with *Vertigo* (5.11a, the equivalent of the F6b/c).

ABOVE: PETER CROFT.

BELOW: JOHN BACHAR (1957–2009).

On the East Coast, the legendary site was the Shawangunk Ridge, an enormous rock face to the north of New York City. It was discovered in 1935 by Fritz Wiessner when he noticed the rocks in a flash of lightning during a thunderstorm. Under his influence and as mentioned earlier, the Gunks soon became the centre of free climbing before the chaos of the Second World War.

Towards the mid-1960s, John Stannard revived Wiessner's philosophy. When revising the equipment on the routes, he chose to leave all the good pitons in place while at the same time developing the use of nuts. Stannard wanted at all costs to avoid what was becoming a real plague in places such as Yosemite such as the damage made to the rock by successively hammering in pitons and removing them. In 1968, the first free ascent of *Foops* (5.11 or F6c), now an internationally known roof, took place. More so than Yosemite where nuts were used only as protection since 1972, the Gunks soon became the driving force of free climbing in the USA defined by the maximum use of natural protection and the growing pursuit of difficulty. In 1972, the new grade of 5.12 made its appearance with *To have or not to have* and, in 1974, the lead climber Steve Wunsch opened *Supercrack*, which would be rated 7c on the French scale. It was the hardest route in America and at that time was certainly also the hardest in the world.

Between 1974 and 1976, with the generalisation of 5.12, climbing increasingly became a sport, including the complete acceptance of falling but climbing ethic was still rather blurred. Some climbers practised moves by rappel or top-rope while others systematically tackled the routes from the bottom. The same applied in equipping routes, which were either opened whilst climbing bottom-up, or by abseiling and placing pegs or bolts and even the pre-placement of nuts. A new way of working emerged as climbers top-roped the key sections, studied the moves, then set off on the lead with repeated attempts until successful. Sometimes, holds were artificially improved which is still a problem today.

This new mentality was reflected in *Kloeberdanz* (5.11), a former aid-climbing route, successfully freed in 1974 by Steve Wunsch after 15 falls and the use of dynamic movements. The same applied to *Psycho* (5.11), climbed in 1975 by Wunsch again, after more than 20 falls. Since then, a hold having broken in the roof, its level of difficulty has greatly increased, making it internationally famous. It is interesting to note that that, from the early 1970s, chalk also made its appearance in Colorado. The controversy about its use still rages in Yosemite: the chalk bags symbolise the defiance of the 'prophets of purism', as Rob Muir put it and the same debate also arose in Britain.

PETER CROFT SOLOING *TIPS*, 5.11, YOSEMITE.

In the tradition of Henry Barber, in 1975 the first 5.12 appeared in Yosemite: *Hotline* on Elephant Rock by Ron Kauk and John Bachar. Then followed *Wailing Wall*, *Crimson Cringe* and *Tips*, as well as *Hangdog Flyer* (Ray Jardine) and *Tales of Power* (Ron Kauk), which raised the level of difficulty a further notch. But, ultimately, in spite of its reputation as the world capital of free climbing, Yosemite was far from being the only region in the United States where it was practised: Colorado was another and so in particular were the Shawangunks in New York State. During this period, some regulars in Yosemite had acquired a very high technical level. Proof of this was the magnificent solo ascent of the *Nabisco Wall* (which includes *Butterballs*) in 1975 by Bachar, already F7a which is more than 80m long.

It would be unjust not to mention Bachar's contemporary Peter Croft, often considered the king of crack climbing. Born in Canada but mainly active in the United States, he was so accomplished at this type of climbing that he climbed *Astroman* (mentioned earlier) solo in 1987, an incredibly daring performance which he repeated that same year while linking it with the *Rostrum*, another great benchmark at this level of difficulty. Until the recent exploits of Dean Potter and then of Alex Honnold, no one pushed the solo game in Yosemite so far as Croft did. Active since then in the high mountains of the Sierra Nevada, he was more rational than his friend Bachar, which may be why he is still among us. In 1986, their roped party achieved the first enchainment of *The Nose* on El Capitan and Half Dome in under 14 hours.

JOHN BACHAR
AND THE STONE MASTERS

———

In the early 1970s a new generation of strong climbers emerged in California. Less attracted by the big walls of El Capitan than their predecessors, they developed free climbing, with or without a rope. With a touch of megalomania combined with a little self-mockery, they called themselves the Stone Masters. Yosemite was their nerve centre, mainly centred around Camp 4, where they adopted the style known as 'bum climbing', a minimalist way of life on the fringe, totally dedicated to their passion where by their own admission many of them were above all the Stoned Masters…

They included John Long, Tobin Sorenson, Rick Accomazzo and Mike Graham. But the most charismatic of them was undoubtedly John Bachar. Born in Los Angeles in 1957, he dropped out of university to the despair of his father, who did not to speak to him again until many years later when he found out that his son had become well-known and admired throughout the world. Like a Berhault, Edlinger or Güllich before him, he became fanatical about training and diet, inventing among other things the training aid, the Bachar Ladder.

In 1975, together with John Long and Ron Kauk, he opened a new route on the East Face of Washington Column which became the hardest long route there with its numerous pitches of 5.11. Renamed *Astroman*, it is still today a compulsory route for every passionate connoisseur of Yosemite. Spending summer in the Valley and winter in the Joshua Tree desert, he also developed particular skills in solo climbing, so much so that it became his main activity. His ascents of *New Dimensions* and *Moratorium* (5.11, on sight at that) and especially the three pitches of *Nabisco Wall* in 1979 which made him an American legend. For many, his free-solo skills made him the best climber in the world.

He was also directly involved in bouldering. In friendly competition with Ron Kauk for the first ascent of *Midnight Lightning*, situated right in the middle of Camp 4, it was he who drew the legendary lightning bolt on it with chalk. The emblem of a generation, it was mysteriously rubbed out one night in 2013 before being immediately restored. First climbed by Ron Kauk in 1978, then by Bachar, this boulder graded V8, probably the most difficult in the world, would not be climbed again for five years, while the two friends enjoyed climbing it every day, almost as if it was a show with a set time.

In the early 1980s, whilst climbing in Europe was moving inexorably towards well-bolted sport problems, Bachar maintained the very traditional vision that a route must always be opened ground up, never by abseiling and with as little fixed equipment as possible. His theories reached their apogee in Tuolumne Meadows with the *Bachar-Yerian*, only 5.11+ but with only 13 bolts over 90 metres. Today, in the United States, this route is still considered a benchmark in the *banzai* style. It was also at this time that Bachar posted a provocative advertisement, offering a $10,000 reward to whoever could follow him for one full day of solo climbing. Not surprisingly, no one came forward. Invited in 1981 to the German Climbing Meeting at Konstein, Bachar seized the opportunity of teaching the Europeans a lesson by securing the first ascent of *Chasin' the trane* (F7c in the Frankenjura), an exploit repeated the following year by Wolfgang Güllich. But, his 'reactionary' philosophy prevented him from taking part in the adventure of 'pure difficulty', so he was completely absent from this pivotal period.

Unlike Ron Kauk, who came to Europe to get a taste of the eighth grade, to discover new techniques and even to participate in the first competitions, Bachar continued with his career as a solo climber, doing traditional routes. The guardian of the temple of Yosemite, he would not hesitate to break bolts placed in a 'impure' way. He was behind the revolution of the resined sticky soles of the Spanish *Firé* climbing shoes produced by Boreal and he created his own brand, Acopa, in the 1990s. Faithful to his ethic and way of life, even at the age of 50, it was almost natural that his life should end on the rock. He died in 2009 at Mammoth Lakes, when he fell solo on a route which had been climbed a thousand times.

JOHN BACHAR SOLOING *UP 40*, 5.11B, JOSHUA TREE, 1979.

THE 'VALLEY' ALWAYS IN THE LEAD

ONE OF THE MOST ICONIC IMAGES OF ROCK CLIMBING
HISTORY: BILL WESTBAY, JIM BRIDWELL AND JOHN
LONG AT THE FOOT OF EL CAP AFTER THE FIRST ONE-
DAY ASCENT OF THE NOSE, 1975.

In that same year, *The Nose* on El Capitan was finally climbed in the course of a single day. Still a legendary objective for most climbers, *Nose in a day* cleared the way for speed climbing of which this route is the archetype. The main protagonist of this first, Jim Bridwell, known as 'The Bird', is the living symbol of everything the American climbing scene could offer at the time. During his long career of more than four decades as a climber and mountaineer, he has tackled most of the routes on the big walls of Yosemite (*Triple Direct*, *Pacific Ocean Wall*, *Sea of Dreams*, *Zenyatta Mondatta*, to mention but a few), as well as others in the Himalaya, Patagonia and Alaska; always technical projects demanding maximum commitment. His desire for simplicity is based on the precepts of his mentor Frank Sacherer.

Girls too were present in this slice of history but, reading the stories about the Golden Age of the 1960s and 1970s in the cult book *Camp 4*, the Valley seems to have been a very macho place. At first, like the surfing girls on the beach, girls used to wait at the bottom of the rock face for their 'warriors' to return. In those years El Capitan was anything but a holiday resort: it offered a minimum of 30 pitches, crazy weather conditions, aid-climbing that was often dangerous and uncomfortable belays and bivouacs, especially before the invention of modern harnesses and the development of portaledge hanging tents. Nevertheless some of girls made the long journey, at first to accompany their man. This was how Beverly Johnson became the first woman to leave her mark on El Cap in 1973. Having climbed *The Nose* with her then boyfriend, she persuaded another young female climber, much less experienced than herself, Sybille Hechtel, to join her in attempting the *Triple Direct*, a royal connection between the *Nose*, *Muir Wall* and *Salathé Wall*. Hoisting their big rucksack was quite an epic experience, as was finding the way on a route which was little climbed at the time. To lighten the rucksack, every day the girls would chuck out some equipment. Finally on the seventh day they reached the top, so becoming the first female roped party to climb a major route on El Cap. Later Beverley Johnson also made some very serious aid-climbing routes with Charlie Porter. Her moment of glory came in 1978 when she completed the first female solo of *Dihedral Wall* in 10 days. A woman alone in this vertical vastness was a concept which undoubtedly inspired many female climbers, including a certain Lynn Hill. Beverly Johnson sadly died in a heli-skiing accident in 1994.

In 1977 an event occurred in the microcosm of the Valley which was worthy of the best thrillers. A small plane had crashed higher up in the mountains. It was carrying packages of Columbian marijuana and the authorities rushed to the scene to recover as much as possible. But winter had arrived early and was particularly harsh, so some of the marijuana was left behind while the authorities waited for better weather. Alerted by rumours, all the locals who could venture through the snow and ice (including the climbers, of course), set off on a clandestine winter expedition. Suddenly and as if by magic their lifestyle changed from conditions of near-homelessness to that of a nouveau riche consumer society. Their philosophy of a 'spartan' lifestyle was dealt a severe blow but more like frivolous grasshoppers than industrious ants, the money from selling the marijuana swiftly burnt holes in their pockets and life returned to normal on the banks of the River Merced.

HEADING FOR THE EIGHTH GRADE

As the revolution of the 1980s approached, in 1978 Ray Jardine broke the legendary barrier of the 5.13 grade with the stripy crack of the *Phoenix* in a style which is still rejected by the locals: he practised the moves and left his fiendish Friends in place in order to make a complete ascent. For posterity, rather than the few holds he carved into *The Nose*, it is better to remember his great contribution to the development of equipment. This aeronautical engineer was the inventor of 'Friends', the invaluable, innovative mechanical camming device which first came on the market in 1978 under the name SLCD (Spring-Loaded Camming Devices). In climbing the *Phoenix,* he used them secretly. Having patented the device, he launched it commercially, then sold the patent to Wild Country which turned it into a worldwide success. Giving up climbing, Jardine first bought a yacht, then in the last few years became one of the gurus of the 'Lightweight Hiking' movement, advocating very long hikes with as little equipment as possible.

At the same time, two visionaries, Mark Hudon and Max Jones, tackled the major historic routes of the Valley (*Salathé*, *The Nose* and *Mount Watkins*), trying systematically to free climb them, or at least to do as much as possible without artificial aid or nuts. 'Free as can be', as they put it in their famous article 'Long, Hard and Free' which appeared in the *Mountain* Magazine in 1981.

The 1970s ended beautifully with Toni Yaniro who climbed the closed dihedral of *Grand Illusion* on Sugarloaf in July 1979. The severity of the rating, 5.13b/c is equivalent to the F8a/8a+, in other words the first 8th grade route in the world, does not reveal the controversy and scepticism current at the time. A young outsider, 18 years old, Toni favoured extreme muscular training (pull-ups and so on) and in particular, working on custom built wooden replicas of the difficult sections of climbs. What seems quite normal now was not so at the time: a climber would fall, descend again and immediately pull the rope through, starting again from the bottom. By *hangdogging*, that is by practising moves in a fluid sequence mostly belayed from the top, he did not receive the recognition of the other Californian climbers at the time, who were 'full of their superiority over the rest of the world and very condescending towards them', as Toni puts it today.

PAGE 88:

ABOVE: THE REVOLUTIONARY FRIEND.

BELOW: THANKS TO HIS INVENTION, RAY JARDINE

OPENS *PHOENIX*, 5.13A, YOSEMITE, 1978.

—

PAGE 89:

TONI YANIRO CLIMBING HIS GREATEST ACHIEVEMENT,

GRAND ILLUSION, SUGARLOAF, 5.13B/C, 1979.

THE REVOLUTION OF BOULDERING

In bouldering, John Gill's spirit and performances attracted numerous followers. Among these were two names which are sadly almost unknown: Pete Cleveland and Jim Holloway. The former, almost completely anonymously, repeated several of Gill's exploits in the 1960s, particularly in the Black Hills and he opened new classics. As Gill points out with amusement, Cleveland did not like the gymnastic programmes of the master: 'It is important to avoid the kind of training which makes you put on muscle because the aim is to remain as light as possible. The fingers are the weakest link between climber and rock and the direct practising of the difficulty is the best exercise for them.' Being a scientist by profession, he always saw climbing as a leisure activity. Nevertheless, many climbers such as Fred Nicole credit Cleveland with the first 8th grade in history, *Phlogiston* at Devil's Lake in 1977. The route is still rated 5.13a/b (or V9 - see bouldering grades below) first climbed with a top-rope but later as a highball (long boulder problem with no ropes but mats underneath).

Holloway had a more radical lifestyle and he lived in Boulder, Colorado, where in the 1970s he devoted his life entirely to climbing. He started bouldering very young, benefiting from Gill's advice and teaching, particularly his interest in dynamic movements, applying them to his great height (1.90 m). Two 'problems' helped transform him into a legend. The first was *Trice*, which dates from 1975 and was not repeated until 2007. When it was opened, the current system of V numerical grades, popularised in the 1990s by John Sherman, did not exist. Holloway had his own personal rating: JH easy, average or hard. Today *Trice* is rated V12 (or F8a+) according to those who repeated the route: 'V12 is the correct rating, rather high up the ladder. It would probably be V13 in Hueco because is certainly as hard as a V13 in Hueco.' Even better, *Slapshot*, which required two years of trying and special training, also remained unrepeated for 30 years and it too is grade V13.

On the other side of the world, Australia was not to be outdone. Anglo-Saxon influences soon led it to free climbing. Arapiles is an enormous quartzite rock formation to the north-east of Melbourne, Australia which boasts one of the most beautiful rock faces in the world. The Australian rating system is the simplest and the most pragmatic starting at 1 then another one point is added for each increase of difficulty. In March 1975 the maximum was 21 (F6c) when 'Hot Henry' Barber arrived.

Barber revolutionised the norms and revived Australian climbing by achieving twelve 22 and seven 23 climbs, while also removing aid on existing routes. He felt he was on the threshold of 24 and even attempted *Maniac Depressive*, a potential 25 (F7b). On these routes, Barber rejected pitons and bolts as means of protection. When he fell, he descended and pulled the rope down before trying again. His concept of climbing had a decisive influence on local climbers in that he brought modern free climbing to Australia.

THE EULOGY OF FALLING

In the United States, Britain, Australia and East Germany, climbing had long been free. Each had its own rules and each had exceeded the threshold of the French seventh grade and all these Eldorados persuaded French climbers to think again. Inspired by the American legends and their own trips to the United States and Britain, French climbers became aware of the enormous enjoyment to be had from free climbing. Thanks to the development of climbing equipment (including thinner, more dynamic ropes), the last great climbing taboo had been completely removed; falling was more than permitted, it had become indispensable to progress and pushing back the limits. As moves were analysed, enabling difficulties to be deconstructed, progress became all the quicker.

A pioneer of this development, Jean-Claude Droyer would be the first to refine this concept of free climbing. Born in Paris, he cut his teeth at Fontainebleau and on the Burgundy rock faces but soon he focused on the high peaks and north faces of Mont Blanc. In 1971, at the age of 24, he made the first solo (self-belayed) climb of the *Directe américaine* on the Drus; a great achievement. Subsequently he concentrated on the pursuit of pure difficulty on rock. Numerous stays in the US and Britain convinced him of the need for a complete change, having seen the damage caused by pitons which damaged the rock and distorted the reality of the difficulties. To practice what he preached, JCD deliberately chose historic icons such as the *Comici* (opened in 1978) and the *Cassini* (opened in 1979) routes on the Tre Cime in the Dolomites. His achievements have both a historical and a sporting perspective. He demonstrated that these routes were climbable in another way, thus promoting 'clean climbing', using nuts and removing excessive pitons. It was this last aspect, combined with his provocative character, often perceived as arrogant, which attracted a lot of criticism in France in spite of the support of official personalities such as Lucien Devies ('A new ethic is necessary to ensure that joy survives in the Alps'). Scouring the rock faces in the mid-1970s, he opened routes and reached the seventh grade; but in doing so he removed all unnecessary fixed protections, particularly in Le Saussois. In doing this without previous consultation, he caused numerous controversies, particularly among the older climbing icons who could not understand the changes which were taking place in the discipline.

Physical threats, a vandalised car, defaced routes (such as the legendary graffiti of the *Triomphe d'Éros* in the Verdon), this was the price that Jean-Claude Droyer, or *Jesus Christ Dardicule* as he was nicknamed by his southern denigrators, had to pay. Nonetheless, he had a great influence on the new generation who would break all the standards during the next decade and for many he remains the spiritual founder of modern free climbing in France.

PAGE 90:

ABOVE: PETER CLEVELAND.

CENTRE: JIM HOLLOWAY, BOULDERING GIANT.

BELOW: JIM HOLLOWAY ON HIS VISIONARY MASTER-PIECE, *TRICE*, V12, FLAGSTAFF MOUNTAIN, COLORADO, 1975.

—

PAGE 91 :

JEAN-CLAUDE DROYER IN *LES FRÈRES CARAMEL MOU*, 7A+, VERDON.

THE INSPIRATION
OF 'THE SEVENTH GRADE'

More generally, this revelation was inspired by a book which was already old at the time. Written in 1972 by Reinhold Messner, the leading protagonist of competitive climbing of the period, *The Seventh Grade* laid the foundation for new concepts. In it, Messner reflected on the problem of grading difficulty in rock climbing: 'While the sixth grade was seen almost 50 years ago as being the insuperable limit of human possibilities, it does not mean that this limit cannot be surpassed. The irremovable division into six grades of difficulty would mean that routes would have to be re-assessed (that is, downgraded) every 10 years. This chaos in the assessment of extreme difficulties can only increase and get worse in the future if the scale of difficulties is not left open at the top. It is equally presumptuous to claim that the sixth grade is the insuperable limit of free climbing. Of course, we are not dealing here with a scale of accurately measurable values but with assessments. Nevertheless I do not doubt that some climbers will be able to exceed the difficulties of today by several grades...'

So, Messner proposed the opening of a seventh grade which he believed was indispensable to ensure the harmonious development of climbing as a sport. He also emphasised the importance of specific training: 'My training at the time was essentially made up of two parts: first, general preparation and secondly specific training to increase the strength of the fingers. Over the years, we have discovered, at Vieille-Scie, a possible traverse, a circuit which could be repeated until the fingers became stiff and one falls; not serious falls because ones feet are usually only 20 centimetres from the ground. The circuit is about 80 metres long and, in my case, I would continue traversing until I 'fell' from 'exhaustion'.'

Of course Messner did not invent training and there is no doubt that John Gill, for instance, was infinitely superior so far as strength was concerned. Nevertheless, Messner was the first 'classic' mountaineer to systematise training and to write about it.
'The concept of performance and of success also play a major part in this constant pursuit of grander, more difficult routes. The notion of 'success' is partly responsible for the growing trend of climbing as a sport, insofar as the desire to practise this activity usually depends on the success achieved. Lack of success reduces interest in practising the activity. I disapprove of rock-climbing being part of the Olympic Games, climbing against the clock, being judged by points, in other words competitive climbing in which climbers are directly compared but, on the other hand, I am fascinated by the idea of the seventh grade of difficulty. Only then will climbing continue to make progress, progress that is in principle unlimited.'

Messner's visionary concepts did not go unnoticed. In France, it was Jean-Claude Droyer who really opened the debate in an article published in 1975 in *La Montagne et Alpinisme* entitled *Aimer la montagne ('The love of mountains')*. After several trips to the

United States and Britain, Jean-Claude became aware of the great potential of the French climbing areas and he was convinced that 'great mountaineering' is going nowhere with all the technological aids and winter-roped parties: 'A new kind of progress could be made if pitons were only used for belaying and no longer as a matter of course to advance. A new approach with enormous potential…' In the mountains he advocated the removal of pitons on rock faces he thought were excessively equipped, such as the Bonatti Pillar, the East Face of the Grand Capucin and the Walker Spur.

'May mountaineering arouse enough passion amongst climbers that they choose this path, the purest but also the most demanding.' On rock faces he advocated the use of 'Fontainebleau-style' climbing shoes which at the time were not widespread. His provocative mind was clearly revealed when he tackled the case of Le Saussois, the Parisians' favourite school: 'The barely concealed bitterness of some ageing virtuosos was not able to prevent future progress and the young continued to apply their technique and their boldness to develop a more refined, more demanding style of free climbing. And those who most strongly oppose any change are often regulars who only climb in the local massif and are therefore unaware of other climbing areas, especially abroad. The fact that they focus exclusively on 'their' massif easily leads to routine, which is just a step away from sclerosis.' Reaction to these words was not long in coming. Again in *La Montagne*, at the beginning of the 1976, a certain Jean-Marc Troussier of Marly-le-Roy replied in an article entitled *Morale des seigneurs et morale des esclaves ('The ethic of the rulers and the ethic of the slaves')*: 'But who is going to impose his standards? This elite, of course! If I manage with three pitons, others must and can do the same. Fortunately, not everyone wants this, or we would see a world dominated by the climate of the elite and by the specialists, a climate which exists in some climbing schools in the shape of approved rallies (competitions with marked-out climbing routes), timed, a beautiful freedom or a self-discipline or a self-repression, depending on how you look at it. But most climbers prefer the fame and glory of a summit they want to reach at all costs. This does not prevent them from finding over-equipped routes and trying to return them to their original condition; to achieve this all they need to do is miss out some pitons and climb with *clogs*…' The most important thing is that the debate has started. It is interesting to note that most British and American climbers were now using soft French-made climbing shoes, the EB Super-Gratton, which paradoxically were not much used in France. This is clear from the full page advertisements for EB climbing shoes which appeared in *Mountain*. The manufacturer Edouard Bourdonneau received the French award for exports in 1975.

ABOVE: REINHOLD MESSNER TRAINING FOR FREE CLIMBING AT THE ROCCA PENDICE DURING THE MIDDLE OF THE 1960s.
BELOW: PIERRE ALLAIN REVOLUTIONISED ROCK-CLIMBING ALMOST MORE THAN ANY OTHER INVENTION. MAYBE YOU SHOULD GIVE THE FROGGIE MORE APPLAUSE.

Slowly but surely free climbing was taking off and at last the great absentees in this story, women, were beginning to make an appearance.

03

THE AMAZING DECADE

AH! THE 1980s.

FINALLY, BELL-BOTTOM TROUSERS AND HIPPY SHIRTS WERE OUT WHILST IN CAME LYCRA TIGHTS AND FLASHY VESTS. WAS IT REALLY AN IMPROVEMENT? IN RETROSPECT, SOME 30 YEARS LATER, I'M INCLINED TO DOUBT IT...

THE DECADE OF THE 1980S SAW THE TRANSITION BETWEEN A KIND OF CLIMBING 'PREHISTORY' AND THE GLOBALISED CLIMBING OF TODAY. IT ALSO COINCIDED WITH THE PASSING OF THE BATON TO NEW GENERATIONS, WHO PROVED MORE OPEN TO THE EVOLUTION OF ATHLETIC SPORT CLIMBING.

PAGE 94:

PATRICK BERHAULT FREEING LE *BOMBÉ DE PICHENI-BULE*, F7B/C, VERDON, 1980.

–

PAGE 96:

LEFT: GÉRARD MERLIN, HIPPY LOOK, 1980!

RIGHT: IN 1985, THE DRESS CODE REMAINS TERRIBLE...

ANOTHER FRENCH NEW WAVE

The first year of the 1980s was particularly fertile in France. While Berhault was linking solo climbs like pearls in the Verdon (*Solanuts, Mangoustine, Barjots, Roumagaou*), the first F7b climbs were seeing the light: *L'Ange* in Le Saussois by Laurent Jacob, *La Gougousse* in Buoux by Jean-Claude Droyer and the *Boulevard à Mathieux* (Saffres) by Benoit Grison, someone who has been unfairly overlooked by history.

Benoit Grison died in 1986 at the age of 25, alone on Annapurna. In appearance he was the last person one would expect to see solo climbing the most austere rock faces in the world. Frail and childlike, whenever I met him I always thought he looked about 15. Yet, from Alaska to the Andes, his boldness was breathtaking. In 1980 he free climbed the *Directe Américaine* on the Dru with Jean-François Peyroux and soon he had built up an incredible list of achievements. His rock-climbing career was short but for him, free-climbing was an inevitable activity, in the same way as it was for Christophe Profit and Eric Escoffier.

In the autumn, Patrick Berhault solved a longstanding problem in the Verdon: *Le Bombé de Pichenibule*, F7b/c; the lower roof which took on a name of its own. A month later his friend Patrick Edlinger repeated it. Maurizio 'Manolo' Zanolla, the most prolific Italian climber of the time, repeated it on-sight after having failed to do so by a hair's breadth, with a fall of tens of metres. The next year he opened one of the first F7c+ routes, *Il mattino dei maghi* on the rock face of Totoga and, after a long career, he finally joined the select circle of the ninth grade at the age of 50.

While the arguments and antagonisms between the north of France and the southern part of the country were still raging as a result of Jean-Claude Droyer's radical concepts and ruthless removal of pitons, two different events which went almost unnoticed proved to be the portents of profound changes.
The first of these events was the organisation of an international gathering of female climbers in England. This was when the name of a young Parisian physiotherapist, Catherine Destivelle, first came to public notice. As a climber she stood out from the rest because of her boldness and self-confidence. Although girls such as Françoise Quintin and Françoise Lepron, known as *Snoopinette*, were beginning to toy with the seventh grade, it was thanks to Catherine Destivelle and, across the Atlantic, Lynn Hill, that the macho perception of climbing as an exclusively male domain began to change.

The other event was the documentary film *Overdon* made in the Gorges du Verdon by Jean-Paul Janssen with the two Patricks, Berhault and Edlinger. An account of an era, this film was also the start of climbing being covered by the media and the leading participants saw how film would enable them to pass on and share their passion. His meeting with Patrick Edlinger played a decisive part in both their lives: *La vie au bout des doigts* ('Life at your finger tips') and *Opera vertical* were the result. *Overdon* was followed a year later by Laurent Chevallier's *Dévers*, again featuring Patrick Berhault.

ABOVE: BENOÎT GRISON (1963–1986), PIONEER OF FREE-CLIMBING IN HIGH PLACES.
CENTRE: ÉRIC ESCOFFIER (1960–1998), A GYMNAST AT FIRST, THEN A TOP MOUNTAINEER TILL THE TOP OF THE WORLD.
BELOW: THE ITALIAN ICON MAURIZIO 'MANOLO' ZANOLLA ON HIS *ULTIMO MOVIMENTO*, F8B, TOTOGA, 1986.

PATRICK BERHAULT
A STAR IS LOST

For people of my generation, Patrick Berhault first appeared as the forerunner of a new kind of mountaineer and climber, the type whom the 'oldies' called the 'mutants'. My first memory of him was in an article in the 11th issue of the first French independent climbing magazine, *Alpinisme et Randonnée* which we used to devour from beginning to end; the piece was called *A star is born*. In 1979, before the Internet or Facebook, he was an inspiration to many. Youth and boldness are always fascinating and the author of the article often compared Berhault to predecessors such as Winkler and Buhl. In one Alpine summer, this 21-year old from Nice made a breathtaking number of climbs in record times; an achievement most people would be happy to achieve in a lifetime. And, evidently the gods were smiling on him when, early in his career, he miraculously survived a fall of over 800 metres on Mont Pelvoux, enveloped in a protective cocoon of powdery snow.

A little later, taking stock of his prolific season, the young prodigy still insisted on the daily training which gave him confidence: 'Every day, I do 100 pull-ups, a 100 leg presses, 50 on the abs, 50 push-ups... I even run races. It no longer tires me out.' Berhault shortened the times previously taken for the classic difficult climbs and what was most shocking at the time was that he climbed 'without a rucksack and with his EB climbing shoes round his neck, even on the North Face of Les Droites'. Later, although better known for his Alpine achievements, he remained above all a climber, where analysis, lightness and speed in linking routes were the signature of his style. He had read and re-read *The 7th Grade*: Reinhold Messner had inaugurated mountaineering with very light equipment but the Nice-born climber took this even further, lighter and faster, enthusiastically followed by Benoit Grison, Christophe Profit and Éric Escoffier.

It was in the Verdon at the end of the 1970s that Berhault discovered free climbing, following the visits of Ron Fawcett and Pete Livesey. His solo enchainements were already breathtaking, climbing, then down-climbing, one after the other like pearls on a string; then *Le Bombé* de *Pichenibule, La Haine* and the routes of the Loubière and Saint-Jeannet with grades that were alarming. Finally came his masterpiece in 1987, the *Toit d'Auguste*, which required specific preparation in the same way as Güllich had prepared for *Wall Street* and *Action Directe*.

Une étoile est née

De temps à autre, une nouvelle étoile naît dans le firmament de l'alpinisme. Parfois, c'est une étoile filante, qui traverse le ciel à une vitesse fulgurante, puis disparaît en laissant le souvenir d'exploits incompréhensibles d'audace : Georg Winkler, Hermann Buhl étaient de ceux-là, du rang des alpinistes si étonnamment au-dessus de la catégorie des bons grimpeurs qu'ils dépassaient tous leurs contemporains d'une bonne longueur. Aujourd'hui, comme toujours, nombreux sont les excellents grimpeurs ; mais *le* meilleur du moment, celui qui dépasse tout le monde, sans contestation possible ?

Et bien, il semble que pour cet été 79, Chamonix ait trouvé son phénomène en la personne de Patrick Bérhault, 22 ans. Dans la vallée, on ne parle plus que de lui, et pourtant l'on ne voit guère son nom dans les journaux. Il faut dire que son palmarès a de quoi laisser plus d'un besogneux de l'exploit et de la première rêveur. Suivez bien, parce que j'en connais pas mal qui se contenteraient d'achever cette liste de course non pas en un mois, mais en une vie : le 26 juin, le Super-Couloir du Mont-Blanc du Tacul (3 h 30) ; le 30, la face ouest de Blaitière avec Philippe Langlois ; le 2 juillet, la Rébuffat-Terray aux Pèlerins ; le 5, la Davaille aux Droites (5 h 30) ; le 8, la face nord du Pilier d'Angle : d'abord la voie Dufour-Fréhel, sortie par la Boivin-Vallençant (3 h pour la face, 2 h 30 pour l'arête de Peuterey) ; le 10, le pilier Carpentier aux Grands Charmoz (4 ou 5 heures) ; les 15-16, une nouvelle voie aux Drus avec les frères Rémy, entre la voie Allain et la voie des Guides : TD +, libre, 12 pitons, 15 coinceurs ; le 23, le couloir nord des Drus (6 h 30) ; le 27, la voie Bonatti-Zapelli au Pilier d'Angle (1 h 50 pour la voie, 2 h pour l'arête de Peuterey) ; le 28, la seconde ascension d'une voie ouverte par les frères Rémy aux Grands Charmoz, entre le pilier Carpentier et la voie Coqueugniot, avec Françoise Quintin. Ensuite, *descente en escalade* du pilier Carpentier.

Voilà. Evidemment, tout ça en solo, sauf bien entendu quand est signalé le compagnon de cordée. Les temps suffisent, on l'espère, à donner la mesure 5 h 30 pour la Davaille, cela fait presque du 200 m à l'heure... La grande classe, une aisance souveraine dans les voies les plus dures du massif du Mont-Blanc. Et rappelez-vous, ce n'est pas la première fois que nous vous parlons de Patrick Bérhault : l'été dernier, il avait battu (involontairement) un record de chute au Pelvoux, avec 800 m de dégringolade. Nous vous avons aussi cité son nom à propos du Verdon, où il a enchaîné en solo plusieurs itinéraires dans la journée. D'ailleurs, les grandes voies du Mont-Blanc ne semblent pas plus l'impressionner que les falaises du Verdon, il les aborde de manière exactement semblable. Alpinistes, mes frères, qui croyez encore que le couloir nord des Drus est une « grande course » et non une voie d'école, asseyez-vous et tenez bien votre numéro d'*Alpinisme et Randonnée*. Toutes ces solitaires, Bérhault les a fait *sans sac* : corde en bandoulière, quelques pitons à la taille, un bout de chocolat dans la poche, les E.B. autour du cou (parfaitement, même pour la Davaille !). Là-dedans, pratiquement jamais d'assurage, sauf une longueur dans le couloir nord des Drus. Pas par volonté de faire une performance, non : simplement, Bérhault se sent bien, voilà tout ; il n'a nullement la sensation de prendre des risques anormaux. Et il considère que sa sécurité à lui, c'est la rapidité. La classe, je vous disais. Rien d'étonnant qu'il marque une prédilection pour le solo, plus élégant et plus rapide.

Pourtant, comme tous les gens doués, Bérhault travaille beaucoup : entraînement régulier, gymnastique et footing tous les jours, escalade aussi souvent que possible. On le voit souvent, paraît-il, le soir à la Pierre d'Orthaz. Il a d'ailleurs conscience qu'il a encore des progrès à faire, et qu'il peut faire encore mieux. Il est vrai qu'à 22 ans, il a encore tout l'avenir devant lui. Bérhault avait fait la Brenva à 16 ans, mais il s'était ensuite arrêté de grimper ; il a recommencé il y a deux ans seulement... On risque de reparler de Patrick Bérhault !

Patrick Bérhault.

D.R.

Ambitious on the rock face but against competitions, he was happy to sign the *Manifeste des 19* which outlawed competition and he was one of the few to stick to it. Climber, mountaineer, instructor and even farmer in turn, his reluctance to give precise grades was undoubtedly the result of his artistic nature, which later found expression in the Danse Escalade movement; he was a great admirer of Rudolf Nureyev. His *Blues Brothers* duo with Robert Cortijo will forever remain an unrivalled performance of gymnastic choreography. This same spirit is also seen in his films *Metamorphosis* (1987) and *Grimpeur étoile* (1989). Extremely supple in spite of his

stocky appearance, he inspired awe with his rugged features, his calm way of speaking and his muscularity. His endurance and speed were legendary, even at the top of Everest and his nickname 'ET' says it all.

In the collective memory, his name will always be linked with Patrick Edlinger. They come across each other in France in the late 1970s. This was a period between the end of 'traditional' mountaineering and the birth of climbing as a sport, so it was then not easy to leave school and devote your life to rocks and mountains. When they first met in Nice in 1978, Patrick

Berhault was 21 years old and Patrick Edlinger 18. As Edlinger explained 30 years later, 'We had the same vision of life, we made the same choices.'

Together they opened routes in the South of France and climbed Alpine rock faces at remarkable speed; then, as soon as they had climbed down, they immediately launched into a punishing routine of push-ups and pull-ups. Their mantra was simple: never a day without training. Overcoming the lack of equipment which gives this period an aura of nostalgia, they 'borrowed' a car to go to the mountains, slept in freezing cellars instead of hotels and mastered the art of shoplifting in supermarkets to eat, escapades driven by the passion and audaciousness of youth.

Berhault was inclined more towards mountaineering whilst his comrade-in-arms remained passionate about rock-climbing. Nonetheless, they met in the mountains in the winter of 1978, making a legendary round trip in the Oisans region where they climbed the austere and little frequented *Voie des Plaques* on the North Face of the Ailefroide Occidentale: over 1,000 metres of icy slopes, punctuated by a sinister rocky outcrop. The climb from Ailefroide and back was completed in 23 hours. Given the length of the approach in winter, it is likely that belays and runners were reduced to a minimum.
As a result of his new fame, in 1980 Patrick Berhault was invited to the Himalaya by Yannick Seigneur, a leading mountaineer and Himalayan climber over the two previous decades. The objective was the Rupal Face of Nanga Parbat (8,125m), the highest mountain face in the world extending 4,500 metres above Base Camp. This was the same route that Messner had conquered 10 years earlier, which cost his brother his life. But Berhault was inexperienced at very high altitudes: he soon fell victim to acute mountain sickness and had to be evacuated urgently.

At that time, Patrick Edlinger was still enjoying the mountains but he had become more interested again in the sunny limestone rock faces of the South of France. Although their joint adventures had come to an end, they remained in touch and the press sometimes brought their legendary roped climbs back to life. When *La Vie au bout des doigts* appeared, Edlinger immediately became world famous, whilst his colleague Berhault's reputation was confined to a specialist public. Then in the early 2000s Edlinger gave way to younger generations while Berhault's activities were in the limelight. He devised a new concept: Alpine journeys consisting of crossing peaks or rock faces in a massif following a theme decided in advance. From August 2000 to February 2001, he traversed the whole length of the Alps on foot. To start his tour, he decided to repeat the roped party of his youth with his friend Edlinger. From the mountain of Triglav in Slovenia to the crossing of the Dolomites, the two men, now in their 40s, linked together a succession of celebrated routes (Cima Ovest, Cima Grande, Civetta, Marmolada and the redoubtable route of *Le Poisson*, Crozzon di Brenta) like mountain goats, travelling between them on foot even in the pouring rain.

This joint adventure seemed to make Patrick Edlinger relive the past: 'When we met again, it was as if we had parted only the day before, the same conversations, the same habits'. Berhault interpreted this as 'a wish to share things again, just a story of friendship' and while climbing one of the rock faces he suddenly said, as if he had a premonition: "We mustn't let time slip by, it is so precious."

Towards the end of Berhault's life, less focused on pure climbing, he contributed to the new media coverage which he had missed out on when young. He had the aura but not the fame he deserved. On 28th April 2004, tragedy struck on the slopes of the Täschorn in Switzerland. Maybe he was in too much of a hurry to complete his new tour, linking all of the 82 Alpine 4,000 metre peaks. A cornice of snow broke beneath him and, his climbing companion, Philippe Magnin saw him fall to his death. Berhault's fatal obstinacy was perhaps his undoing. He wanted to succeed at any price, believing that by doing so it would be easier to organise his next project, a gigantic traverse of the Andes from north to south. But the snow which had saved his life on Mont Pelvoux 30 years earlier got its own back when it gave way beneath his feet.

There are routes whose heights bear no relation to their historical importance. This is the case with *La Haine* at La Loubière and *Chimpanzodrome* in Le Saussois, the former being eight metres high and the latter barely six metres higher and yet, in the early 1980s, they marked the start of a new era in France and the fact that one was in the far south and the other in the north of the country only reinforced their symbolic opposition. Of the two, it was *Chimpanzodrome* which attracted most attention. Situated on the 'summit' of Le Saussois, it is a smooth, overhanging limestone bulge, displaying the range of white to grey-black shades that are characteristic of the local limestone along the banks of the Yonne.

The possibilities of the route were first spotted by Jean-Claude Droyer, true to form in his visionary role of the time. He had even jokingly named it the *Berostakhano*,

THE ROUGH LIFE OF A PRO CLIMBER: PATRICK BERHAULT 'TUCKED-IN' IN HIS SLEEPING BAG DURING A BIVVY IN A RUIN, VERDON.

an ironic tribute to the achievements and especially the Stakhanovite training of Patrick Berhault. Unfortunately Droyer did not have the necessary physical resources for this very gymnastic climb. From the end of the 1980, other big Fontainebleau names ('Bleausards') such as Jérôme Jean-Charles and Jacky Godoffe have attempted it but in spite of a few clean holes, improved by years of aid-climbing pitons, the first free climb was still waiting to happen. In due course this route would become *Chimpanzodrome*. At Le Saussois, April is the ideal period for this kind of challenge; winter is over but the air is still cool. The man who felt ready to tackle *Chimpanzodrome* was Jean-Pierre Bouvier, by then nicknamed *La Mouche*. In spite of being so short (1.62 metres), his fingers worked wonders. At the beginning of the year he had already made the first ascent of the *Médius* on Montagne Sainte Victoire, an incredible climb on a slab 40 metres high, first climbed by Guyomar, which, although rated F7b+ by *La Mouche*, is perhaps still the hardest F7c in the whole of France. Swiftly, Bouvier top-roped the moves, then the sections. Using two ropes with two belayers to minimise the risk of falling to the ground, he was close to succeeding on his second attempt at a lead. Then a recalcitrant jammed rope at the finish prevented him completing the climb. But the next day he did it and this says it all about his potential, because in just two days he had made the first ascent of a world-class top level climb.

In *Le 7ème degré en France* ('The Seventh Grade in France', *Montagnes* magazine, June 1981 issue), Jean-Pierre Bouvier clearly spelled out the new rules of the game and listed 39 seventh grade routes. And yet, *Chimpanzodrome* was not the first route of this level in France. A few weeks earlier, Patrick Berhault had set his sights on a white

LEFT: JEAN-PIERRE BOUVIER FREES *CHIMPANZODROME*, F7C+, LE SAUSSOIS, 1981.

RIGHT: STILL IN SAUSSOIS AND 'LA MOUCHE' AGAIN WITH HIS OWN *SHEIK YERBOUTI*, F7C+, 1982.

bulge in one of his favourite climbing sites, La Loubière, in the mountains overlooking Monaco. The route was very short, the size of a modern highball with a violent lunge on a vertical flat which involved a big compression effort. Many unsuccessful attempts followed and this is probably why the route was called *La Haine*, meaning 'hatred'.
Once Berhault had reached the flat, the next movements were just a formality and the toughest route in France and potentially in Europe, was born. Following the very tight French rating system where F7b was already the top, Berhault proposed a rating of F7b+ which would later more reasonably be raised to F7c+. The eighth grade was imminent but it would not be in that year.

Since then, these two 'milestones' have become classics. In 1985 *La Haine* was climbed solo by Alain Ghersen, probably the best boulderer in the world. As for *Chimpanzodrome*, it was another year before it was repeated by Alain Le Bihan and, a few minutes later, by J-B Tribout. The first solo ascent was by Marc Le Menestrel (1984) while the first on-sight was by Jerry Moffatt in the same year: 'I had hitchhiked from England with Ben Moon, then we had slept for a whole week at the foot of the cliff in spite of the cold and damp. I had decided to try *Chimpan* on my birthday. To be as light as possible, I only took a harness belt and an 8.5 mm rope. I was so excited and over-motivated that I literally ran up the route. That same evening we were hitchhiking south and when night fell we found ourselves stuck by the autoroute. It was snowing, I climbed into my sleeping bag and slept on the verge, the evening of my happiest birthday ever.' In 2001 Jean-Pierre Bouvier carried out a solo climb of *Chimpan'* to celebrate the 20th anniversary of his first ascent.

...AND BUSY TIMES IN EUROPE

In May 1981 the German magazine *SportScheck* organised an international meeting at Konstein, an obscure German rock face. Among those present were Ron Fawcett, Wolfgang Güllich, J-C Droyer, Marco Troussier, Jean-Pierre Bouvier and Laurent Jacob, all dressed in red jackets, the colour of the sponsor. The guest of honour, John Bachar, wanted to demonstrate to the Europeans that he was indeed 'the best climber in the world' and, verging on the theatrical, he was more than happy to hang repeatedly from overhangs with one arm to impress the public. Then, in the Frankenjura, he opened an unconquered route which was provocatively renamed *Chasin' the Trane* (a reference to the saxophonist John Coltrane). In the Verdon he top-roped *Le Bombé de Pichenibule*, rating it 5.12+. Nevertheless this was a kind of last gasp for American climbing and its champion. Blocked by a conservative ethic in the face of European pragmatism, the US merely looked on as the level in Europe was about to shoot upwards. Just a few metres to the left of *Chasin' the Trane* was *Wall Street*, which would be the first F8c and set back a few dozen metres, *Action Directe* awaited its moment of glory.

As time went by the climbing atmosphere became increasingly excited, especially in France. The English-speaking countries were still bogged down in questions about ethics, equipment, refusal to use bolts and so on. Spain and Italy were not yet exploiting their full potential. Only Germany was on the same wavelength; hence the creation of *Boulder*, the first (albeit short-lived) magazine devoted exclusively to climbing as a sport. But in spite of climbers such as Wolfgang Güllich, Kurt Albert, Wolfgang Kraus and others who followed in the footsteps of the late-lamented Reinhard Karl, the German climbing scene was still small while in France, a whole new generation of ambitious climbers appeared, unencumbered by complex ethics.

In 1982, driven by competitiveness, grades moved upwards so suddenly that there was soon an F8a+ (*Autoroute du soleil* in Buoux, F7c+ today) and even an F8b (*Fenrir* in the Verdon, F7c+ today) in France. But this surge was soon corrected by those making repeats and which meant that a 'real' eight was still awaited in France.

LEFT: KONSTEIN MEETING, MAY 1981, FROM LEFT TO RIGHT: HEINZ MARIACHER, JÜRG VON KÄNEL, MARCO TROUSSIER, JEAN-CLAUDE DROYER, RON FAWCETT, JEAN-PIERRE BOUVIER AND JOHN BACHAR.
RIGHT: 1981 AGAIN, KURT ALBERT (1954–2010) COVERING THE FIRST ISSUE OF *BOULDER*, ON *SAUTANZ*, FRANKENJURA, FIRST GERMAN IX- OR F7B+.
—

PAGE 105:
THE YOUNG GERMAN STEFAN GLOWACZ CLAIMING THE SECOND ASCENT OF *THE FACE*, X- OR F8A/8A+, ALTMÜHLTAL.

LEFT: THE GREAT KURT ALBERT FREE SOLOING *FIGHT GRAVITY* (8+ UIAA OR F7A+), RICHARD-WAGNER-FELS, FRANKENJURA.

RIGHT: BELAYED BY JIBÉ TRIBOUT, ANTOINE LE MENESTREL MAKES HIS WAY ON THE TERRIBLE ONE-FINGER OF *CRÉPINETTE* AT THE EAUX-CLAIRES, ONE OF THE FIRST F8A IN FRANCE DURING SPRING 1983.

–

PAGE 106:

QUITE A PIECE OF HISTORY: RON FAWCETT AND HIS DETERMINED MOUSTACHE PERFORMING THE CRUX *OF SCHWERKRAFT* (IX- OR F7B+)AND BELAYED BY A SMILING WOLFGANG GÜLLICH! CASTELLWAND, ALTMÜHLTAL.

As to on-sight, Patrick Edlinger was the most successful, reaching F7c with the *Polka des ringards*, also in Buoux. At the time, 'on-sight' had a clear, precise meaning: no quickdraws in place, no prior inspection and no getting information from one's partner below. Under this regime, a few catastrophes were only avoided by a hair's breadth.

Between the end of 1982 and spring 1983, the epicentre of climbing returned to France. First there was the appearance of *La Vie au bout des doigts* ('*Life at your fingertips*'), a cleverly-titled documentary which was a great success worldwide. Patrick 'Le Blond' Edlinger became world-famous, as did climbing. Then in spring 1983 the first unquestionable F8a climbs took place. Edlinger made light of *Ca glisse au pays des merveilles* at Les Confines de Buoux, which he first climbed on a top-rope before tackling it in the lead. The route was first repeated by Marc Le Menestrel. It never became very popular because of the risk, there being just four anchors over 25 metres and several potential ground falls. It was abandoned altogether because Les Confines became off limits.

At Eaux-Claires near Angoulême, Fabrice Guillot overcame the bouldering problems of the *Crépinette* while Marc Le Menestrel, celebrating his 16th birthday, opened the *Rêve de papillon* in Buoux which is still very popular today. A little later, in Germany, it was a young Englishman who hit the headlines: Jerry Moffatt opened *The Face*, a very big F8a, perhaps the hardest route at the time. It was repeated the following year by an equally unknown 19-year-old, Stefan Glowacz.

PATRICK EDLINGER
...BEFORE HE BECAME 'LE BLOND'

In the minds of many, Patrick Edlinger is the very symbol of rock-climbing? Before he became one of the icons of the 1980s, celebrated for his public performances, Patrick Edlinger was already a promising young climber.

In Toulon, Robert Exertier was both his friend and his first photographer: 'I met Patrick Edlinger at the Ailefroide camp site in the summer of 1976. He was 16 and he was there with his parents and his sister. They always spent their summer holidays together, climbing and mountaineering as a family.

'It was then that I started climbing with him and continued to do so regularly for six years, so I have been able to follow his development. I lived near Toulon and Patrick lived at La Seyne, nearby. He learned to climb with his parents, then with Christian 'Kiki' Crespo and his friends who were part of the climbing group of the Toulon MJC (Maisons des Jeunes et de Culture). At the age of 13 he had applied for membership of the CAF (Club Alpin Français) in Toulon but he had been rejected because he was considered too young to climb. In the same year the members of the climbing group of the MJC accepted him and they soon realised that their new pupil was a prodigy with an exceptional gift.

At 16 he already knew how to climb naturally, automatically finding the best positions of the body and the perfect poise on the rock face and within a further year he was moving with incredible suppleness and fluidity. He already had all the qualities needed to become one of the best climbers but he was unaware of this because he had no one to compare himself with. He only discovered his potential gradually as he climbed. He decided to leave school and began climbing and training every day. After a year he had made incredible progress and reached the level of the best climbers. It was an extraordinary period: everything went right for him and he was surprised at his achievements. He was already very interested in the aesthetic aspect of movement. Anyone fortunate enough to climb with him could watch a superb display as he performed a magnificent choreography on

the rock, his movements looking easy and perfectly fluid so that it seemed as if he was making no effort at all. He combined an aesthetic approach to movement with perfect efficiency in the difficult passages. He was as interested in mountaineering as in rock-climbing and his aim was to become a mountain guide.

PAGE 108: FIRST PHOTO SHOOTING EVER FOR THE YOUNG PATRICK EDLINGER, 17 YEARS, LA PIADE, TOULON, 1977. PAGE 109: PATRICK EDLINGER WITH EBS AND HEADBAND ON *CAPOUERA*, F6C, BAOU DE 4 OURO, TOULON, 1981.

Since his roped companions from Toulon and Marseilles were not always available, he sometimes had to climb alone. At that time I was studying in Nice and I was also climbing with Patrick Berhault, whom I had met in Baou de Saint-Jeannet. Neither of the two Patricks was yet famous and they did not know each other. I thought it would be a good idea if they met and climbed together so they could share their enthusiasm, skills and experience and perhaps they would perform miracles together. In 1978, I arranged this meeting, during a climbing weekend at Saint-Jeannet with Patrick Edlinger, Hervé Pichoux and Nicolas Bergasse. We went to visit Patrick Berhault at his mother's house in Nice. Patrick Edlinger was then 18 years old and Patrick Berhault 21. Their first meeting went very well and they were immediately keen about the idea of climbing together, which they did for four years. Their joint achievements in the high mountains and rock faces were exceptional. During the winter of 1979/1980, they climbed the *Davaille* route on the North Face of Les Droites, the *Super Couloir* on Mont Blanc du Tacul (a winter first) and the *Voie des Plaques* on the North West Face of the Ailefroide Occidentale (a winter

first), each in record time. They remained friends all their lives. When they met, Berhault had muscular strength and endurance greater than that of any other climber, as well as unwavering willpower. He was already free climbing almost all the routes of Saint-Jeannet, including the *Mafia* which was the benchmark. Being three years older than Edlinger, he had that much more experience on rock faces and mountains. Edlinger was an expert in the art of finding the most delicate balance, of putting all his weight on minuscule footholds, of moving with incredible ease on the rock face and of reading it with exceptional skill. Under Berhault's influence, he understood that to make progress it was necessary to increase his strength and endurance. When training together, each shared his experience with the other. After 1982 and the success of his films, Patrick Edlinger chose to climb less often in the high mountains and to specialise in rock-climbing, the discipline at which he was best. His films show him climbing with sequences of magnificent movements carried out with perfect precision. He was not trying particularly hard to impress Jean-Paul Janssen's camera, it was just his normal way of climbing, as he did every day. He was an artist.'

Another witness of these early years was Gérard Merlin, known as 'Nate', who was then a famous climber in the Calanques (among others, he opened *Triple Direct*, F7a+, one of the first grade F7 climbs before 1980). In the autumn of 1979, the two of them went with a group of friends, including Robert Exertier, on their first journey to Yosemite. There they climbed classic routes: *Royal Arches*, *Middle Cathedral*, the *North West Face* of Half Dome and *Triple Direct* on El Capitan (hence the name of the route in the Calanques). 'We chose *Triple* because *The Nose* was too busy with other parties and since there were three of us with Hervé Pichoux, we drew lots to decide which sections each one of us would climb. Patrick drew *The Nose section*.' Having pitched their tent at Camp 4, they met Ron Kauk and were able to enjoy Bachar's 'circus act' which he performed on *Midnight Lightning* every evening at the same time. In spite of a few attempts, the boulder was still too hard for Edlinger but he was already well into his training period with Berhault so that every time Nate came across him, he saw his muscles were noticeably bigger.

The following year they set off together with Michel Ricard for the Hoggar Mountains. After a rough crossing of the Mediterranean in which they were dreadfully seasick, they drove to Tamanrasset at the wheel of an extremely ancient Peugeot 204 with 240,000 miles on the counter. Fortunately Nate, a future hill-climbing racing driver, was also a good mechanic and he plugged all the leaks. They made firsts on the Adaouada and the Stoppers. Nate climbed in the lead with loads of pitons, Hexcentrics and stoppers, the must-haves of the time and Patrick followed, trying to open as many passages as possible. At Patrick's request, Nate had knocked together a home-made exercise system: every evening the little Peugeot also acted as chinning bar, so not a day's training was missed.

Shortly afterwards, Patrick Edlinger came back to this area with Patrick Berhault to film *Oversand*, one of the films in Jean-Paul Janssen and Laurent Chevallier's trilogy, a seminal forerunner of the later film *La Vie au bout des doigts* which would make him famous.

PAGE 110: TRAINING SESSION THANKS TO THE PEUGEOT 204 WITH THE HOGGAR PEAKS IN THE BACKGROUND, 1980. PAGE 111: 'THE BLOND ANGEL' IN MEDITATION AT THE BELAY, HOGGAR, 1980.

LEFT: PATRICK EDLINGER HANGING FROM ONE ARM 1981 ON THE *BEDA* ROOF, BUOUX, A NOW WORLDWIDE KNOWN IMAGE.

RIGHT: THE AMERICAN LEGEND, RON KAUK ON *FAME AND GLORY*, 5.12C, TUOLUMNE MEADOWS, YOSEMITE, 1988.

By the beginning of 1984, Le Saussois was back in the limelight. A few metres to the right of *Chimpanzodrome*, the Le Menestrel brothers and J-B Tribout tackled a typical boulder problem resulting from old piton holes: *Le Bidule*. Marc was the first to climb it, followed almost immediately by his brother and J-B. It was the first F8a+ in France and there was no harder route anywhere until, in the same year, Wolfgang Güllich took the lead again in Germany with *Kanal Im Rücken* in the Altmühtal (grade 10 UIAA, corresponding to the French F8b). At the time some people felt that this route was just another F8a+ but with the benefit of hindsight after various repeats, the rating was confirmed as F8b.

In spring, accompanied by the young Ben Moon in his dreadlocks phase, Jerry Moffatt flashed *Chimpan*, quickly repeated *Le Bidule*, then rushed to the Verdon where he just missed an on-sight climb of *Papy on sight* (F7c+). As with the visit of Ron Fawcett and Pete Livesey in the previous decade, an Englishman had come to impress the French on their own territory but he was keener on beer and hallucinogens than on warming up exercises and he had to take a year-long break because of injured elbows before returning in full force.

Now at last, rock-climbing in France and Europe was about to have their first female rock star. In 1985 Catherine Destivelle conquered *Le Bombé de Pichenibule*, the first woman to reach this level (apart from Lynn Hill but she was not yet known on the European side of the Atlantic). Then she appeared in the film *E Pericoloso Sporgersi* before going on to win the first climbing competition in Bardonecchia.

While some climbers, such as Destivelle, Louisa Iovane, Glowacz, Godoffe and the young Didier Raboutou, opted for the European limelight, others worked on more distant areas. Patrick Edlinger was one of these. After his spectacular climb of *La Boule* on Montagne Sainte Victoire (the second French grade F8a+), which appeared on the cover of the first issue of the magazine *Vertical*, he set off on an extensive tour of the United States. He is still the only star well-placed enough to arrange a trip accompanied by a photographer (Gérard Kosicki) with a book contract in place (*Rock Games*). On this occasion he swiftly tackled the classics such as *Sphynx Crack*, *Rainbow Wall* and *Grand Illusion*, showing that the French style can easily adapt to trad climbing.

ABOVE: BEN MOON DURING HIS 'DREADLOCKS' ERA.
BELOW: PATRICK EDLINGER'S DYNO ON *LA BOULE* (F8A+, LES DEUX AIGUILLES) MAKES THE FRONT COVER OF *VERTICAL* FIRST ISSUE IN 1985.

JERRY MOFFATT
A WHIRLWIND DEBUT

Jerry Moffatt first made a prominent appearance on the international scene with an article which has become part of rock-climbing history. It appeared in the English magazine *Mountain* (no. 92, summer 1983) with the innocent title: 'What we did on our holidays'. For Jerry, then aged 20, talking about the holidays was a joke in itself, since it is hard to think of him doing anything else but climbing. In this case, the word 'holiday' was stretched to cover more than seven months touring the United States.

With Wolfgang Güllich, Jerry was the first person who systematically followed the radical concept of being a full-time climber. They travelled all over the world, tackling the toughest challenges, irritating the envious locals and then returning home. Güllich usually left his mark by opening the hardest route in the country they were visiting (*Punks in the gym* in Australia, for instance), while Jerry specialised in on-sight climbs.

The American John Bachar had a similar international approach, repeating *Le Bombé de Pichenibule,* then opening *Chasin' the Trane* in Frankenjura (both F7b+) in 1981. This internationalism was unusual at the time: most of the leading climbers, such as Jean-Pierre Bouvier and Patrick Berhault in France, Toni Yaniro in the States and Ron Fawcett in England travelled a bit but they usually stuck to their home ground whenever they wanted to achieve a personal best.

All these climbers were notable for having long careers. In spirit, they were reminiscent of Royal Robbins, Gary Hemming, Tom Frost and John Harlin, the great American names of Yosemite in the early 1960s. Justly confident of their superiority, they came to Europe and revolutionised Chamonix.

As is often the way in England, Jerry's adventure began and ended in Sheffield. For 20 years this city was the home of the hottest climbing scene in Europe, although how it became so remains a mystery.

In September 1982, Jerry set off for the United States with Chris Gore, a prominent English climber of the 1980s. At the time climbs such as Rifle, City of Rocks, Hueco, New River Gorge and even Smith Rock were still undiscovered. In those days the American dream consisted of the Shawangunks, Colorado, Joshua Tree and Yosemite and that was it.

The start of the journey was depressing: they arrived in New York in pouring rain, then hitchhiked to the Shawangunks. As the rain continued to fall, the first few days were spent bouldering on the piers of an old railway bridge near the cliff. The first steps were laborious: 'The 5.11 seems atrocious, will I ever do a 5.12?' But the routes were gradually conquered on the way to the legendary fissure, the aptly-named *Super Crack*, probably the first F7c in the world, freed in 1974 by Steve Wunsch. Some bold placing of Friends and a few desperate jams opened the door to his first flash.

The opposite of Güllich's Sylvester Stallone-like appearance, Jerry Moffatt was skinny and gaunt, not visibly muscular, with the faintly glamorous look of the period: EBs, tennis socks, football shorts and a bag of chalk dangling down to mid-thigh. Even in still photographs, the style which would make him famous is apparent: somewhat rudimentary placings and summary foot movements but with fiendish energy and muscle tone, driven by an iron will, whatever the run-out.

The rest of the American journey continued in the same vein. After three days of non-stop travelling, Colorado and its

Eldorado Canyon finally emerged on the horizon. In just two days they climbed the two local monuments, both 5.13c but very different from each other: *Psycho*, a short-roof boulder requiring acrobatic movements and *Genesis*, a great pitch ending with a confusing sequence of notches and underclings, opened by Jim Collins and never repeated until then in spite of numerous attempts.

Probably encouraged by his achievements in these new areas, it was in the Californian desert of Joshua Tree that Jerry achieved his winter successes. After a few weeks of boulders and intensive training sessions, he felt he was ready to tackle the masterpieces. The perfect crack of the *Equinox* (5.12c), running for over 20 metres across a granite mushroom boulder, towering in the desert, was the first opportunity for an on-sight first, the stuff of every climber's dreams.

Then, Jerry Moffatt met the expert of the area, John Bachar, with whom he tackled *Moonbeam*. This was a short, challenging overhanging crack, a project Bachar had been working on for two years. After a few runs and in spite of an extremely painful fingerlock, both men were close to success. But the American had a secret weapon: new, revolutionary Spanish climbing shoes: called 'Firé', they had resin rubber soles, making the EB look completely obsolete. So in the end it was the American, spurred on by his competitive nature, who secured the first. As soon as he had climbed down, he agreed to lend his new shoes to Jerry. With this technological boost, he too succeeded in conquering *Moonbeam* on the eve of his departure and he never wore EBs again.

The last stage of the programme was to have been the inescapable Yosemite. But in this particularly freezing March, the Valley looked more suitable for cross-country skiing and ice-climbing. So they cut their holiday short and went back home.

In 1983, back in Britain and much encouraged by the successful tour, Jerry immediately left his mark on the English climbing community by scoring two major successes on Cloggy (Clogwyn Du'r Arddu) in Wales: the solo of *Great Wall* and the first ascent of the wall to the right of it. This had been a long-term project of the climber-painter John Redhead, who planted a bolt there (which was very controversial at the time) and christened the route *Tormented ejaculation*. But he was unable to exit it because of its extreme exposure. After four reconnaissance rappels and one rest day, Jerry removed the bolt and flashed the route, relying only on rotten nuts. Immediately he renamed it *Master's Wall*. Today it is still seen as the embodiment of boldness, not to say recklessness verging on suicide.

Like Patrick Berhault, who stunned the Alpine world during the summer of 1979, Jerry was a young troublemaker who definitely ousted the old guard, personified by Ron Fawcett, while heralding the arrival of a new generation. Again like Patrick, Jerry had all the ingredients for creating a legend: a few brilliant exploits in a time short enough to capture the spirit of a period. Soon he made other trips to Germany and France, planned in the same style and equally successful. The first time I met him, he and Ben Moon were living in Apt, camping at night under a bridge. Staying nearby with Jibé, we must have looked very middle class in our rented caravans on a camp site.

Since then, 30 years have passed and Jerry has survived everything: car crashes, leaving the track on his bike many times, terrifying solos, repeated tendonitis and surgery, various banned hallucinogenic substances, dreadful breakfasts consisting of beer and fish and chips and last but not least, the biggest danger which can distract even a climber with nerves of steel: women! Now a passionate surfer, he tells all this and more in his gripping autobiography, *Revelations*.

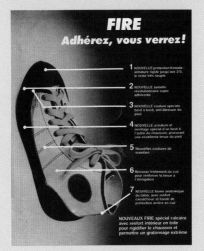

FIRE
Adhérez, vous verrez!

1 NOUVELLE protection frontale armature rigide jusqu'aux 2/3, le reste très souple

2 NOUVELLE semelle révolutionnaire super adhérente

3 NOUVELLE couture spéciale bord à bord, anti-blessure du pied

4 NOUVELLE armature et montage spécial d'un bout à l'autre du chausson, procurant une excellente tenue du pied

5 Nouvelles coutures de maintien

6 Nouveau traitement du cuir pour renforcer la tenue à l'élongation

7 NOUVELLE forme anatomique du talon, avec renfort caoutchouc et bande de protection arrière en cuir

NOUVEAUX FIRE spécial calcaire avec renfort intérieur en toile pour rigidifier le chausson et permettre un grattonage extrême

PAGE 114: JERRY MOFFATT IN HIS FRENCH ERA: ON THE FINAL MOVE OF *LE SPECTRE DU SURMUTANT*, F8B+, BUOUX. **PAGE 115**: NEVER SURRENDER! JERRY WINNING THE 1988 FRENCH SEYNES MASTER. **PAGE 116**: 1987, AFTER AN ELBOW INJURY, JERRY MOFFATT COMES BACK STRONGER THAN EVER AND POCKETS THE THIRD ASCENT OF *LE MINIMUM*, F8B+, BUOUX. **PAGE 117**: FIRÉ, THE REVOLUTION OF THE MID 1980s.

CATHERINE DESTIVELLE
ROCK QUEEN

What is an icon? A sacred image worshippedby everyone and this is what Catherine Destivelle has become. Today the public has crowned her the ambassadress of the mountains, not just of rock-climbing. She can very simply convey the beauty of the high peaks and the passion of mountaineering. But it was through rock-climbing rather than mountaineering that she became famous.

From a large family, her parents took her to the forest of Fontainebleau as a young child, first just to romp around on the rocks like all children of that age. Then as a teenager she learnt the subtleties of sandstone, thanks to the CAF and the legendary 8.23 train from the Gare de Lyon to Bois le Roi. French rock-climbing and mountaineering owes a tremendous amount to this SNCF railway line which has enabled so many generations of climbers to develop their talent and vocation.

Soon Catherine's physical skills and above all her enthusiasm and daring, made her stand out from the rest, not only on the boulders of Bleau but also on rock faces and in the Alps where, unknown to her parents, she climbed the north faces of L'Oisans and the Ailfroide at the age of 17 with her companion of the time. Then at the age of 22, she went through a period of doubt and lack of motivation. She was a strong climber, still an amateur, a trained physiotherapist as well as an inveterate late-night poker player. As she writes with great humour in her book *Danseuse de Roc*, she started putting on weight as well as smoking like a trooper, disastrous for an asthmatic. Fortunately this period did not last long and her love of the open air took over again.

Her life was changed when she met the filmmaking mountaineer Lothar Mauch. He saw her potential immediately, as a pretty girl who was a champion in a discipline which had yet to become glamorous. As with Patrick Edlinger, it was through a film that she became known to the general public. Made in the Gorges du Verdon by Robert Nicod in 1985, *E Pericoloso Sporgersi* alternated pure performance, such as the legendary *Le Bombé de Pichenibule* free, with sequences included for their charm, such as the scene in which Catherine and Monique Dalmasso, wearing simple low-cut swimsuits, scamper through a field of poppies pursued by a lecherous shepherd.

Now Catherine was both a film star and a rock-climbing professional. The years which followed were marked by her rock-climbing successes: she confirmed her talent by being one of the first women to conquer the eighth grade and one of the first competition stars (Bardonecchia, Arco, Lyon, Snowbird), soon joined by Lynn Hill and Isabelle Patissier. She was also filmed in spectacular places such as the American West, Mali and Thailand.

It is interesting to compare her achievements during this rock-climbing period with those of Lynn Hill and Isabelle Patissier. With hindsight, Lynn Hill probably had the biggest impact on the history of rock-climbing, notably through her free ascent of *The Nose* on El Capitan and her success winning competitions. But, Catherine has proved much more versatile with her mountaineering achievements, a discipline in which Lynn has never felt comfortable.

In the 1990s, bored with the restrictive world of competitions, Catherine focused increasingly on mountaineering, in particular on soloing the great north faces and tackling many firsts for women which had yet to be achieved. Through meeting the American Jeff Lowe, a pioneer of modern ice-climbing and dry-tooling, she broadened her horizons on Trango Towers and attempts on Latok in the Karakoram.

In the Alps, she made a solo climb of the *Bonatti Pillar* on Les Drus, followed by opening a new route on its West Face involving 11 days of aid-climbing and solitary camping at high altitude, an unprecedented feat in female mountaineering.

Like all the great male mountain climbers of the late 20th century, she too would complete her trilogy. Over two years, for the first time ever, a woman climbed the north faces of the Eiger, the Grandes Jorasses and the Matterhorn in winter and solo, probably her most important achievement. The Matterhorn was particularly notable: she followed in Bonatti's footsteps, choosing his direct route of 1965 which marked his farewell to high-altitude mountaineering.

Her next logical step was to return to the Himalaya where she had already had a taste of high altitude on Trango and Latok. With her new companion, Erik Decamp, an experienced mountaineer, she made a bold attempt on the Makalu West Pillar, then a successful conquest of an 8,000er with Shisha Pangma followed by an attempt on the dangerous South Face of Annapurna. There were not many successes but some very ambitious attempts.

The birth of her son, preceded by an unfortunate accident in Antarctica in 1996 which stopped her in her tracks, led her to reflect on the extreme dangers of these great massifs outside Europe as well as the physical effects of high-altitude on the body. Nonetheless, she ended the 1990s with a final impressive solo in the Dolomites: the direct Brandler-Hasse on the North Face of the Cima Grande of Lavaredo. By now she had established herself as the greatest female mountaineer of the 20th century.

Since then, she has spent her time sharing her love of climbing and open spaces, making films, writing books and publishing them. In 2007, the full-length film *Au-delà des cimes*, which had an unusually large budget and wide distribution for a film about mountains, was both a nostalgic summary and glorious crowning of her career as a mountaineer. In the eyes of the public she has come to symbolise the joyous, feminine aspect of ice, snow and rock.

PAGE 118: CATHERINE, FIRST FEMALE ROCK CLIMBING STAR. PAGE 119: AN IMPORTANT AND SYMBOLICAL FIRST FEMALE ASCENT OF THE 1980s: CATHERINE DESTIVELLE IN 1985, *BOMBÉ DE PICHENIBULE*, F7B/C, VERDON. PAGE 120: ONE OF THE MOST SPECTACULAR AND DIFFICULT F8A IN BUOUX: CATHERINE ON *LA DIAGONALE DU FOU*, 1988. PAGE 121: ON *L'ANGE EN DÉCOMPOSITION*, VERDON.

TRIVIALISATION OF THE EIGHTH GRADE

The younger Europeans were not to be outdone. Jerry Moffatt had made a series of trips to Joshua Tree the previous winter and then it was England's turn to give him a run for his money. As a symbolic climax, Antoine Le Menestrel solo climbed the hardest route in Britain, first opened by Jerry: *Revelations* (F8a+). During this journey with Jibé Tribout, after several solo sessions on the nearby gritstone, Antoine climbed *Revelations* fairly rapidly. While Jibé continued to work on *Revelations*, establishing the key starting movement, Antoine saw the solo potential: 'At the foot of *Revelations*, as soon as I saw it, I realised that I was irresistibly attracted by this route and that I would climb it solo'.

Encouraged by Jibé, Antoine Le Menestrel spent several days working on the details before setting off on his solo climb, observed by the confident eye and the camera of his companion. As if by magic, the difficult holds happily seemed to stick to his fingers. Here is an extract from his diary: '8 August 1985, 9 a.m. I don't know, perhaps it's too much for me? But I feel so strong, I feel good, I'm no longer afraid, I'm on my way... In the afternoon J-B and I arrive at Raven Tor; it is crowded but the weather conditions are perfect. Usually I do some warm-up exercises but I know I shan't be able to do them immediately because of the many climbers around and I need privacy for my warm-up. I am not in perfect form but I feel relaxed. I belayed Jibé whilst he tried it but he could not do it. Jibé belayed me one more time as I practised the moves, then I moved the rope to one side, still hanging from the piton. I was calm as a glass that slowly fills with bubbles but at the foot of the route I tell myself it is impossible, that I shall crack up, yet I know all the moves, I am mouldable and the stone is my sculptor. I am comfortable, I no longer feel any adrenaline rush, it is relaxing and soothing and my fear of not being able to do it is gradually fading away as the shadows get longer and the climbers are scattering on the cliff. Towards 4 o'clock, I feel it: now is the time, everything is ready, I am at the foot of the route, my head is empty, my body is filled with concentration. J-B spots me for the first moves and is going to take pictures. Move follows move in a perfect sequence; no hesitation, no superfluous moves, no tension: right up to the top my concentration is total. I climb as if inspired, as I have never climbed before. A sling round my waist enables me to climb down to the arms of Jean-Baptiste. Our friendship had become even closer. I am no longer aware of anything except that I am happy.'

This was also the first time that an eighth grade had been climbed solo. In the same summer, taking advantage of the relative coolness of the early mornings and the last traces of dusk in Buoux, his brother Marc Le Menestrel climbed what everyone thought was the first F8b, *Chouca* but it would eventually be downgraded to F8a+ and in any case Güllich was then climbing at the same level without anyone knowing. Marc repeated his exploit on the West Face with *Les main sales*, a definitive F8b and also *Le Fluide enchanté* at Mouriès. At the top of his game when only 1F8, Marc was the first to climb many routes of this grade and what is more he was extremely quick when opening them.

A 'BOLT OF LIGHTNING' FRANÇAIS IN THE SUMMER OF 1985 AS ANTOINE LE MENESTRAL SOLOES *REVELATIONS*, BRITAIN'S HARDEST PITCH.

A PARIS GANG
THE GROUP EFFECT

In 1982 a group of young Parisian enthusiasts from all backgrounds were climbing at Bleau and in Le Saussois and they soon became lifelong friends, known as the Paris Gang.

Life in the Le Menestrel family was centred on rock-climbing. The father, Jacques, had been a famous climber in the early 1960s and he dragged his wife along with him in all his exploits. Marc, 15, Antoine, 17 and their young sister Séverine were almost born with climbing shoes on.

To make a bold comparison and using the words of President Jacques Chirac about his prime minister Alain Juppé, we thought that Marc Le Menestrel was 'the best of all of us'. He was young and physically very talented. Naturally he stood out as the youngest of the group with his angel face and the skills of a child prodigy. Ambitious, he never doubted that in the years to come he would push the grades upwards as he looked for challenging new routes. Photographs, sponsors, tough routes, trips and nomadic episodes, Marc lived the life of a professional climber before deciding that on its own it would not fulfil him completely. So at the end the 1980s he returned to studying again, then discovered the tough world of big business working for Elf before returning to his first love in Bleau where he attracted the limelight on the bouldering scene. Today, Marc is a researcher and a distinguished teacher in the fields of decision making and ethics. As a Visiting Professor at Pompeu Fabra University in Barcelona, he is located in the centre of the leading region of high-level climbing and he certainly takes advantage of this.

Antoine Le Menestrel, Marc's elder brother, is less exuberant, more reserved and more sensitive. At the age of 17, he hitchhiked to Britain on his own to try his hand at the test-pieces of the period, such as *Right Wall* in Wales, enlisting climbing partners on the spot. He was not as strong as his brother but this was compensated for by his complete commitment every time his feet left the ground. This mental strength enables him to excel both in on-sight and in perseverance. He is the most uncompromising and determined of us all.

The rest is history: from *La Rage* to *Ravage* and his solo of *Revelations*, Antoine would inspire many climbers in the years to come. Not at ease in competitions, he much preferred doing new routes, often with Fabrice Guillot, before he found his true vocation as an artist in 'dance climbing', founding the Compagnie Lézards Bleus. He performs regularly, even on the walls of the Palace of the Popes at the Avignon Festival, where he coined the phrase 'poetic climbing': 'Climbing becomes poetic when successful moves are not the only objective. I turn my climbing into pictures: I have little time to climb between shows of facade dancing and each climb is like a gift bringing me to life again. I take each climbing day as it comes, without an objective to be achieved at any price. When a climbing route calls me and I respond to the invitation. I climb without thinking of the summit, I forget the summit. I climb with my heart and not my muscles. Step by step, the summit comes towards me. Free climbing is the pursuit of creativity in the gestural adaptation to the constraints imposed by the rock face, in other words inventing your signature as climber.'

1982, THE YOUNG (14 YEARS OLD) MARC LE MENESTREL ON *CAPTAIN' CROCHET*, F7B, ONE OF THE NUMEROUS LAURENT JACOB CREATIONS IN BUOUX.

Jibé Tribout was aware that he was not the most gifted climber but on the other hand his commitment to work and training were unequalled. His famous mantra: 'An extra attempt is never wasted' enabled him to conquer the most difficult routes in the world which would have put off most climbers. Coming from a prosperous background and loving a challenge, nothing scared him. For example, before he came to know us, he arrived at a Burgundy cliff face equipped by the sports association FSGT. He ignored the no-parking signs and parked his parents' Golf GTI right at the foot of the cliff face, then freed the last obstacle, which he immediately renamed it *Les bourgeois font la loi* (*'The bourgeois make the law'*).

One can imagine lively discussions round the fire between the socialist Le Menestrel brothers and Jibé Tribout. An indefatigable collector of first ascents, he was always ready to do anything to secure more. One day, an English climber even sabotaged his own lifetime project by coating the holds with lubricating oil just to prevent Jibé snatching the first from him. Today he is the head of a company marketing outdoor products; his passion for climbing has remained intact and he has passed it on to his sons.

Laurent Jacob was in a way like an elder brother to us all, because of his size, his age and his experience. He had been immersed in the climbing world from an early age, his father having been a famous mountaineer who took part in the 1971 French expedition up the Makalu West Pillar in the Himalaya. Years later, this enabled us to benefit from the expedition's stock of brand new pitons. From the 8,000 metres they had been intended for, fate brought these pitons to the cracks of the Buoux cliffs. As a teenager, Laurent was not particularly interested in rock-climbing and when his father took him to Le Saussois, he much preferred fishing in the Yonne river. But eventually the sport took hold and, to what effect. His devilish foot technique, his size and his comparative lack of strength led him to invent the Egyptian or drop knee position. Since then, generations of climbers have been able to conquer otherwise impossible routes but as a result knee surgeons have acquired some new patients.

A brilliant pioneer, there are many places where the routes known as *Voies Jacob* are still considered benchmarks. As a medical student at the time he was climbing, he eventually became a world famous doctor, specialising in natural methods of better aging. He is the author of the book *Devenir centenaire* (*How to become a centenarian*) and he practiced medicine in Hong Kong for many years before returning to Switzerland.

Fabrice Guillot listened a lot to Gothic rock bands such as The Cure and Joy Division, with an appropriate expression completely out of tune with everyone else. He specialised in short routes, bouldering moves, especially with very small holds, micro-holds, so small that they required the use of fingernails which no reasonable person would have dared envisage. He showed what he was made of when he tackled *Crépinette*, one of the first F8a grades in the world. Without turning professional, like many others, he became a route-setter for several distinguished competitions then, like Antoine Le Menestrel, he founded a dance-climbing company, Retouramont. Becoming more interested in choreography, he 'used a city's vertical surfaces as a stage' with performances such as *Réflexion de façade* or *Clairière urbaine*.

As for me, who had no climbing roots, having first been introduced to the sport by the master J. C. Droyer in person, I tried to follow the others in tackling difficulties, taking advantage of their energy, then getting out while the going was good, sometimes on unlikely solo climbs. With my ironic prose, I was the 'intellectual' of the group, this status being reinforced by my glasses with their very thick lenses which Jean-Paul Sartre would have envied. Fortunately the members of the group persuaded me to change my appearance radically so that I was noticed by girls — at last!

We had several base camps: the Le Menestrel family house in the Paris suburbs, Jibé's parents' holiday house in Burgundy, not far from Le Saussois and, when we discovered Buoux, the 'bories', then the copse on the Claparèdes plateau which we used as a camp site, far from the ecological standards of today.

PAGE 124:

1984, ANTOINE LE MENESTREL ON THE STARTING DYNO OF *LE BIDULE*, SAUSSOIS, F8A+.

—

PAGE 125:

DAVID CHAMBRE ON FREE SPACE SOLO MODE AT LE SAUSSOIS, *TROYENNE*, F6C, 1984.

—

PAGE 126:

ABOVE: A HAPPY JIBÉ TRIBOUT IN VERDON DURING A 1982 *ENDLESS SUMMER* CLIMBING TRIP.

BELOW: MARC LE MENESTREL.

ANTOINE LE MENESTREL PERFORMS HIS *CÉLÉBRIS-SIME CROISÉ* OF HIS *ROSE ET LE VAMPIRE*, F8B, 1985.

–

PAGE 128:

ABOVE LEFT: LAURENT JACOB SE DÉPLIE DANS *SUPER CRAMPE*, 7A+, LE SAUSSOIS, 1983.

ABOVE RIGHT: FONTAINEBLEAU 1983, FABRICE GUILLOT PERFORMS ON ONE OF THE FIRST FB8A, THE *SURPLOMB DE LA VALLÉE DE LA MÉE*.

BELOW: 1983, SCENE FROM THE DAILY LIFE ON THE UNOFFICIAL BUOUX CAMPSITE OF PLATEAU DES CLAPARÈDES...

Now and again we would be joined by Marc and Antoine's little sister Séverine, their cousin Cyrille, Frank Scherrer, who had the body of a Greek god (see the photograph of our camp site) and our future coach, Laurent Darlot, a talented artist as well as a Fontainebleau climber. Others who came included Jacques Schneider, later a famous mathematician and the brothers Stanislas and Nicolas Richard who, every morning at dawn, would take refuge in their Renault 4L to find the silence they needed for their transcendental meditation. Last but not least was Corinne Labrune, who would become Jibé's wife and a famous climber in the late 1980s.

Our unknowing sponsors during those first years in Buoux were the ironmongers for bolts and the Intermarché (for everything else) in Apt, Marc and Antoine being the most reckless at the dangerous sport of shoplifting. Laurent had even made himself a special coat with deep inside pockets, perfect for storing smoked salmon and a good bottle of wine. It is true we were loud and sometimes arrogant but we were never lazy; rather we were over-enthusiastic in giving the best of ourselves. We never withdrew into ourselves but were always driven by the desire to emulate the exploits of the other climbers of the time.

This intense period culminated in the winter of 1984 with our first 'sponsored' trip to the American desert of Joshua Tree. Climbing partners quickly formed, sometimes changing from time to time. With Jibé, we were already the among the few actually climbing as a career, ready to spend two months in Chamonix watching the rain fall, sitting under the canopy of our Trigano tent at La Pierre d'Orthaz. This was how we started our roped party and we had good times, all the better because we survived them.
The Tribout-Jacob pair had multiplied the routes at Mouriès. During the hot summer of 1982, Laurent Darlot, who adored his suntanned body and liked wearing as little as possible, would go shopping at the local supermarket. There he could be seen pushing the trolley wearing only flip-flops and a G-string, catching everyone's eye while we carefully remained a good five metres behind him.

The rivalry between Marc and Antoine, not expressed but latent, meant that they did not often climb together. Antoine spent a lot of time with Fabrice or Jibé (for instance, on the famous trip to Britain in the summer of 1985). During that time Marc and I climbed a lot together, even in places as far away as Japan. Then, inspired by Eric Escoffier (who paid a heavy price for it) and Didier Raboutou, Marc decided he wanted to drive sports cars. He turned out to be as bad a driver as Didier and was involved in several accidents, fortunately without serious consequences.

Most of us were trying to become part of that first generation of professional climbers and we gradually gave up our university studies. Then came media exposure, various failures or successes of each of us in competition and the inevitable distractions of our love lives which loosened the cohesion of the group and each of us went his own way. 'The group effect', so dear to sociologists, had faded away but this did not affect our friendship and our passion for climbing. It is interesting to see that since then, few top-level climbers have repeated this experience of living together, individualism being the norm today.

'RAVAGE MOI'

The new grade of F8b soon became commonplace on the crags in the south of France: for instance, *La rose et le vampire* (Buoux, A. Le Menestrel), *Les braves gens…* (Verdon, J-B Tribout) and *Simulacres* (Cimaï, J-B Tribout). In March 1986, after countless attempts to repeat the legendary starting crux, Antoine Le Menestrel succeeded in enchaining *La Rose* and *La Secte* to *Bout du Monde* in Buoux. This produced *La rage de vivre,* without any doubt the first French F8b+. A year earlier, on the solid sandstone of the Australian Arapiles, Güllich had again been ahead of the French at this level of difficulty with *Punks in the gym*, a project bolted and almost achieved by the Swiss Martin Scheel. Naturally all this is subjective; it is a delicate matter, if not illusory, to compare half-grades of difficulty with scales based on different rating systems, on rock faces as far away as the Antipodes. It is only with the passing of time (now decades!) that the numerous repeats by new generations, more objective and detached from the emotional context of the period, have made it possible to make progress with these classifications. Also, history prefers to remember only the most famous names.

As far as women climbers are concerned, they were fairly few in number but very active. Next to Lynn Hill, who had already reached the F7c+ level in 1984, there was of course Catherine Destivelle but also Christine Gambert, born in Lorraine, as well as the young 18-year old Isabelle Patissier from Lyon. Outside France, the German Andrea Eisenhut, the Italian Luisa Iovane and the Australian Louise Shepherd were prominent. In the mid-1980s European women were beginning to tackle F7c routes (*Katapult* and *Magnet* in the Frankenjura), then the athletic and indisputable F7c+ (*Chimpanzodrome*, Christine Gambert, November 1985). Catherine Destivelle returned to the limelight in April 1986 with *Fleur de rocaille* in Mouriès, soon repeated by Isabelle Patissier. This was the first woman's F8a but the alternative rating system puts it closer to a F7c+, no more difficult than *Chimpanzodrome*, although there are no routes more difficult to compare than these two. The first female F8th grade is generally attributed to Luisa Iovane in 1986 with *Come Back* (Valle San Nicolo). In the following year Christine Gambert and Lynn Hill joined her with the celebrated climb of *Rêve de papillon*.

At this time competitions began following each other at an increasingly frantic pace (see box), attracting even those originally opposed to them who suddenly changed their minds (including me). Meanwhile Antoine Le Menestrel spent the summer of 1986 at the very heart of the Bâlois Jura, concentrating on a bolted route some 15 metres high which had already been unsuccessfully attempted by Wenzel Vodicka. Antoine grew lyrical: 'My breath, like a hurricane, devastated my strength, my muscles were liquefied by the power of my breath. I became a blazing breath climbing up the rock face. This devastation within me changed me. My moulted skin remained hanging on the holds. I climbed as I breathed.' This eventually led to *Ravage* in Chuenisberg and he rated it a grade F8c. Although later reduced to F8b+, it was definitely a new step up in difficulty. His brother Marc reached the same level the following winter in Buoux with *Le Minimum* using his 'cacagnolet', a square micro-hold (or shitty little hold) which eventually broke, thus making it even harder.

ABOVE: LUISA IOVANE ON HIS 1986 MASTERPIECE, *COME BACK*, F8A, VALLE SAN NICOLO, ITALIE.
BELOW: MARC LE MENESTREL GIVES EVERYTHING ON HIS *LE MINIMUM*, F8B+, 1986, BUOUX.

THE FIRST COMPETITIONS

YALTA 1982, PATRICK EDLINGER (CENTRE, IN BLUE) AND BACK BEHIND, EDDY BOUCHER AND LAURENT JACOB.

The spirit of competition has always existed in mountaineering. By the 1F9th century, mountaineers were already competing to be the first to conquer the legendary peaks of the Alps such as the Matterhorn and then the last unclimbed faces, the most famous of course being the North Face of the Eiger.

With the increasingly individual nature of rock-climbing in the last century, it was inevitable that climbers should want to compete with each other more directly and radically than through a first ascent or rating.

The first competitions were organised by the Communist countries of the former Eastern Bloc and in particular the Soviets. Initially they were mainly speed races, for which very soon there were real local, regional and national championships. In the early 1980s the Soviets also began to invite West European countries, coinciding exactly with the first generations of pure rock-climbers. The Fédération Française de la Montagne (French Mountain Federation) responded positively to this invitation in 1982 and sent three leading climbers, Patrick Edlinger, Laurent Jacob and the outstanding Parisian Eddy Boucher. They were accompanied by Yves Ballu, then the mountain expert at the Ministry of Sport, who believed that 'climbing is just a sport like any other'. In Yalta, on the Black Sea, the challenge was to climb a moderately difficult route as fast as possible, belayed by a long rope, then abseil down. In spite of their technical superiority, the French never managed to win but they had started the debate. Two years later a new team travelled to Yalta which included Jacky Godoffe who acquired the taste for it and subsequently, on top of his bouldering skills, won many podium places in modern speed climbing competitions.

1985 was a decisive year in Western Europe. In France the FFM declared itself definitively in favour of competitions but it was Italy which started the ball rolling. At the beginning of July, 60 Italian, French, Swiss and German competitors, dozens of journalists and several thousand spectators gathered in Bardonecchia. The sum of 30,000 francs, a fortune at the time, would be awarded to the winner and half that amount to the female winner. And the Italian mountaineering legend Riccardo Cassin was a member of the jury. It was a young, unknown German who was victorious: Stefan Glowacz took the style and difficulty events (but not the speed one). The female winner was Catherine Destivelle.

Yet not much earlier she had signed a symbolic manifesto, *Le Manifeste des 19,* which stated loud and clear that the essence of rock-climbing lay in the pursuit of technical

difficulty and ever increasing commitment: 'Perhaps tomorrow there will be competitions and competitors wearing numbers cavorting in front of the television cameras. But there will also be climbers who continue to practise the true discipline of rock-climbing. Climbers who will be the guardians of a certain spirit and a certain ethic.'

Of all the self-appointed idealists who signed this manifesto, which included the Paris gang, most would soon change their mind and take part in competitions, with the notable exceptions of Patrick Berhault and Jean-Pierre Bouvier. We parodied this situation at a meeting organised by Michel Béal, the 'guardian' of the climbing community at the time, by having our photograph taken with our coats inside out, as turncoats. Be that as it may, this first event was an overwhelming success both with the public and the media, showing that competition could be commercially viable.

Now that the Pandora's box had been opened, the race for sponsors and television coverage was on. The following year, a competition circuit was organised in France and Italy, these two countries being at the forefront of progress, while in Britain and Germany the more traditional approach to rock-climbing, linked to a stricter ethic, slowed down changes in attitude. The questions of support and the rules of the game were still the subject of earnest debate. As artificial climbing walls were still an infant technology, competitions still relied on natural rock which obviously had to be adapted to the event and 'DIY' solutions were disliked because of their environmental consequences. In addition, weather conditions could be treacherous. So it seemed that in the short term, resin was bound to win. As to the rules of the game, these too would be refined; taken into account were the number of holds touched or held, the height reached and whether the routes were on-sight or not. The winner was established by counting the points or by direct elimination: it was a developing sport in which new rules were invented as it went along.

LEFT: THE *TURNED INSIDE-OUT JACKETS* PICTURE OF THE *MANIFESTE DES 19* SIGNATORIES. FRONT ROW, LEFT TO RIGHT: FABRICE GUILLOT, CATHERINE DESTIVELLE, DAVID CHAMBRE. SECOND ROW: ANTOINE AND MARC LE MENESTREL, JIBÉ TRIBOUT, LAURENT JACOB AND ALAIN GHERSEN.

RIGHT: FIRST EUROPEAN AUDIENCE FOR A COMPETITION, BARDONECCHIA, SUMMER 1985.

THE YOUNG STEFAN GLOWACZ TOWARDS HIS HEADS
FOR GLORY, BARDONECCHIA 1985.

The first large-scale competition on a wall took place in Vaulx-en-Velin, in the suburbs of Lyon. The holds felt more like plastic than resin, the route marked was sometimes risky and some climbers even made use of the edges of the belay plates since it was not specifically forbidden. Here again, there was joy for some and disappointment for others as a hierarchy developed. Some stars, well-established on rock, found they were on a sticky wicket as young unknown climbers, such as Didier Raboutou, Robert Cotijo and Isabelle Patissier, began to emerge.

Climbing on artificial walls became an important area for those who wanted to make a living from climbing by attracting the attention of manufacturers who might sponsor them.

The summer of 1986 was another Franco-Italian one. With the support of the town of Arco, on the shores of Lake Garda, Bardonecchia became Sportroccia, a tournament in two stages with a combined classification. Even Patrick Edlinger took part and this stirred up a horde of young pretenders who became even more determined to 'set the record straight'. Over 100 competitors gathered on the shores of Lake Garda. Foreshadowing the future Rock Master competition which would make the name of Arco famous throughout the world, the organisers did a fine job, building a real 'tent village'. In this region of Trentino a solid culture of rock-climbing activities had developed, inspired by the ghosts of all the *maestri* of the Dolomites.

Patrick Edlinger's presence was an event in itself. The only true star of the discipline since *La vie au bout des doigts*, he always steered clear of most of the other top climbers and the least that could be said is that they were eager to get even with him. From the start of the qualifying events, the overall tension and nervousness of those involved was tangible. After a few cold sweats, a F7b slab and chipped two-finger moves it soon became a punishment for some of the participants. Marc Le Menestrel was unsuccessful and went back to the academic research he enjoyed, while Glowacz swayed so much that he ended up slipping and had to continue at a slower speed (the number of attempts within the allotted time did not matter). For those who had already made a reputation, it was also an occasion to examine their current hopes and expectations and to face the possibility of relegation to the second rank.

As to the women, there was less suspense because at 14 the number of participants was smaller and there was an enormous gap between the top five, Catherine Destivelle, Lynn Hill, Isabelle Patissier, Christine Gambert and Luisa Iovane and everyone else. For the time being, it was still Catherine Destivelle, a heroine to the Italians, who dominated the situation but it already seemed that the American Lynn Hill had the potential to dethrone her. Spectators thronged to watch the men's final but this ended like a damp squib: on a short roof a few holds had been badly cut and the favourites fell like flies. Naturally a 'bleausard' would be in the best position to tackle such a boulder section and it was Alain Ghersen, a climber little known except in specialist circles, who succeeded in conquering it in double-quick time. Behind him Jacky Godoffe, another leaping 'bleausard' and the Belgian Arnould t'Kint played their cards right and succeeded, while Edlinger, Glowacz and Raboutou served only as foils. But something became apparent during this first stage in that to put on a show, spectacular routes were required, a statement of the obvious which is still valid today. At Bardonecchia, the organisers had learned their lesson and later offered longer, more challenging routes.

BARDONECCHIA 1986 FINAL, PATRICK EDLINGER
GRABS THE BELAY CHAIN AND TAKES THE GOLD.

–

PAGE 134:

ABOVE: LUISA IOVANE, ITALIAN.

CENTRE: STEFAN GLOWACZ, GERMAN.

BELOW: CATHERINE DESTIVELLE WITH HER RIVAL AND
FRIEND, THE AMERICAN LYNN HILL.

A week later, for the second stage, it was rumoured that Patrick Edlinger had lost six kilos between the two events. In the first round, on a F7b roof, he had made it a point of honour not to let his knee touch the rock like most of his rivals who were puffing away painfully: 'It's a matter of class,' he said. After Arco not many people would have bet against him in a match with the 'Rest of the World'.

At the same time, although Lynn Hill was the only one to finish the last route, Catherine Destivelle won the event, thanks to convoluted regulations which added all the routes together to arrive at the combined classification. But the great duel between them had started, a duel which would last for many years until Catherine returned to her beloved mountains. In the final, all eyes were on Alain Ghersen, who was best placed for the final victory. Unfortunately as some killjoys remarked, he climbed 'with the Panda on his back', a reference to the little Fiat Panda which would be the winner's prize. He was too tense and failed on a route which all the other favourites climbed easily.

Even without Jerry Moffatt, Britain caused a sensation. It was the first appearance of Ben Moon with his 'offbeat' look (dreadlocks and tights full of holes, all guaranteed unwashed for three years). His style, both bounding and sparse, the opposite of Glowacz, caused a sensation right to the last metre of a superb final which was very technical and complex. But he rushed too much and missed the last undercling. He was not the only one, since none of the other top climbers of the time, Steulet, Glowacz, Raboutou, Godoffe, Tribout or the Le Menestrel brothers, did any better.

Then, like a good suspense novel, it was Patrick Edlinger himself who knocked out the competition by not missing the miraculous hold. Much to the annoyance of his rivals, especially the other French climbers, Edlinger had struck a great blow. Not only did he win the event but the disappointing performance of the Arco winners enabled him to pocket the victory in the combined competition, the only one which mattered to the media. The legend continued and enabled him to make only rare appearances in competitions. Every time, whether successful or not, this exceptional climber created a tension and an atmosphere wherever he went, a phenomenon rarely repeated since.

A few days after this, it is said that some of the big names returned to this competition rock face, now deserted by the crowds, to touch the famous undercling again and check why they had not seen how they too could have done it. Some weeks later, the Grand Prix de France was held at Troubat in the Pyrenees. Again it was a popular success with an unknown Savoyard climber, Gilbert Ogier, outwitting the professionals of the time and Lynn Hill asserting herself as a great champion for the years to come.

But these events were at the mercy of the weather. The upper echelons of the climbing world gathered in Haute-Savoie in 1987 but there on the cliff of Le Pas de l'Ours at Le Biot, uninterrupted rain caused turmoil and the event was cancelled because the site had become a swamp. This unfortunate occurrence, as well as the need for a more regular calendar, led investors to prefer events on artificial walls, usually in covered sports halls.

EUROPE PREACHES THE GOOD WORD IN AMERICA

In the mid-1980s there were a few exceptional climbers who were not French, such as Wolfgang Güllich, Stefan Glowacz, Jerry Moffatt and Ben Moon but in general the French had conquered the world of climbing. They were the best both on rock faces and in competition, the most active and the most widely covered by the media thanks to Patrick Edlinger, while France itself had the greatest concentration of hard routes and bolted cliffs. So it was that the French imposed their style and grading scale.

In just a few years, with the notable exception of Lynn Hill who soon realised Europe's potential to enrich her climbing techniques, the Americans were no longer in the limelight as they had been for so long. Admittedly Alan Watts was developing Smith Rock but otherwise, pioneering places such as Yosemite had become 'dead' as far as free climbing was concerned. Climbers were at each other's throats as soon as a new bolt was put in and even the heroic John Bachar was considered a reactionary. He came to blows with his fellow climber Ron Kauk in the Camp 4 car park because he had chopped bolts placed by abseil on Kauk's *Punchline*. Then Kauk (again abseiling) opened the well-known *Peace* in Tuolomne which Bachar had attempted earlier from the bottom.

The leading European climbers only went to America as a pilgrimage honouring what had inspired them when young. Now it was the European magazines which made young Americans dream: the Buoux legend had temporarily replaced the Yosemite one. The lack of new climbers entering the field in America meant that the few US climbers who came to Europe were crushed in competitions and stunned by the levels of difficulty, as well as encountering a climbing style and rock faces that they were not used to. I was extremely embarrassed when Ron Kauk visited us and said: 'You Europeans are so strong.' Ron Kauk had been my idol when I was young, the hero of *Midnight Lightning*, *Astroman* and the Tower of Uli Biaho and his photographs in *Yosemite Climber* had been an inspiration to me. Later Ron became very open to new developments in Europe and adapted so well as to complete a sportsmanlike F8c. Hats off to him. Today his son Lonnie, brought up in Yosemite, has taken up the baton, still in the same spirit.

Given the European supremacy, it was natural that a Frenchman, Jibé Tribout, would definitively and symbolically put the nail in the American coffin. In November 1986, Jibé was in Oregon, being shown around by Alan Watts on his local Smith Rock. On an interminable wall with belays which also required very precise footwork, he freed the line *To bolt or not to be*. The name of this route alone was a statement in itself. Its grade too was significant: F8b+ on the French scale or 5.14a on the American one. For the first time the 5.14 barrier had been broken. Two years later, the first big competition took place in the United States. It was organised by Dick Bass, a millionaire entrepreneur who is passionate about mountains (he was the first American to conquer the Seven Summits, the highest peaks in each continent). The support was to be the climbing wall in the Snow-

A POWERFUL NEWCOMER, THE AUSTRIAN GERHARD HÖRAGHER.

LEFT: SNOWBIRD 1988, THE CLIMBING WALL OF THE FIRST US COMP WAS HOSTED BY THE LUXURIOUS THE CLIFF LODGE.

RIGHT: RON KAUK, ALWAYS IN COMMUNION WITH THE ROCK AND NATURE.

bird Ski Resort in the Rockies and Dick Bass invited the best European climbers to the event. But there too, despite of the emergence of a new generation of American climbers including Scott Franklin (*Scarface*, 5.41a, Smith Rock, 198F8), Jim Karn and Robyn Erbesfield, the battle would be among the French. In an atmosphere which could be described as epic, because of the heated arguments between the *Spécialistes* (described later), Patrick Edlinger settled his scores with the two Parisians, Jibé Tribout and Marc Le Menestrel, by being the only one to reach the top, while Catherine Destivelle survived the qualifying sessions and beat her rivals Lynn Hill and Isabelle Patissier. Irritated by losing, Jibé drowned his sorrows in alcohol and ended up with a monumental hangover.

Everywhere in Europe, impatient young enthusiasts were creating their own challenges in their own countries, particularly in the south of France. To mention just a few names: Isabelle Dorsimond and Baron Arnould t'Kint flew the Belgian flag at the Rochers de Freyr. In Italy Luisa Iovane and Andrea Gallo ascended *Hyena* in Finale Ligure (one of the first F8b+ grades in 1986 after Manolo had reached F8b at Totoga in the same year). Gerhard Hörhager and Beat Kammerlander were active in Austria as Andrea Eisenhut was in Germany. Switzerland was not to be outdone thanks to Philippe Steulet, Martin Steel (who opened many great technical routes in the Rätikon, such as *Acacia* and its numerous compulsory seventh grade pitches) and the Czech migrant Wenzel Vodicka, who had secretly crossed the Iron Curtain and now made a living on the cliffs as he satisfied his passion for climbing.

PATRICK EDLINGER
HE WORE THE YELLOW JERSEY

Patrick Edlinger's climbing achievements have already been described but another aspect, rarely mentioned, is that he was an outstanding competitor. Jibé Tribout competed against him several times and as he pointed out: 'Like all great athletes, Patrick had the ability to be 100% when it mattered most'. As a number-one media star, he was never a normal competitor. On his rare appearances, he was always in the unspoken role of defender.

The first time I saw Patrick was in May 1983 at Le Saussois, at an international gathering organised by the Fédération Française de la Montagne. As well as the cream of French climbers, Wolfgang Güllich, Ron Fawcett and the Australian Kim Carrigan were there. *Chimpanzodrome* was a benchmark route and everyone knew that Patrick had come to climb it on-sight, which had never been done before. He got out of his car and, without doing any warm-up exercises, he went straight to the foot of the route, where a small crowd was waiting for him. He set off, passed the first anchor, reached the runner of the second, became tangled in the karabiners, fell, climbed down, then walked away immediately, all without saying a single word and in a silence so deafening it still echoes in my ears.

The tone was set and he did the same again at Bardonecchia in 1986 and at Snowbird in 1988. The difference was that he won these two important events in an incredibly tense atmosphere without any difficulty. In Munich in 1989 the victory was decided in a super-final, again between him and Jibé, who remembered the situation: 'We found ourselves alone in the isolation room. We did not look at each other, it was more a psychological contest than anything else and in the end he won. He was a really great competitor.' Sometimes the pressure was such that he would blow a fuse. Thus in the Master de Nîmes, three months after Snowbird, after a never-ending wait, he chose the wrong moves and fell after two metres. Although the levels of difficulty are much higher today, no competitors today have ever been subjected to the degree of tension which existed in those early contests. Patrick Edlinger was more of a defender than a normal competition climber. He did not compete in the newly developing circuit of World Cups, only using these events to reaffirm his status as 'best climber' and to confirm that his level was still in line with his media exposure.

Until 1994 he made a few more appearances, for instance at Serre-Chevalier, where one of the headlines in the magazine *Grimper* read: 'God is among us'. Then the following year he had an accident in the Calanques and fell 18 metres to the ground, suffering a cardiac arrest. This prevented him from climbing for a while.

At this point his life took other directions. He became involved in journalism, becoming editor-in-chief of the short-lived magazine *Roc'n Wall* from 1997 to 2000. He took up line-fishing which became a new passion, he rediscovered bouldering in Bleau and Annot and he ran a guest house in the Verdon. Then he had to face the cruel loss of Patrick Berhault: 'He was my double and I was his. He was the brother I never had.' Sadly he only survived him by eight years. At their peak in their youth, the two Patricks were like invincible gods but the fragility of the human condition tragically caught up with them later.

With much courage and lucidity he described the difficulties he faced in the last years of his life in his posthumous autobiography, written with Jean-Michel Asselin. He had planned to sail round the world in a yacht but the Verdon where he had blossomed and found happiness for so long did not let him go.

PATRICK EDLINGER (1960–2012) MENTALLY PREPARING BEFORE THE BARDONECCHIA FINAL, 1986.

THE INDIVIDUALITY OF THE BRITISH

Meanwhile, things were also moving in Britain where there were quite a few colourful characters on the scene. Besides Jerry Moffatt and Ben Moon, there were John Redhead, Chris Gore Andy Pollit, Johnny Dawes and John Dunne.

A Yorkshireman with gypsy origins, John Redhead climbed mostly in North Wales, ranging from the impressive coastal cliffs of Gogarth to the rugged rock faces of Llanberis. Perhaps surprisingly, as a teenager in the 1960s, he made his made his name as an artist. Self-taught, his paintings were exhibited in art galleries and he made a decent living from them. In the early 1980s Redhead became a specialist in what might be called mental climbing, making fist ascents in traditional style using just nuts for protection; difficult naturally and also very committing. Here 'boldness' was really a euphemism for what at the time was thought of as a potentially fatal fall, a kind of roped solo. In the purest British style, these routes were not created to become popular but rather to make an impression on the mind, as was expressed by their evocative names such as *Margins of the Mind*, *The Bells! The Bells!* and so on. As another painter said: 'John Redhead's climbs are the greatest artistic performances one can imagine'.

Although these routes corresponded to the French seventh and eighth grades, the approach to them was more spiritual than competitive. Unlike his contemporary, Ron Fawcett and later Jerry Moffatt, Redhead did not train or climb intensively before climbing. His was an approach inspired by meditation, reflecting his relationship with the rawest aspect of nature: the mineral quality of the rock. Interestingly, he has studied the pictorial art of the Ancestral Puebloans on their sacred cliffs in the south-west of the United States.

Among the stories which have made him a legend is *The Indian Face* affair, which reflects his dual role as an artist and climber. First climbed by Johnny Dawes (another legend of this kind of climbing) and situated on the imposing and remote Welsh crag of Cloggy in Snowdonia, *The Indian Face* is a steep slab over 40 metres high where a repeat is a remarkable event – it has only been repeated fewer than 10 times in almost 30 years. The rating, E9, English 6c, a first at the time, does not reflect the near deadly risk of attempting a lead. One of the climbers who repeated the route described its difficulty as '100% mental'. Dave MacLeod, one of today's best-known 'trad' climbers, originally abandoned the project after much reflection, believing the risk of a fatal fall was too great but he returned to complete it. Another climber remained on the face for four hours without moving before eventually having to unrope so that his only belayer could climb to the top and rescue him by throwing him the rope.

Before it became Johnny Dawes's masterpiece, Redhead had opened the lower part under the charming name of *Tormented Ejaculation*. He then attempted the rest of the route, still following his ethics of starting from the ground, without abseil inspection but having miraculously survived a 20-metre fall on a micro-nut, even he had deemed it necessary to put in a bolt. Dawes said he had 'placed a bolt like a dog pissing to

SMALL IN STATURE BUT IMMENSELY TALENTED: JOHNNY DAWES PERFORMING HIS *OFFSPRING*, E5 6B, BURBAGE SOUTH, PEAK DISTRICT, 1985.

mark his territory'. Later it was removed by the no-less-famous Jerry Moffatt to create his *Master's Wall*, mentioned earlier. When Redhead returned to inspect the route by abseil, he accidentally broke a small crucial hold. In response to those who accused him of wilfully damaging it, he returned to paint the broken hold very artistically, exactly the same as the broken-off piece which he then delivered to Dawes's house.

Johnny Dawes is also a real character. Besides *The Indian Face*, the first E9 (the E stands for 'extremely severe'), he also opened legendary routes which are still challenges today: *Gaia, End of the affair* and later (1990) *The very big and the very small*, a terrifying, dark slab in a slate quarry which sums up his leaping style, arising from his small size: dynamic, balancing moves, micro-footholds and elegant weight transfer.

Another rather unique character is John Dunne. His achievements on gritstone, such as *New Statement* (E8 7a, 1987) and *Parthian Shot* (E9 6c, 1990) or with a 'sport' route such at *Magnetic Fields* in Malham (1988, the first British F8b) made him famous. His appearance seemed incongruous because his excess weight did not correspond to the morphological stereotype, which is closer and closer to anorexic. He has shown that lightness is not the ultimate or the only solution. At the cancelled competition in Biot in 1987 when it poured with rain and everybody was bored, I saw him win a yoghurt-eating competition (binge eating) which was just-not-done by the Continental ascetics, who counted how many grains of rice they ate each day.

It was now the era of Margaret Thatcher and deregulation but many still managed to take advantage of the system, receiving subsidies for shared dwellings, particularly in Sheffield which had the advantage of being close to the Peak District and its craggy limestone cliffs such as Raven Tor, and the Yorkshire crags of Malham and Kilnsey. Having visited some of these 'houses', let us say that domestic chores were not an absolute priority: a vacuum cleaner was never seen and as the climber Alain Ghersen put it, 'Washing up is bad for your hands'. On the other hand, beer and fish and chips were always plentiful.

Martin Atkinson is a case apart. He was definitely plump when he discovered rock-climbing and he did not share John Dunne's theories, so he started by losing over 20 kilos. Having become one of the best climbers in Britain, he started travelling and became good friends with us, the French. Like us, he loved solo climbing but he did it the English way, on-sight. One day in Buoux on *Camembert Ferguson*, a F7a overhang 30 metres above the ground, Martin started climbing in the wrong direction. He hesitated and changed arms as everyone below, horrified, started to scream 'To the left Martin. LEFT! LEFT!' Fortunately the story ended well.

In fact we appreciated him so much that his photograph is on the cover of the *Le huitième degré*. Later he became involved in business and took over the management of the company Wild Country, well-known for making Friends.

Having started his career with Jerry Moffatt, Ben Moon succeeded him in the pursuit of extreme difficulty. After just missing the title in Bardonecchia in 1986, he paraded his dreadlocks (finally replaced in the 1990s by a platinum blond hairdo) on all the projects of the moment. Very competitive, he loved climbing in France and solving remaining problems. Thus in 1989 he redpointed the old aid-climbing route in Buoux, *Les Barouilles* and immediately renamed it *Agincourt*, after the battle in which the English defeated the French during the Hundred Years War. It was one of the first French F8c grades.

He defeated the French again by conquering the *Le Plafond* in Volx, another F8c, thus becoming the first climber to climb two routes of this level. This short overhang and its left-hand notch, so difficult to hold, should have gone to the Aix climber Alex Duboc who had made countless attempts and was perfectly prepared but he never managed to conquer it. So it was Ben who snatched it from him and renamed it *Maginot Line*. Several years later, Jibé Tribout gave him a taste of his own medicine when he called the connection *Le Super Plafond* (leaving by *Terminator*), opening *La Lune dans le caniveau* ('The moon in the gutter'), a sly reference to Ben's surname. When Patrick Edlinger repeated the route, he removed the plaque on which 'Le Plafond' was still written and sent it to Ben as a tribute.

Although Alex Duboc never climbed *Le Plafond*, he accomplished a magnificent performance for the time, linking on the same day three F8b routes of the Cimaï, *Sortilèges*, *Simulacres* and *Treblinka*. As for Ben, he made the best use of his special skills, namely fingers of steel on very short routes and in 1990 he appeared as a serious contestant for the world's first grade F9, Hubble and its terrible undercling on Raven Tor, near Sheffield.

PASSING THE TORCH

In 1984, rumours were going round in Bleau that there was a Goliath wandering in the forest, who quickly solved most problems while eating only nuts and Mars bars so as to have energy without the weight. While the first part of the rumour was correct, the second was just a myth. This man was Alain Ghersen.

An outstanding 'bleausard' (more on this later) and the surprise winner of Arco 1986, Alain soon focused on mountain climbing. It was a perfect destiny for this little Parisian who, after carrying out several impressive solos in the Alps, joined the select Compagnie des Guides de Chamonix before becoming a teacher at ENSA (École nationale de Ski et d'Alpinisme).

In 1987, Alain boldly joined together three disciplines, bouldering, rock-climbing, and the classic mountaineering so dear to Walter Bonatti, by linking three icons solo: *Carnage*, 'bleausard' f7b, *Le Bidule* in Le Saussois and finally *L'Arête de Peuterey* on Mont Blanc. This he achieved in 49 hours from Paris to the summit of Mont Blanc, with a f7b at Bleau, an F8a+ route then the full Peuterey Ridge. Quite original! Alfa Romeo lent him a sports car for the occasion and as usual, the greatest risks he took were on the road. Alain had the unfortunate habit of driving his usual Renault 5 'coach' as if it was a Porsche but the power of the engine did not match his bold overtaking manoeuvres. One day when we were travelling to Bleau, he was stopped by the gendarmerie for three offences: 1: Going through a red light, 2: Speeding and 3: Not wearing a safety belt. He just about avoided being fined for insulting the police. The fines were always sent to his

LEFT: JIBÉ TRIBOUT OVER-FOCUSED ON *LES SPÉCIA-LISTES*, F8B+, VERDON, 1987. CHECK OUT THE PINK SOCKS, A TESTIMONY OF THE DRESS CODE OF THIS ERA…
RIGHT: ALAIN GHERSEN WINCES BUT HOLDS *LE BIDULE* BETWEEN AN EXPRESS BOULDERING SESSION IN FONTAINEBLEAU AND AN ALPINE SOLO IN THE MONT-BLANC RANGE. 1987.

grandmother's address and she was harassed by bailiffs as a result but her grandson was never at home… Preferring short, intense routes by nature, Alain was less patient on longer, continuous routes. Hanging from the rope, he had extraordinary conversations with his forearms, speaking to them as if they were two different people and shouting at them for getting tired too quickly. His latest challenge is certainly his boldest: having failed to complete his studies when young. Now, at the age of 40 he has started reading philosophy at university.

In 1987, magazines were full of hard routes, impressive exploits and reclassifications as well as new names. Patrick Berhault reached the peak of his rock-climbing career with the first ascent of *Toit d'Auguste*, a very short single-finger pitch which had stopped him for several years. Shortly afterwards it was repeated by two Swiss climbers, the Nicole brothers aged 17 and 19 who were then still unknown. The on-sight level was also progressing, probably because it was often part of competitions. This meant that to stand out it was vitally important to appear over and over again, as Didier Raboutou, Robert Cortijo and Stefan Glowacz did. The first indisputable F8a climbed in this style was secured by someone who remained slightly on the fringes: Antoine Le Menestrel with *Samizdat* and its vanishing column on the Cimaï. After Luisa Iovane, Christine Gambert and then Lynn Hill had climbed the first F8a grade after several attempts, they were joined by Catherine Destivelle who carried out an impressive series in Buoux, then pushed the bar up one notch in 1988 with *Chouca* in Buoux (F8a+) before being overtaken by Isabelle Patissier (*Sortilèges*, F8b). The story became more exciting as the performance gap between men and women soon diminished, then stabilised, a sign of maturity.

At the same time a juicy controversy, so typically French, was developing between Jibé Tribout and Patrick Edlinger over *Les Spécialistes*. The popular film of that name, representative of a certain kind of French cinema in the 1980s, was inspired by the challenging 15-metre overhang of this isolated route. The route was bolted by Jacques 'Pschitt' Perrier during a technical reconnaissance climb. Jibé spent a good deal of the summer in 1987 at La Palud-sur-Verdon where he concentrated on what he thought could be an F8c. Motivated more than ever to finish first, he spent a great deal of his resting time immersed in the frozen water of a torrential spring to tone his body and lose weight. He had to leave the area briefly and since he had noticed that a key hold was loose he took the precious piece of rock with him to make sure that no one could try the climb before him. When he got back, he stuck it back in place with some epoxy glue (it was not a man-made hold since it already existed before, a subtle distinction) and finally, *Les Spés* was conquered. Jibé proudly thought that this was the first ascent of the toughest route in the world. Then the following March Patrick Edlinger repeated it, so easily according to him that he immediately downgraded it to F8b+, having found it no harder than his *Are you ready* in Chateauvert, free-climbed at the same time. Slightly irritated at first, Jibé became increasingly angry and through the magazines he demanded that Patrick Edlinger justify the grade he had given it. This was settled at Snowbird two months later and in the end history will remember that the first F8c was *Wall Street*, opened in Frankenjura by the unparalleled Wolfgang Güllich.

WOLFGANG GÜLLICH
ALL FOR THE F9

—

In the late summer of 1992, a BMW was being driven erratically and too fast on a German autobahn between Nuremberg and Munich. Exhausted after a series of media appearances, at dawn the driver dozed off, the car left the road and hit the concrete wall of a retention basin with fatal consequences.

This was how Wolfgang Güllich lost his life just before his 32nd birthday, at the height of his fame, he who more than anyone symbolises the title of this book. No one embodied the constant pursuit of difficulty better than him and eventually he reached the ninth grade.

It could be said a little unkindly that, like James Dean and Ayrton Senna, his premature death inevitably made him a legend. But through his actions and his climbing philosophy he had already acquired the aura of a pioneer by the late 1970s.

Of all the great climbers of modern times, he was the one who was best at adapting his climbing style both to his strong points and weak ones. Initially, far from the top level in on-sight climbing and in competition, he was the first to undertake specific training tailored to precise objectives. He invented the Campus Board to improve finger strength and tackled routes in the Franconian Jura, already attempted several times, which involved dynamic movements with one finger only. He also made use of the deadpoint in a lunge, arriving at the targeted hold when the trajectory was at its peak and the speed was zero. His first ascents of *Ghettoblaster*, *Wall Street* and *Action Directe* were all milestones in their day.

His range was wide, both in the types of climb and geographically. From the frozen cracks of Patagonia to the Nameless Tower in the Karakoram range and the rounded forms of Mount Arapiles in Australia, he left the twin imprint of his originality and his performance on all five continents.

After briefly dabbling in tennis, he fell completely in love with climbing while still a teenager. Taking advantage of his remarkable physique, he first made his name with free ascents of the most difficult routes in Germany's Palatinate, namely *Superlativ* (F7b) and *Batman* (F7b). Then he travelled to the United States, where he was among the most active non-Americans to repeat the Yosemite test pieces. On the east coast he conquered the legendary *Supercrack* in the Gunks and in 1982 he was the second to ascend *Grand Illusion*, often considered the first F8a in history. He was now among the very best of those who feel they must open routes to explore new perspectives. He was always an indefatigable traveller who tried to leave his mark wherever he went; for instance, in Australia with the legendary *Punks in the Gym*, an F8b+ in 1985.

Nevertheless it was in Frankenjura, not far from the scene of his fatal car accident, that he made his legendary reputation. He tackled short routes on austere rocks with compulsory movements, real bouldering problems which were very challenging in terms of reconnaissance and preparation. These included *Wall Street* (F8c, 1989) and of course its neighbour *Action Directe* (F9a, 1991). Today, repeating the 16 movements (or fewer, depending on the method) of the 12 metres of *Action Directe* is a great moment for every ambitious climber. So far no French climber has repeated it and the radical nature of the first lunge has proved insurmountable for many.

But Wolfgang will not only be remembered for his on-sight performances or competition appearances. What defined him most as a climber was the number of routes he opened, combined with specific training. As a result, the famous Campus Board he designed became a benchmark, immortalised by photographs showing him pulling himself up with a single finger on its rails. It was this preparation which enabled him to conquer *Action Directe*: 'Eleven days of trying but months of training'.

He has often been criticised for only opening short and very specific routes (involving pure strength and single finger moves), in other words, a limited range. On rock faces this may

be true but elsewhere he was an extremely versatile climber. This is apparent from the great routes he opened with his friend Kurt Albert in Patagonia (*Riders in the Storm* on Torres del Paine, 1991) and in the Himalaya (*Eternal Flame*, Trango Tower, 6,250 metres, 1989) which are still considered benchmarks of difficulty and climbing ethics. Striking too was his command of free solo-climbing, immortalised by his photographer friend Heinz Zak in the famous cracked roof of *Separate Reality* in Yosemite. This horizontal crack six metres long, climbed in 1986, will always be remembered. Some years later, Heinz Zak decided to climb it solo too, as a tribute to his mentor.

Güllich will be remembered for adding several grades to the system: the first F8b (*Kanal Im Rücken*, 1984), F8b+, F8c and F9a. These routes will always be the subject of controversy, in particular the first three, where routes of similar difficulty were also proposed elsewhere. What remains certain is that very few climbers embodied the spirit of free climbing as he did, not to mention his determination to turn climbing into a top-level sports discipline.

Towards the end of his life he was caught up by his own fame as for instance, with Ron Kauk, he was Sylvester Stallone's double in the unforgettable film *Cliffhanger*. Having decided to become a professional climber, he had to accept numerous engagements at conferences, sponsors' receptions and exhibitions. Like the handful of other 'rock stars' such as Patrick Edlinger, he had to juggle these responsibilities and doing so made him nostalgic for the total freedom of his early years.

His grave is in the cliffs of the Frankenjura he loved so much and his statue there is always decorated with flowers and climbing equipment put there by admirers from all over the world. He summed up his own philosophy as follows: 'To open a route, first you study it, then spend a few hours in the pub and only then do you climb it.' Wolfgang Güllich is no longer a climber but now he is a legend.

PAGE 147: ENTER THE LEGEND: THE LATE GERMAN WOLFGANG GÜLLICH (1960–1992) ALL IN CONTROLLED DYNAMICS ON HIS *ACTION DIRECTE*, F9A, 1991. PAGE 148: WOLGANG GÜLLICH, FIRST ASCENT OF *SYPHON*, X OU F8B, FRANKENJURA, 1990. PAGE 149: MOMENT OF GRACE FOR WOLFGANG ON *SEPARATE REALITY*, 5.12A, YOSEMITE: FIRST FREE SPACE SOLO ASCENT, 1986.

This acceleration of performance was the result of an approach based on training. Originally empirical, training gradually progressed from the pull-up bar and indoor beams to specific programmes inspired by other athletic disciplines. Pioneers in this were the French climbers Alain Ferrand and Gilles Bernigole, who transformed his loft in the Paris suburbs into a training wall for climbers. But although the French were dominant at the time, it was the German, Wolfgang Gülllich, who left his mark most widely, always in a very contained style, tackling near-impossible routes with challenging boulder sections. Gülllich had strength and talent in equal measure and he favoured dynamic movements, as John Gill had earlier.

Didier Raboutou arrived on the scene in the mid-1980s. Coming from the south-west of France, he was already a very talented skier when he took up free climbing with the same competitive spirit. After quickly repeating and opening benchmark eighth grade routes, he distinguished himself in the first important official competitions. From the very start it was his style which stood out. Rather short, he developed an incredibly precise, calm climbing style, with astute gripping of holds, exact footwork to the millimetre, little change in rhythm, even a certain slowness; in this way he advanced inexorably, like a steamroller.

Although rather reserved, especially verbally, he was one of the first climbers to develop a completely professional approach, notably towards competitions which he took part in while other top climbers were still divided on the subject. He competed in the first one, SportRoccia at Bardonecchia in 1985, then at the next in Vaulx-en-Velin in 1986. For 10 years he was one of the main competitors in both competitions. He reached his peak in 1989 when, at the age of 27, he won the legendary Arco Rock Master and finished second in the first World Cup. Strangely enough, he never won a World Cup or World Championship although apparently destined to do so, even at a time when these competitions were dominated by the French. Gradually he gave way to François Legrand and the Petit brothers.

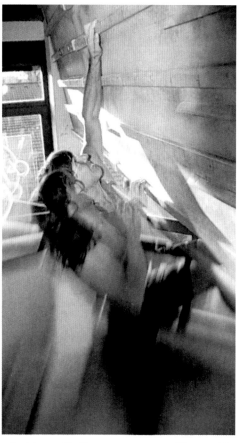

THE FAMOUS *GÜLLICH BOARD* AND ITS INVENTOR, ALLOWING VERY EFFICIENT TRAINING FOR STRENGTH AND CONTROLLED DYNAMICS.

—

PAGE 151:
DIDIER RABOUTOU ON *LE GENOU DE CLAIRE*, 7C+, VERDON, 1986.

IN THE COMPETITION ARENA

At this time, international authorities were more and more keen on organising and regulating an activity which was becoming increasingly popular with the general public. Federations were created and mountain organisations which already existed were officially recognised. The International Climbing and Mountaineering Federation (UIAA) drew up regulations, although these were often contested. The competitions now being held in famous stadia were sometimes rather amateurishly organised but the possibility of climbing becoming an Olympic sport was an appealing thought for many a climber.

So for example, in January 1988, the Ecco Grand Prix was organised on the banks of the Seine. It was the first time that an artificial climbing structure had been erected in a stadium as large as the Palais Omnisports de Bercy and the objective was of course to fill the 15,000 seats. It was a private competition like the Masters but it had the advantage of approval by the FFME (Fédération Française de la Montagne et de l'Escalade). The competition was made possible by the involvement of a major sponsor, the world's leading temporary employment agency. The Federation was already hoping that climbing would be accepted at the Barcelona Olympic Games in 1992.

Only 15 women and 18 men, intended to represent the world elite, were invited to the competition and they were encouraged by the size of the prizes: 30,000 francs (4,500 euros) for the winners. The total budget of the competition, one million francs (160,000 euros), was far beyond anything which had been seen before.

Designed by Jean-Marc Blanche, the wall was an impressive example of an artificial indoor structure. It was a grand arch, pure white, adorned with esoteric details: hieroglyphs, broken egg shell shapes and a giant arrow. Antoine Le Menestrel and Fabrice Guillot set the routes which reflected their approach which were complex, sometimes puzzling and never depending on pure strength.

An accurate reflection of the times, 95% of the participants were Europeans and two-thirds of them were French. Favourites such as Didier Raboutou, Lynn Hill and Catherine Destivelle soon asserted their supremacy. Only the duel between the two 'best female climbers in the world', with Isabelle Patissier judging the result, added a touch of suspense. The American's aggressiveness made all the difference. As for Didier Raboutou, he was victorious in a superb final against the aesthetic climber Robert Cortijo with his metronomic style, the only competitor to put any pressure on him.

Cortijo was nicknamed 'Corto' partly because he was short, as was Didier Raboutou but while Raboutou climbed like a machine, Cortijo revealed a certain genius in his climbing style. With his remarkable suppleness, he could secure the most unlikely on-sights. He was a little whimsical and often seemed to be living on another planet. I remember driving with him in February 1991 while the radio reported the latest developments in the Gulf War which was then reaching its climax. Corto suddenly asked innocently: 'What's all this about golfers fighting each other?' In spite of disappointing number of participants (9,000 spectators but fewer than

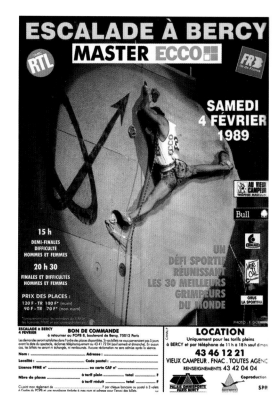

ROBERT CORTIJO PORTRAYS THE OFFICIAL POSTER OF THE 1989 BERCY MASTER.

—

PAGE 153 :

CORTO, QUITE AN ARTIST, BETWEEN SHADE AND LIGHT.

4,000 of them paying), Bercy continued to organise this symbolic event. The formula was repeated over the next two years, using the same wall assembled differently. In 1989 the event was a preamble to the first UIAA World Cup. Didier Raboutou and Lynn Hill were again the winners, defeating Jibé Tribout and Jerry Moffatt and Isabelle Patissier and Nanette Raybaud respectively.

In 1990 it was the same old story, although Patrick Edlinger, still the uncontested star, stayed away. A reconnoitred route was added to the on-sight final. Complex calculations resulted in Jibé finishing behind Moffatt and Glowacz, instead of winning as he had expected. As for Lynn, she won a historic hat trick.
The event never managed to fill the Palais Omnisports at Bercy and it attracted little media coverage, so the profits it made were disappointing. When Ecco announced that it was withdrawing, it killed the event immediately. After the World Championships at the Zenith arena in Paris in 1997, Bercy hosted climbing events for the European Championships again in 2008 and the World Championships in 2012.

In 1989, the first federal national championships enabled the UIAA to move up to the next level: it organised a World Cup with several European stages and detours to the United States and what would soon be the former Soviet Union. The stage, which was held in the valley of La Riba, brought to light Catalan climbing gems such as Siurana and Montserrat, not to mention the talent of Carlos Brasco. It revealed the geological and human potential of a nation which would play a major part in the future: Spain.
Although the Frenchmen Didier Raboutou and Jibé Tribout were regulars on the podium, it was a surprise guest who snatched the top place in the 1989 IFSC Climbing World Cup, the Englishman Simon Nadin. It was the same on the women's podium: the Marseillaise Nanette Raybaud defeated Luisa Iovane and the young American Robyn Erbesfield. France was still the most powerful country overall (with climbers such as Robert Cortijo, Jacky Godoffe, Alex Duboc, the budding star François Legrand, Patrick Edlinger – when he took part – and Corinne Labrune) but globalisation was inexorably taking place. In 1998 Yuji Hirayama caused a sensation at Nuremberg when, through a successful lunge, he became the first person who was neither American nor European to win a major competition. More than symbolic, this victory was the affirmation of the universal potential of modern rock-climbing.

04

TIME
FOR NINE

AS THE 20TH CENTURY SLOWLY CAME TO AN END, THE UNSTOPPABLE CLIMBING TRAIN CONTINUED ITS MAD PROGRESS. NOW RECOGNIZED BY INSTITUTIONS AND THE GENERAL PUBLIC AS A RESPECTABLE AND UNDERSTANDABLE SPORT, IT STILL RETAINED SOME OF THE FLAVOUR OF ADVENTURE WITH ITS AURA OF 'EXTREME' ACTIVITY'. DURING THIS TRANSITION PERIOD, MORE AND MORE CLIMBERS IN SEARCH OF RECOGNITION MAY, THEREFORE, HAVE FOUND THEMSELVES TORN BETWEEN THE RATIONALITY OF THE COMPETITION RANKINGS AND THE CALL OF THE GREAT OUTDOORS.

PAGE 154:

LYNN HILL CRUISING *THE NOSE*, EL CAPITAN, YOSEMITE.

–

PAGE 156:

JERRY MOFFATT ON *LIQUID AMBAR*, 8C+, PEN TWRYN, 1990.

1990 saw two impressive achievements by British climbers on their home ground. Jerry Moffatt was back in full force and he secured *Liquid Ambar* on Lower Pen Trwyn on the Welsh coast. Its initial F8c grade was refined over the years and stabilised at F8c+. Ben Moon secured *Hubble* (named after Hubble Space Telescope) on Raven Tor which was an even higher grade. Was it the first F9a? This question was asked recently by the present generation. It was a very short route which marked a break, as so often in the past with, for instance, *Chimpanzodrome*, *Bidule*, *Kanal*, *Wall Street* and *Agincourt*. Ben's analysis of this phenomenon is clear, spiced with a little provocation: "A short problem is more radical, either you can do it or you can't, you know this almost from the start. For a long route, you can work at it, learn the moves by heart and complete the route. It is less a matter of level than of hard work. It is also the reflection of a particular effort, especially if it is abroad. But I believe that a short route is more important. You've reached the level or you haven't. The pioneers of each level are strong climbers who therefore prefer short routes. It's afterwards that things start getting tougher and long routes make their appearance!"

BEN MOON ON *HUBBLE* AND HIS TERRIBLE UNDER-CLING! F8C+, F9A OR f8B+? RAVEN TOR, 1990.

THE MONUMENTAL 'ACTION DIRECTE'

Also in 1990, Lynn Hill, having barely recovered from her accident at Buoux, contradicted a statement by Jibé (see below) by climbing *Masse critique* on Cimaï, near Toulon. In doing this, she became the first woman to climb an F8b+ (equivalent to the magical figure of 5.14a in America). It was a route which included boulder sections as well as being fairly long. With his usual tact, Jibé Tribout who had made the first ascent, had predicted that a woman would never be able to do it which he had said to both spur her on and tease her.

A year later, Wolfgang Güllich confirmed Ben's theory: at 12 metres, *Action Directe* had become the most famous example of the short, difficult route requiring special training. Although now recognised unanimously as the first ninth grade route, its illustrious opener gave it a prudent UIAA grade of XI, equivalent to F8c+/F9a. It was originally bolted in the early 1980s by Milan Sykora and remained a project for many years. Güllich used his famous Campus Board to prepare for it and strengthen his one-finger hold technique. After numerous attempts he was successful in mid-September 1991, a year before he died. Several distinguished climbers (Moon, Tribout, Rouhling and Nicole, to name but a few) tried to repeat the route but before 2000, only one was successful, the former East German climber Alexander Adler in 1995 (who lost eight kilos for the occasion). Since then there have only been 17 proven ascents; 16 officially recognised with that of Scotsman Richard Simpson which has been questioned for lack of proof. Amongst them, the most memorable is probably the 2014 Alexander Megos one-day ascent. In view of current developments, a first on-sight is imminent or at least a flashing since all the moves are easily available on the Internet.

With the benefit of hindsight, Ben Moon's concepts were also contradicted by a series of longer, extreme routes based on continuity and inaugurated by Alexander Huber's routes (see insert). In fact, Ben worked long and hard on a long project at Kilnsey but not in his usual explosive style. In the end he had to abandon this route which was finally conquered by Steve McClure in 2000 who named it *Northern Lights* (F9a).

Although levels of difficulty and endurance required to climb the most recent extreme routes are very much higher than those needed in the 1990s, the intrinsic level of the most difficult moves has hardly evolved. This is the opinion of large number of today's leading climbers.

Hubble has not been repeated very often in 25 years and then only by British climbers. The first repeat was in 1992 by the young Scott, Malcolm Smith, an 18 year-old with fingers of steel, then by John Gaskins, Steve Dunning and Steve McClure. Adam Ondra, who made several unsuccessful attempts, suggested that it might be the first F9a ahead of its time: "The first F8c+ in the world could easily be rated F9a… These English are so strong!" More recently, he saw *Hubble* more as 'the first boulder 8b+ in history', in view of the fact that there were no runners on the first crux part. So, Ben Moon was indeed far ahead of his time in achieving what is now the first F9a in the world. To mark the fact, the 2015 collection of his clothing brand Moon Climbing includes T-shirts with the inscription 'First F9a, 25th anniversary'.

It must be admitted that 'old school' routes of the 80s and 90s are rated very harshly today compared to their current counterparts, which are often less challenging and less brutal in style. There is also the effect of climbing web sites: while 20 or 30 years ago the tendency was to downgrade another person's route, today the trend is to add plusses to grades so that climbing them sounds more impressive.

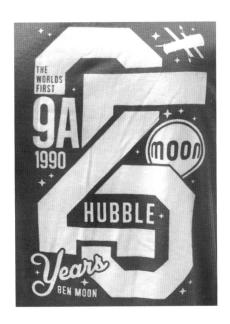

'HUBBLE FIRST 9A' T SHIRT, MOON CLIMBING 2015.

—

PAGE 158:

AN EQUATION FOR HISTORY: WG + AD = F9A!

A WOMAN AT THE TOP OF THE WORLD

As a result of training for competition, the on-sight level also rose and in 1992 Jerry Moffatt claimed the first F8b with *Serpentine* in Australia. Later this level was questioned and downgraded to F8a+ and the same happened with *Space Camp* at Saint Pé d'Ardet, climbed by Raboutou in 1991. But a year later this grade was unequivocally awarded to *Liaisons dangereuses* in the Calanques, climbed by Elie Chevieux. In 1993 the F8b grade became more widespread with successful climbs by Yann Ghesquiers, Stefan Glowacz and the Italian Severino Scassa. Then Elie Chevieux added the little + with *Les Massey Ferguson* (F8b+), again in the Calanques.

At this time, Lynn Hill was reaching the men's level. She was the first woman to secure an eight (*Simon*, F8a, Frankenjura, in 1992) and she had long been planning to tackle *The Nose*. Her first free ascent of *The Nose* was the major climbing achievement of the late 20th century, irrespective of sex.

LYNN HILL
IT GOES BOYS!

—

A living legend, Lynn Hill transcended all bias against women climbing and her name is at the highest level in the climbers' pantheon of the 20th century. A child of the 1960s, from an early age she was involved in civil rights and the struggle for equality between men and women. She thrived on the dynamism emanating from America's West Coast.

She discovered climbing as a teenager in California in the mid-70s. Her training as a gymnast and her exceptional physical and athletic condition compensated for lack of height, being a 'mere' 1.57 metres. Soon she found her way to Yosemite where she joined the libertarian fringe community of Camp 4. She described it as terribly macho in her autobiography, *Climbing Free: My Life in the Vertical World*, published in 2002. All her life she fought against sex discrimination and the attitude of 'males' to the performances of the best women climbers. She responded with numerous first ascents.

At the start of the 1980s Lynn was already nearly the best in the world, having reached grade 5.12d in 1979 (*Ophir Broke*, Colorado). With her then companion, John Long, one of the founders of the Stonemasters group of climbers, she roamed the American west from Joshua Tree to Las Vegas, taking on small jobs to support her climbing.

A long period on the East Coast enabled her to build closer ties with the American climbing elite. Back in the Shawangunks, New York State, which she used to visit in her youth, she secured the first ascent of the *Vandals* (5.13a) in 1984, unquestionably the first women's F7c+ in the world. But in order to move up this new level of difficulty, she had to reconsider her traditional ethic and work on her technique, as climbers had long been doing in Europe.

PAGE 160: LYNN HILL EXITS THE *GREAT ROOF*, 5.13C, ONE THE MOST DIFFICULT CRUXES WHEN FREEING *THE NOSE*. PAGE 161: INTO THE HEART OF *THE NOSE*.

Europe beckoned and in 1986 Lynn was invited to an international meet in the Gorges du Verdon and then to the Italian Rock Master competitions. For her, it was the discovery not only of a new culture but also of limestone, a rock well-suited to her size and approach. Although she was defeated in Italy by Catherine Destivelle, her great rival at the time, she learned fast and a few weeks later she won the Grand Prix of Troubat in the Pyrenees. (At that time competitions were held on natural outcrops.) Having decided to make climbing her living, she dominated the evolving competition circuit for the next six years, now also climbing on artificial structures: she won the Rock Master event at Arco five times and had many victories in the World Cup, competing most of the time as an outsider against European climbers, in particular the French climbers Catherine Destivelle and then Isabelle Patissier.

Meanwhile, having realised that her potential was best expressed in modern sport climbing on bolts, she spent a lot of time in Europe, especially France. She even bought a house in the Luberon and so became our neighbour. The good food and good wine she found in France certainly played a part in this because, seeing a lot of her, we soon realised that, as well as being an exceptional athlete, she was also an epicurean.
In 1989 she miraculously escaped death in Buoux after making a beginner's mistake, a badly tied knot. She survived a free-fall of 25 metres before ending up in a tree which saved her life, escaping with 'only' a shattered elbow and a broken foot.

Always keen to set herself 'larger than life' challenges and rather bored with the competition circuit, in the early 1990s she decided to return to her roots: Yosemite and El Capitan in particular, where the most famous route, *The Nose*, was still waiting to be freed after several unsuccessful attempts. This was a challenge indeed, not a female challenge but a universal one, which motivated her even more. After a first abortive attempt in 1993, she secured her first great victory in just four days completing 34 pitches, thus solving the final problem of the thin crack in the Great Roof and the very contorted moves of the following pitch, *Changing Corners*, which was settled at 5.14a/b (F8b/c). Malicious gossip suggested that her small size and thin fingers had been decisive advantages but as Lynn retorted: "The essence of climbing is to adapt one's skills to the rock and not the other way round". As well as the rating, it was her famous cry of "It goes, boys!" which put the magnitude of her exploit into perspective again.

The following year, on *The Nose* again, she took advantage of her knowledge of the moves, the strategy to adopt and especially her exceptionally good physical condition to repeat a free ascent in under 24 hours. In preparation, she had achieved on-sight climbing up to F8a and, further, made a first free ascent of the 12 pitches *Mingus*, F7c+ in the Verdon. More than 10 years would elapse before anybody, man or woman, would equal her achievement and repeat *The Nose* free.

There were other symbolic female firsts in 1998 those being the two American legends *Midnight Lightning*, the classic boulder of Yosemite and, *To Bolt or Not To Be* at Smith Rock, the first American 5.14a.
Lynn is undoubtedly the person who has contributed most to the development and popularisation of climbing in America, attracting wide media coverage and arousing the public's enthusiasm as Patrick Edlinger had done in France. In 1995, after the triumph of *The Nose*, she decided to share her experiences, taking part in various travels and expeditions to the four corners of the earth. She also organised 'adventure' climbing courses where she was generous with her advice. Then at the age of 42 she gave birth to a son, thus realising one of her dearest wishes which her intense sporting activity had delayed for a long time. While still continuing to climb, she devotes her time to him, seeing the opportunity for new challenges and adventures as a mother.

ALEXANDER HUBER
MADE IN GERMANY

—

"Without humility you cannot invest yourself in a long, difficult project." This was Alexander Huber's approach to the preparation necessary for success on extreme routes. Regarding one of his masterpieces, *La Rambla* which he did in 1994, he was quite a visionary: "If, in a few years, other climbers can climb all the pitch, so much the better. That day I shall be happy that I resisted the temptation of chipping the rock". Initially the young German allowed himself to be tempted by national competitions but without much enthusiasm. In 1997 he said: "I am really fascinated by rocks while resin leaves me completely cold but, to win the World Cup, one would really have to work hard to beat the French".

Alexander made a name for himself during the 1990s through a series of extreme routes which were much longer than those of Wolfgang Güllich and Ben Moon. His first ascent of *Om* in Germany in 1992 was recognised as the second F9a in history. Two years later he opened another F9a, *Weisse Rose* but what he really wanted to do was to explore new territories in Catalonia. After *Action Directe* and before *Biographie/ Realization*, *La Rambla* in Siurana was undeniably one of emblems of the past 20 years. This 40-metre long route is notable for the incredible scale and natural beauty of the rock but it is also remarkable for its historic interest.

It was opened by Huber as an F8c+; he placed a belay in the middle of nowhere after a few holds broke off and refused to chip holds to continue. Dani Andrada considered a way out and placed the bolts but wasn't able to free the whole thing. Then, Ramonet managed a first free ascent in 1996 at F9a. Recently reclimbed it is considered to possibly be F9a+ and if so the first one in history but that's not confirmed officially. This could possibly be the same grade as *Open Air* in Schleirwasser, Austria, which Alexander Huber did in 1996. He believed it was the hardest route ever but it was 'only' graded F9a. It was not repeated until 2008 when it was climbed by the young but already experienced prodigy Adam Ondra. Not known for exaggeration, he believed that the route deserved to be a F9a+, which retrospectively would have made it the hardest route of its time.

Huber (like his brother Thomas) proved to be a very versatile athlete. In 1995, he started a long love affair with El Capitan where he successfully conquered *Salathé Wall* free. Some saw this as a first free ascent because of a variation on the route by Skinner and Piana's 1988 ascent below the headwall which left some trying to repeat it perplexed. His brother did the same in the following year. In 1998, on the *North America Wall*, they opened *El Niño* which had free pitches of up to F8a+ and they also freed *FreeRider*. It was the same story in 2000 with *Golden Gate*, then *Corazon* in 2001 and finally the famous aid-climbing route *Zodiac* in 2003. His knowledge of El Capitan, combined with his Alpine experience, encouraged Huber to tackle the speed record of *The Nose*, the route most covered by the media in America. Challenging the greatest specialist of this discipline, Hans Florine, the brothers had to climb the 900 metres in less than three hours. Preferring the technique of the second jumarring instead of moving together, in 2007 the two brothers were the first Europeans to hold the record twice, albeit briefly. Their second time was two hours 45 minutes 45 seconds.

Back in the Alps, in the Mont Blanc Massif, Alexander Huber climbed the *Petit* route on the Grand Capucin, F8b and, in particular, the Tre Cime in the Dolomites with *Bellavista* and *Pan Aroma*, two F8c climbs to the top of the Cima Ovest. In 2013 in the Sonnwendwand (Austrian Tyrol) he opened *Nirwana*, F8c+, one of the hardest long routes of recent times. He is a bold soloist who has pushed the boundaries extremely far, both on cliffs (*Kommunist*, F8b+) and at high altitude (*Voie des Suisses* on the Grand Capucin and most importantly the *Directissime Brandler-Hasse* on the Cima Grande, also on the Tre Cime), all solo.

It was only a step from the long routes to the mountains where Huber, now in his 40s, followed in the footsteps of Güllich and Glowacz. His new climbing areas were the Himalaya (the 8,000 metres Cho Oyu) and Karakoram (the West Face of Latok II and the first free ascent of *Eternal Flame* on the Nameless Tower of Trango) and Patagonia.

Like his fellow-countryman Fred Nicole, Elie Chevieux is an unusual character, reminiscent of Antoine Le Menestrel in his on-sight involvement and for allowing his intuition and creativity to play a major part in his climbing. In other words, he has pure talent and is not keen on planned training but nevertheless he has excelled in competition as in 1993 for instance, when he won the Arco Rock Master.
After hanging up his climbing shoes, he became a photographer. In 2003 he set off on a immense tour of Asia, backpacker-style, reaching Japan by way of Russia, India, Nepal and Afghanistan. It was in that war-torn country that Elie found himself unwittingly involved in the news. In 2004, his death by lynching in Kabul was reported throughout the world. His father thought that, "...he certainly died for the sake of one more photograph", while the head of the Afghan security service hinted at drug trafficking. While funeral tributes poured in, it fortunately turned out that the information was wrong and that Elie was actually in Pakistan. Since then he has followed his three passions, travel, photography and climbing. As he says, "I love setting off but I also love coming back. There is no true travel without coming back".

THE SWISS ELIE CHEVIEUX.

–

PAGE 169:
THE BRITISH DEREK HERSEY (1956–1993), FREE-SOLOING ON ELDORADO CANYON, COLORADO.

In an era of climbing globalisation in which the French were slightly losing ground, Jibé Tribout could proudly boast that for the second time in his career he had made the first ascent of the hardest route in the United States, inaugurating a new grade, 5.14c or French F8c+, in doing so. After *To Bolt or Not To Be*, it was again at Smith Rock but on the austere East Face of Monkey Face that *Just Do It* unrolled its 43 metres, adding its name to the growing list of 'long' routes. With its radical, challenging name, it has become one of the legendary routes of the climbing world, one for which people travel thousands of miles to add to their list of routes climbed. To celebrate his victory he organised an alcohol-fuelled evening with American friends, including a pull-up competition which he proudly won but at the cost of double tendonitis of the elbows. Out of the limelight, the same grade of difficulty was achieved by Tadej Slabe in Osp in Slovenia, which had only just shaken off the Soviet yoke.

In those days, all over the world and especially in America, there were still 'climbing bums', moneyless, pilfering drop-outs, mad bolters, often homeless, who lived from hand-to-mouth. They wandered around bouldering and opening their own routes, far from sponsors, living a 'dirtbag' life as 'rock-climbing vagabonds'.

In most cases, their names were unknown except to a few initiates but their achievements were sometimes spectacular and always driven by passion. For instance, there was Derek Hersey, an unemployed English youth who had cut his teeth in the Peak District and then emigrated to Colorado in the 1980s. Living from hand to mouth, he was nicknamed 'Dr Death' around Boulder because he solo free-climbed all the classic routes of the region, from the sporty short pitches to the great routes of the *Diamond*, the East Face of Longs Peak. Dr Death called his chalk bag 'my bag of courage'. He had plenty of it until the fatal day in 1993 when he slipped free-soloing the *Steck-Salathé* route on Sentinel Rock in Yosemite and fell to his death.

THE CLIMBERS REBEL

As far as competitions are concerned, the results are never very exciting to talk about because as the years pass, they become mere lists of dates and names, getting longer with the growing number of events. Nevertheless, they chart the emergence (or decline) of some countries while also stimulating the overall rise in the level of difficulty. Although Wolfgang Güllich and Alexander Huber were exceptions, in general it is hard to be a professional and look for sponsors without taking part in competitions at some time or other.

Some professional athletes who were keen to have more control over their career and finances went their own way. At the time I wrote: 'Many climbers are already envisaging a division between an amateur system, under the control of the UIAA and the federations and a self-managed professional circuit. Is this utopia or a prophecy?' Well, the answer was quick to come, it was utopia.

JIBÉ TRIBOUT OPENING THE HARDEST US PITCH, JUST DO IT, 5.14C, SMITH ROCK, 1992.

It was in September 1988 that ASCI (the Association of Sport Climbers International) was founded. At the famous Arco Master, a few rebels from all countries (Patissier, Destivelle, Moffatt, Atkinson, Steulet, Glowacz, Tribout and Raboutou among others) tried to put the world to rights as they sat on the terrace of the Café Trentino by setting up an international association to defend the rights of competition climbers. Since the objective of ASCI was to form the basis for a professional circuit in opposition to the federal amateur system championed by the UIAA (with its vision of Olympic participation), it was quickly decided to use a ranking system, like that of the ATP in tennis. The classification was to be based on the amount of money earned, as is the case with golf and not by position.

But this was still a little premature. The first great battle took place in Leeds in May 1989 during the first UIAA World Cup. To prevent the suppression of qualifying for the Open, the climbers threatened to strike and soon obtained what they wanted. Then there were a few upheavals mainly regarding the rules of the game, in particular the fundamental question of the way of assessing the height measured.

The following two years marked the apogee of the ASCI with the creation of the World Master Tour as a counterpoint to the UIAA World Cup. Nanette Raybaud and François Legrand were the winners in 1991. Better funded and better covered by the media intheir respective countries, the prestigious events of the WMT such as Serre-Chevalier, Arco and La Riba seemed to mark the beginning of a true professional era in which private organisers held all the trump cards.

Yet, this did not happen, because by the following year the balance of power had tipped in favour of an international state system, led by the most influential federations at the time, the Italian and the French ones. With such motivated leaders as Marco Scolaris, still today president of the IFSC (International Federation of Sport Climbing), it is reasonable to attribute this reversal of the situation to the lack of cohesion of the climbers themselves.

In 1990 Martin Atkinson handed over the presidency to Jibé Tribout, who quickly discovered the difficulty of balancing climbing with presiding. In the latter role he found himself facing the most varied problems. One was that, administratively speaking, ASCI did not actually exist, a fact which had been carefully concealed from the other official authorities. There were no statutes and the headed writing paper had the address of Jibé's parents' pub and Jibé himself, who had never been officially elected, started receiving membership cheques to be paid into a hypothetical ASCI bank account. In order to finance itself and with the agreement with the organisers, ASCI suggested taking a percentage of the money paid to the climbers but this idea never came to anything because it was unpopular with the climbers, who were delighted that such a force of opposition existed to defend their interests but were not at all keen to invest time and money into it. Relatively speaking, climbing lacked the charismatic visionary, megalomaniac visionary of a Bernie Ecclestone in Formula 1.

A few years later, Jibé was quite open about the matter: 'The climbers had been disappointing; the first national teams had been formed but those concerned then sat on the fence trying to please everyone, never really becoming involved while giving in to the strong pressure of their federations. I left in disgust during a meeting of CICE (the committee in charge of competitions within the UIAA, on which ASCI had finally succeeded in getting a seat) when it was decided to make an overall reduction in the amount paid to climbers during the World Cup, on the pretext that climbers earning money was not good for the future of the sport. So I stopped immediately.' By 1992 the ASCI no longer existed except for its permanent ranking system and this too disappeared when UIAA took it over. As a result, there is now an annual World Cup, organised in stages, plus biannual Championships, as it the case with most major federal sports.

ASCI Association of Sport Climbers International

Jean Baptiste Tribout, Président
35, rue Etienne Marcel
75001 Paris France
Tel. 33 90 79 56 23
      33 (1) 42 33 49 00
Fax. 33 (1) 42 33 33 15

Andy Brown, Secretary
Great Britain
Tel. 44 943 870327
Fax. 44 943 870509

SHORT-LIVED OFFICIAL ASCI HEADER.

STEFAN GLOWACZ
FROM PLASTIC TO ANTARCTICA

For 30 years, Stefan Glowacz has been one of the most famous characters in the world of rock-climbing, widely covered by the media. Younger than the German generation of Kurt Albert and Wolfgang Güllich, he made a name for himself at an early age with the first repeat of *The Face*, the first German X- (F8a), opened by Jerry Moffat and also through several benchmark climbs of 5.13 in the United States, such as *Phoenix* in Yosemite and *Rainbow Wall* in Colorado. The first competition in Bardonecchia in 1985, highly rated both for difficulty and style, was made for him. The feline fluidity of his moves, his good looks and long hair made him the logical winner and a star. And this was just as well because he was absolutely determined to live off climbing. He was one of the first climbers to make a living from his sponsors.

In the following years he was a leading competitor in major competitions, notably as triple winner of the Arco Rock Master. He also travelled a lot, to Australia (first repeat of *Punks in the Gym*, Australian grade 32 and opening of *Lord of the Rings*, 31, in the Arapiles), Japan, the United States, France and Spain. He achieved his first F8c in 1992 with *Agincourt* in Buoux and he was considered the best on-sight climber at the time. In 1993, his 'second life' started. Suffering from recurrent knee problems which required several operations, he decided to retire from competition and concentrate on more adventurous, almost Alpine climbing. With the first ascent of *Des Kaisers Neue Kleider* in the Kaisegebirge, eight pitches including two F8b+, he was also the first to complete the Alpine trilogy of the three hardest multi-pitch routes. The trilogy was completed by *Silbergeier* (F8b+ seven pitches, Rätikon) and *End of Silence* (F8b+, 11 pitches, Berchtesgaden) and it has been one of the most attempted challenges of the last 20 years. Stefan was the first to complete it in 2001.

Meanwhile he widened his horizon even further, often with the late Kurt Albert, tackling the big walls of Greenland (including the thousand metres of the famous *Moby Dick*) and cliffs on Baffin Island, in Antarctica and also in Mexico (first ascent of *El Gigante*). In the last few years he has been more a mountaineer than a rock-climber (first ascent of Cerro Murallon in Patagonia). He loves exploring and publicise still unclimbed faces, such as the rocky outcrops in deepest Siberia in winter or a giant cavity in Oman with Chris Sharma. As a shrewd businessman (he started the Red Chili climbing shoes business) and the father of triplets, his early passion for climbing has always remained strong and creative.

PAGE 172: THE GERMAN STEFAN GLOWACZ, PICTURED HERE IN THE UK IS COMFORTABLE ON ALL STYLES. PAGE 173 ABOVE: DON THE FAMOUS ROOF OF *KACHOONG*, 21 OR F6C, ARAPILES, AUSTRALIA. PAGE 173 BELOW: THE ROUGH LIFE OF BUM CLIMBER! PAGES 174-175: STEFAN GLOWACZ PERFORMING THE MOST ICONIC BOULDER ON EARTH: *MIDNIGHT LIGHTNING*, V8, CAMP 4, YOSEMITE.

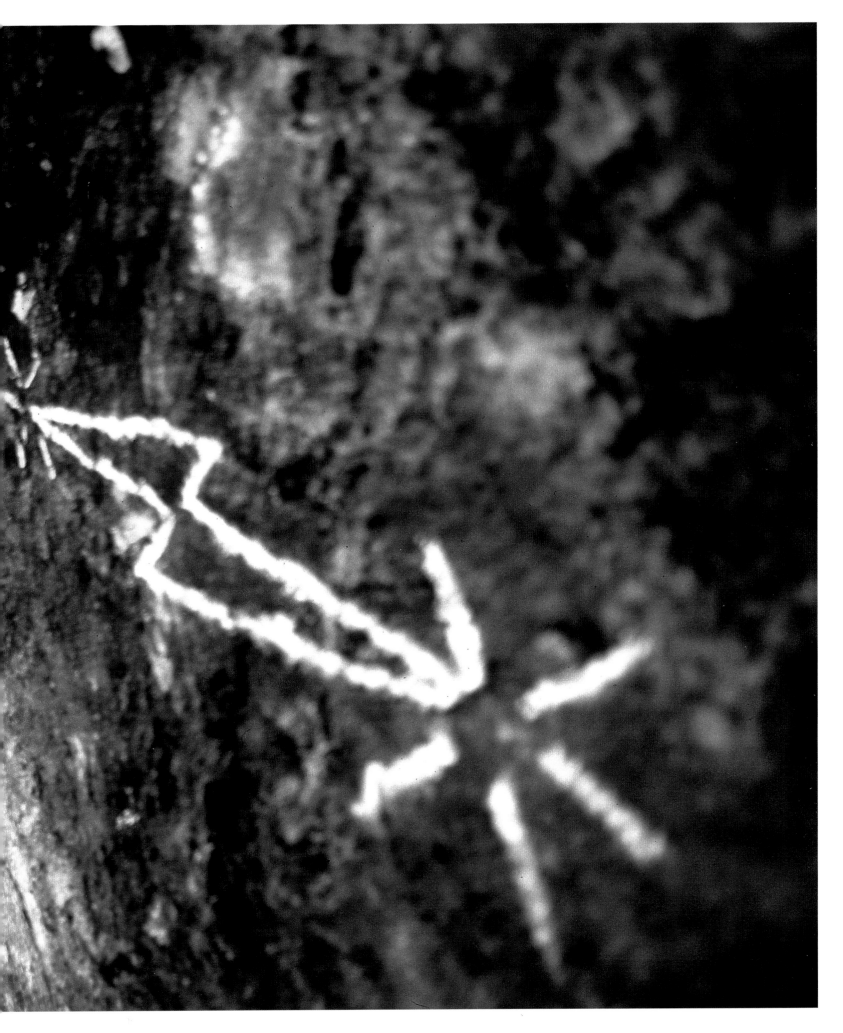

CHAMPIONS OF THE WALLS

Another climber who stands out for his amazing list of achievements is François Legrand, known at the as *The Big*. Three consecutive victories in the first World Championships (1991, 1993 and 1995), five times winner of the World Cup (the annual classification based on several stages) in 1990, 1991, 1992, 1993 and 1997, four Arco Rock Master titles, plus of course the European and French Championships: his supremacy in the early 1990s was overwhelming.

Born in 1970 into a family of mountaineering enthusiasts, François very early on covered his bedroom walls with climbing stars, including Edlinger. After a terrible fall in Buoux which required a long period of recuperation and regenerative body-building, in 1988 he finished second behind Jacky Godoffe in the first senior French championships. More motivated than ever, he secretly gave up studying to go and spend a (harsh) winter in Buoux where he rubbed shoulders with the climbing elite of the time. It was during this period of intense rock-climbing that he developed his steely determination whilst also thinking about the best way to apply his progress to competition. He became very interested in training techniques: "I did some more or less analytical research into climbing moves in order to discover ways of solving problems of body movements and this enabled me to find positions adapted to almost every situation in relation to my skills. Everyone has their own strong points and not everyone does a move the same way and in any case, people do not experience difficulties in the same way. Knowing more about the subject has enabled me to anticipate difficult moves and to position myself correctly, accelerating at the right time while respecting the climbing rhythm." In addition, Legrand had an extraordinary ability to memorise holds and moves. When sharing a flat with Yuji Hirayama, they installed a climbing wall in the living room and spent entire days training the equivalent of 20 pitches on a crag. Having retired from competition, he has become a coach, training the French teams of young climbers amongst others.

Changes were taking place among the female climbers. Lynn Hill started (very) slowly to take a step back and Catherine Destivelle had moved to the mountains. Isabelle Patissier, after her double victory in the 1990 and 1991 World Cups and her marriage to Nicolas Hulot and subsequent divorce, became a successful rally driver. She was the first woman world champion in her category in the Paris-Dakar Rally in 2004.

The female counterpart of 'The Big' was Robyn Erbesfield who won four consecutive World Cups. Small but muscular, she took over as America's representative when Lynn Hill turned to more traditional climbing. Born in Georgia in the deep South, she discovered climbing by accident through her then boyfriend. When she moved to Boulder, Colorado, her level went sky high. As a training fanatic, within a few months she went from being completely unknown to winning a stage in the World Cup. Like François Legrand, Robyn was the great champion of the early

FRANÇOIS LEGRAND AKA THE BIG.

—

PAGE 177:

ABOVE: ROBYN ERBESFIELD.

BELOW: LIV SANSOZ IN THE VERDON GORGE.

1990s: she won the World Cup four times in a row, from 1992 to 1995. In fact, she said that she owed a lot to François as far as training was concerned. It was in France that she achieved her best rock-climbing performances with an on-sight F8a+ at Lourmarin and F8b+ elsewhere after several attempts, the second woman in the world after Lynn Hill to reach this level. She married the Frenchman Didier Raboutou in 1993 and became World Champion in 1995, succeeding Susi Good of Switzerland (another of the first women to have conquered F8b+) who had taken the first two editions.

Among the most dazzling characters was the American Katie Brown who, in spite of her minute size and weight (1.50 metres and 33 kilos), would crush the opposition. After just two years' climbing, she became Junior World Champion in 1995 at the age of 15. In the following year she won the X-Games and Arco Rock Master, the most important competitions.

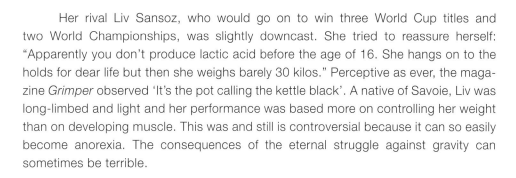

Her rival Liv Sansoz, who would go on to win three World Cup titles and two World Championships, was slightly downcast. She tried to reassure herself: "Apparently you don't produce lactic acid before the age of 16. She hangs on to the holds for dear life but then she weighs barely 30 kilos." Perceptive as ever, the magazine *Grimper* observed 'It's the pot calling the kettle black'. A native of Savoie, Liv was long-limbed and light and her performance was based more on controlling her weight than on developing muscle. This was and still is controversial because it can so easily become anorexia. The consequences of the eternal struggle against gravity can sometimes be terrible.

She has secured several classic on-sights such as *Omaha Beach*, an F8b on her favourite cliffs on the Red River in her native Kentucky. Since then she has been less in the public eye, making a few expeditions and long routes. Today, a happy 35-year old, she has given up top level climbing but as she says: "I have climbed in places I dreamt of and I have done everything I wanted to. Not everyone can say that."

YUJI HIRAYAMA
A CLIMBER FROM THE EAST

—

When some of us travelled to Japan with Marc Le Menestrel in 1987 as the first Western climbers to find out about sport climbing in Asia, we were invited by the local newspapers to sponsor the first official climbing competition in the country. We were very impressed by the talent of the winner, a young climber, just turned 18 and naturally unknown. He was Yuji Hirayama.

Since that first competition, Yuji has become a true legend. He is probably the most versatile high-performance climber of the last 20 years with hard routes on-sight, bouldering, competitions, big walls, traditional climbing and speed-climbing; nothing has escaped him. Many considered him the best climber in the world because he is the best all-rounder, effective and aesthetically stylish. His influence on today's generation and the inspiration he provides is enormous.

Of course the Japanese had been distinguished mountaineers before him, especially in the Himalaya and later in the Alps but, normally, these made rather laborious group ascents or risky solo climbs. Yuji was encouraged by the first free-climbing generation in Japan and also by the visits of stars such as Jerry Moffatt and Stefan Glowacz. This immediately gave the young man the idea of travelling. He realised that his future would benefit from discovering those places where climbing was developing so fast in the United States and Europe, particularly the South of France.

After his first stays in Yosemite and then Buoux, his level swiftly rose to F8b. He had not yet reached the top level of the best climbers in the world but he was already the best climber in Asia. Now he set off to climb the rock faces of Europe from his base in Aix-en-Provence where, in 1989, he shared a flat with François 'The Big' Legrand. The main room was completely converted into one big training wall and intensive training on it paid off well. A first victory in the World Cup in Nuremberg boosted his growing fame. His feline, technical style, combined with excellent intuition were working wonders. But although he won the prestigious Arco Masters, he remained in The Big's shadow during the 1990s as far as competition results were concerned.

Then followed a more indulgent Spanish period as well as a few injuries but he pulled himself together both physically and mentally, helped by intensive yoga. His moment of glory finally came at the turn of the millennium. He won the World Cup in 1998 and again in 2000. These successes transformed his status in his native country. Beyond the closed rock-climbing community, he became a real star of Japanese sport with all its advantages, but with the pressures and media coverage associated with it.

The following years revealed new facets of his talent. Leaving the world of competition, he distinguished himself with the first on-sight of *Mortal Kombat* in Castillon (2000); this was then considered an F8c but Yuji himself very honestly assessed it 'rather as an F8b+'. He then achieved an unequivocal on-sight F8c first ascent: this was *White Zombie* in the Baltzola cave in the Basque Country in 2004, in preparing for which nothing was left to chance. He spent three weeks practising by climbing neighbouring rock faces and one hour each day studying the route with binoculars. This shows how much things had changed since the early 1980s when for an on-sight, any prior view of the slightest inch was absolutely forbidden.

He had another unfortunate injury during a trip to the United States with François Legrand. While pulling up to climb back up the rope after a fall, one of his fingers was caught in a loop of the rope; silly things can happen even to the best.

As far as top-level difficulty is concerned, he has cleared the bar of F9a several times and, back in Japan, he reached 5.15 (F9a+) by redpointing *Flat Mountain* (this is what his name 'Hirayama' means). He threw himself into bouldering, a field which had never been his speciality and, still in Japan, reached V14 or rather the 5th Dan: a little known fact is that Japan has its own rating scale for bouldering, which is the one used for martial arts.

PAGE 179: YUJI, THE MOST EUROPEAN OF THE JAPANESE CLIMBERS.

But what turned him into a real legend were the great Yosemite cracks. From the start he had a particular aptitude for climbing on bolts, flashing *Sphinx* (5.13c) in Colorado. On El Capitan he free-climbed *Salathé Wall*, *Golden Gate* and *El Niño*, only just failing to climb them on-sight. In the case of *Salathé,* he surprised everyone by announcing in 1997 that he wanted to climb it in this way. Then, even more surprisingly, he set about breaking the speed record of *The Nose*, in 2002 starting a battle with the Huber brothers which was widely covered by the media. He broke their record twice in 2008 by climbing it in two hours 37 minutes five seconds, leading the entire route and most of the time climbing simultaneously with his partner Hans Florine.

Today, in his 40s, he is exploring new climbing areas such as Mount Kinabalu in Borneo where at an altitude of over 4,000 metres he recently opened an F8c. He is also a shrewd businessman who owns some the finest indoor climbing centres in Japan, which benefit from his reputation.

PAGE 180: YUJI HIRAYAMA STAYS FIT, EVEN IN 2015! PAGE 181: YUJI ON KALYMNOS ISLAND, GREECE.

FRENCH SUPREMACY

Now, the climbers who had excelled in the previous decade were joined all over the world by a new generation, trained on climbing walls: Boone Speed in the United States, Guido Kostermeyer, the Bindhammer brothers, Marietta Uhden in Germany, Malcolm Smith, Mark Leach, John Gaskins in England, Elie Chevieux in Switzerland, Gerhart Horager and Klem Loskot in Austria, Christian Core, Christian Brenna, Luca Zardini, Severino Scassa in Italy, Jean-Paul Finné and Muriel Sarkany (future World Champion) in Belgium, Patxi Arocena, Carles Brasco, Pedro Pons, Dani Andrada in Spain, Martina Cufar and Marco Lukic in Slovenia, Daï Koyamada in Japan, Garth Miller in Australia and Salavat Rakhmetov (pioneer of the first bouldering competitions) and Elena Ovchinnikova in Russia.

Many of them were French: Laurence Guyon (Rock Master 95), the brothers François and Arnaud Petit, Yann Ghesquiers and François Lombard (winner of the 1994 World Cup and of two Rock Masters), were the most active in competition climbing. François Petit was the prototype of the young talent, not overawed by his elders. Between 1991 when he won the French Championship at the age of 16 and in 1999, when he won the World Cup, he concentrated mainly on competition: "In the past it was all about doing increasingly hard routes while today it is training to win competitions. For me, climbing started in 1988 with Jibé Tribout. Before that, there was nothing".

In 1994, a month after Jibé had conquered the F8c+ *Superplafond* in Volx, he opened *Bronx* in Orgon. This route of similar difficulty, worthy of a large artificial wall, had until then stopped even the best and, just to make a point, François Petit did it several times in a row. His older brother Arnaud, also outstanding in competitions (he won the World Cup and European Championship in 1996) was more open to climbing on real rock and later he joined Stéphanie Bodet (winner of the first edition of the Bouldering World Cup in 1999) to climb rock walls around the world.
Throughout the 1990s, the Difficulty World Cup (which annually rewards the consistency of the best climbers) was always won by French climbers, with the exception of one men's title (Hirayama 98) and six women's titles (shared between Robyn and Muriel Sarkany). But this crushing supremacy was not to last.

PAGE 182:
ABOVE: FRANÇOIS PETIT.
BELOW: THE SLOVENIAN MARTINA CUFAR ON *CHIQUITA*, 8B, MISJA PEC, OSP, SLOVENIA.

—

PAGE 183:
FRANÇOIS LOMBARD IN HIS LOCAL AREA BRIANÇONNAIS ON *BALLADE D'ENFER*, F7B ON TÊTE D'AVAL.

A NOT SO NATURAL ROCK AFTER ALL...

A recurrent problem is the chipping of holds and, more generally, tinkering with the rock which becomes particularly relevant where levels of difficulty are concerned. People point the finger at certain famous sites such as Orgon in France or Fork Canyon and Mount Charleston in the United States but these are just the result of a long evolution. In Bleau there is an ancient chipping tradition, particularly in the Cuvier area with famous boulders such as *Carnage*, the first f7b in 1977. In the same era, Ray Jardine chipped holds on the *The Nose* on El Capitan in order to free climb it. Most of the holds in Le Saussois, to mention an example of just one rock face, are holes made by pitons placed by previous generations. In Buoux, the holes sometimes need a very thorough cleaning before being declared fit for climbing and, just to provoke, Jacky Godoffe would screw a short-lived succession of artificial fluorescent holds on the smooth surface of the *Os à Moëlle*. When the first competitions were still taking place on natural sites, rock faces were often massacred with hammer bits and trowels.

These bad examples have sometimes inspired other bolters to treat entire rock faces in this way and at all levels, to make them easier or to create new routes. In Annot, for example, which is famous for its natural boulders, routes have been created on entirely smooth surfaces and this with the approval of the Town Hall, which is keen to attract more tourists. After all, climbers (and particularly foreign climbers with money to spend) are also potential tourists and consumers.

Many big names are against the practice. In the words of Alexander Huber: "Rather than chip the rock, I prefer to wait to make progress so as to give it a true rating, not one which reflects the present top level of climbers but one which corresponds to a sequence of natural holds". Ben Moon is of the same opinion, as is Fred Nicole who has said: "The climber must adapt to nature and not nature to his fantasies". They point the fingers to French 'DIY' climbers such as Marco Troussier, François Legrand and Fred Rouhling, to mention only the most famous. But whenever one starts bolting, the line between consolidation and improvement is very narrow, as is that between picking out little pieces and carving a hole, especially with the arrival of synthetic products such as epoxy resin...

Antoine Le Mestrel said that: "Holds are the weak points in our discipline. They can be broken, enlarged, filled or carved. They are at the mercy of the goodwill of the opener and of the climbers."

All over the world, the 1980s and 1990s saw questionable practices being carried out, both on boulders and cliffs rock faces as well as on all kinds of rocks, particularly on the limestone cliffs of Europe.

AMERICAN FORK, ONE OF THE NEW AMERICAN SPORT CLIMBING CRAGS OF THE 1990s.

NEW DEVELOPMENT

After 1995 and the Akira 'bombshell', things calmed down a little in extreme climbing. In 1996 Alexander Huber did not dare to add a little + to the F9a of his *Open Air* but it was something which Adam Ondra did not hesitate to do after his first repeat of this route several years later. Meanwhile Fred Rouhling continued to concentrate on Les Eaux-Claires. Four years before Tom Cruise's similar move in *Mission Impossible 2*, he invented the crossover of *La Rose et la Vampire*, with his feet in the void and his back to the rock. It was *L'autre côté du ciel* which led him to make his memorable statement: "Of course it is natural. Naturally drilled!"

Some routes, not necessarily the hardest and most overhanging, become legendary, such as the masterpiece of the famous Austrian redhead, Beat Kammerlander's Voralpsee Spee, only F8c+ but 80 dream moves.

LEFT: THE AUSTRIAN BEAT KAMMERLANDER.
RIGHT: BEAT KAMMERLANDER ON *SPEED*, F8C+, VORALPSEE, ONE OF THE MOST BEAUTIFUL PITCHES IN EUROPE.

THE AKIRA CASE

Here is an example which should have remained a Franco-French debate (for Les grosbif this means that the French just wanted to argue among themselves) but thanks to the little symbol following the number it became an international affair, taking the form of a real thriller with a suspect, accusations, investigations and counter-investigations over almost 20 years.

In 1995 when Fred Rouhling announced that he had opened a F9b in an unknown cave in the very heart of the Charente, he was far from being unknown. Earlier on when studying at Luminy University in Marseilles, he had explored the Grotte de l'Ours, opening the first F8c of the Calanques with *UFO* and conquering the *Directe des Spécialistes* in Verdon, giving an F8c to this famous route of the 1980s. In 1993 he even made the first French F9a at a time when examples of this grade worldwide could be counted on the fingers of one hand.

It was *Hugh* at Eaux-Claires, a white overhang, an old route with climbing aids which Fred had cheerfully carved, then modified, among other things to 'create' the enormous median lunge which, although it was not the hardest move, established his reputation: "It's obvious that the hold at the start of the lunge and the one where it finishes are not ideal but, it should be understood that I bolted it before the development of climbing walls. This type of wide move where two good handholds were some two metres 40 apart was something quite innovative at the time". At the time, chipping or tampering with the rock to make holds was normal practice and not one to be criticised, after a decade of 'aided' or carved chipping from Buoux to Orgon or at Smith Rock and Mount Charleston in the United States.

Soon, climbers repeating it like Jean-Minh Trinh-Thieu reported contradictions between the declared grade of difficulty of the starting section and the reality. Even more so than *Akira*, *Hugh* in the course of time became a regular subject in the climbing discussion forums on the Internet, such *Camptocamp*, where people would debate matters at length for page after page. The main question asked was whether these potential repeaters were actually trying the same route.

On *Camptocamp*, his main critic used the name LocalCharente who led a police-like investigation, supported by photographs and videos, in order to denounce alleged irregularities by Fred Rouhling such good holds altered to make them flat after the ascent, a new mono-finger appearing afterwards and each side blaming the other, edited videos not validating the ascent and so on. One of the main weaknesses of these forums is the anonymity given by using a pseudonym, which makes accusations and slander much easier.

On the other hand, an unknown local man using convincing arguments to accuse a famous climber who is also a professional (in that he derives an income from his activities) is in an unfair situation. It is always much harder to prove someone has cheated than the other way round and relatively easy for the accused (in this case Fred Rouhling) to appear as a persecuted victim: "I am glad that the participants in the forum have unmasked the author of these defamatory statements and made him admit that he was the sole source of this slander". (The name of LocalCharente was eventually revealed: Philippe David.)

Just a virulent as the *Akira* business, if not more so, was the *Hugh* controversy, again centred on Fred Rouhling. *Hugh* was finally repeated by the Italian Alessandro 'Jolly' Lamberti who confirmed the F9a rating, then again in the following year by Pierre Bollinger who showed amazing perseverance: "Having realised that this route did not suit me at all, I decided to work on my physical condition in order to climb it. Rouhling had made it his toy with his acrobatics". Then it was repeated again in 2002 by Daï Koyamada. Yuji Hirayama, who accompanied him, remarked rather perceptively at the time: "*Hugh* is harder than all the F8c+ climbs I have tried. Its grade is out of the world... for the moment".

Akira follows the roof of a dark, humid cave across a stretch of 15 metres before a face climb exit. As a result, a large part of the climb takes place without karabiners, as a very long boulder problem with the rope only being used towards the end but, the relatively high roof makes the crux bits very difficult (Fred used a ladder to get into place). Because some holds are fragile he strengthened them with epoxy resin. The cave was very close to Fred's family house and in 1995 he often stayed there because his wife Céline was convalescing there after a serious accident.

In 2004 journalists of the American magazine *Climbing* came to investigate on site. Asked about the keys of his success and why he had not conquered a harder route since, he explained it as follows: "Three reasons: route, style and time. It is very hard to find a route which is exactly at your limit and is exactly in your style and to have unlimited time to do it. I have never found another route meeting all these conditions". To prove his achievement after the event, the Frenchman repeated sections of *Akira* in front of the journalists.

Suggesting a F9b in 1995 without any witnesses was bound to attract criticism. Ben Moon strongly disapproved: "A F9b, that's rubbish. It's stupid to think you are three grades ahead of everyone else. You don't just claim that your route is a F9b without asking anyone's opinion. I bet that if tomorrow I was to say that I had conquered a F9c and taken photographs just anywhere, I would be in most magazines if the pictures were good. But it would prove nothing. It is important to see people climb and not to be alone when you are working on a route." Alexander Huber shared Ben Moon's opinion: "The rating seems crazy to me. If he has reached that level, he is far ahead of all the other climbers in the world." Later in 2006 he added: "One thing should be clear, we all want to believe the other climbers but, if this is not possible, I cannot validate their ascents because the history of mankind has taught us that we cannot believe everything without question. Chris Sharma has climbed and earned his credibility. Fred, in my opinion, has not earned his, he is the centre of too much controversy."

FRED ROUHLING

—

PAGE 186:
FRED ROUHLING PERFORMING THE BIG JUMP ON *HUGH*,
FIRST F9A IN FRANCE IN 1993, EAUX-CLAIRES.

On the other hand, those who criticised did not travel to the cave to check but others such as Jibé Tribout and then Dani Andrada made this effort a few years later. Coached by Fred himself, Jibé managed to carry out all the moves of the ceiling except one and he found the exit methods much easier but he was still impressed by the level of difficulty of the route: "We tried without a crash pad and those who go and see it one day will realise that it is an enormous commitment because the roof is very high and there is an unpleasant boulder under the crux. Apart from consolidation, the route was untouched at the time and if holds were chipped, this was done later. As to the rating, I had F8c+ at the time and the route seemed to me very hard but perhaps feasible. When Fred tried he was using more difficult methods than me, I was using easier ones but he did not like them. He obviously preferred his own. F9a already seemed a good rating to me but F9b was definitely too high, especially since historically one does not jump grades because it is impossible to understand such a leap. As a result, it tainted the rest of his career. He either regressed, or the route was overrated. The only mistake was to rate it so high. But this does not mean that Fred is not a super strong climber."

Interviewed by *Grimper* in 1997, Fred admitted that he did not favour the easiest methods but chose the one he preferred: "In rock-climbing, the grade of a route is based on the easiest moves. As for me, I go where the route seems the most imposing. I love impressive routes and beautiful profiles and I am not interested in knowing if I shall be able to Shunt the crux or not. When I have found the right moves, I finish and I no longer question my methods."

Later, in 2004, he admitted that if he had to do it again he would not have give *Akira* an F9b so as to avoid all controversy. Nevertheless, the grades of all his other first ascents in Eaux-Claires, such as *Kami* or *Archipel*, have been confirmed by repeat ascents. Naturally if one was not speaking of the hardest routes in the world at the time, these stories would be academic, apart from the quest for truth by the accusers and the legitimate defence of his honour by Fred Rouhling.

Since 2000, Fred has done a lot of bouldering in order to add an impressive list of 'bleausard' and Swiss grades, initially established by Fred Nicole, as well as 'rediscover' Eaux-Claires. Then, after moving to Haute-Savoie, he conquered new ninth grades such as *Mandallaz Drive* (F9a), *Salamandre* (F9a+), *Empreintes* (F9a+), acquiring a few critics on the way but also loyal supporters such as the best French climber today, Romain Desgranges, European Champion in 2013. Today he runs an indoor climbing hall which is part of a massive sports centre near Annemasse. But in the end, he remains for many what he was at the beginning: an outsider, a rather solitary climber in his extreme achievements. It is obvious that to take credit for the hardest routes in the world without confirmation by others would not be possible today. Ondra's and Sharma's lists of achievements have never been questioned because they were always carried out in front of other people, almost live and they are always very cautious about grading their routes before they have been repeated.

As to *Akira*, it has never yet been repeated…

A FRAGILE HERITAGE

Today, the bolting of cliffs (or by now the first re-bolting) has benefited from the existence of fast, battery-powered drills which have made it possible to establish secure routes much more easily and in much less time. Hilti, Bosch and Ryobi have become part of the climber's vocabulary. But bolting has a price and it involves the increasingly important concept of civic responsibility. The bolter has the choice of working on his own and at his own expense or to enrol as members of joint plans, which are to some extent subsidised. But globally, the DIY solution which was still the rule not long ago has become increasingly marginal. In 1991, the Access Fund was created in the United States. It is a non-profit making organisation whose main objective is to preserve the vertical heritage from bans (and from inconsiderate climbers). Indeed, many sites in the US are situated on private property and the Access Fund sometimes buys them off the owner.

In Europe, conflicts of interest often arise when a nature reserve is involved or an exotic bird is in the wrong place from the climber's point of view.

Wonderful discoveries of new climbing areas are being made all over the world. Examples in the US include: Rifle (Colorado), Red River Gorge (Kentucky), Rumney (New Hampshire) and the Hueco boulders in Texas. Meanwhile the Spanish have been exploring neighbouring Morocco (the Todra Gorge), Sardinia has appeared on the climber's map and the Thai islands are becoming a much favoured exotic destination.

DANIEL DU LAC RIDING, HUECO, TEXAS.

BUOUX, CEÜSE, SIURANA
END OF THE MILLENNIUM CLIFFS

Buoux will always remain a seminal rock face, not only for modern rock-climbing in France but also internationally. The gem of the Luberon has been explored for centuries, in particular by climbers since the 1960s, among them the legendary 'blacksmith' Raymond Coulon who made his own pitons. In the late 1970s, matters gathered pace, first with the free-climbing of the 'classics' and the recurrent north/south confrontation in which Jean-Claude Droyer always played the part of the 'baddie' from the North. The softness of the limestone mollasse and its numerous holes encouraged a frantic opening of routes in which many climbers took part, such as Patrick Edlinger, Bruno Fara's Lyon gang and our own little gang. We were young, keen Parisians enjoying the Luberon sun, so things could not be better for us. We spent happy times on those limestone outcrops as well as bivouacking in the wild and in the dry-stone shelters on the Claparèdes plateau, sometimes playing cops and robbers with the Bonnieux constabulary, especially at the time of the first climbing bans.

PAGE 190:

HRH CEÜSE UNDER THE SNOW.

—

PAGE 191:

ABOVE: THE AIGUEBRUN, BUOUX MAIN CRAG.

BELOW: STAYING AT LA PLAGE (THE BEACH) IN BUOUX DURING WINTER TIME REQUESTS A STRONG MOTIVATION!

SIURANA, SIURANELLA AREA, SPAIN.

Buoux soon became the victim of its own success, closely followed by the media. There was the documentary *La Vie au bout des doigts* of course but also articles in several magazines including some widely read in Germany. (Fara, known for his lack tact and good taste, opened a few routes with explicit names: "*Germanophobie* will express our resentment towards thoughtless foreigners whose behaviour led to the banning of the rock face for a whole year and sometimes even forever in the case of the *Confine.*" This was in 1984; the west face was finally opened again in 2010, after a ban of 27 years.

During the 1980s, Buoux became an international hotspot. The international crème de la crème met up at the camp site of Les Cèdres d'Apt, the French version of Camp 4, which was run with a rod of iron by the unforgettable Lucette. For the impoverished, there were the joys of winter camping or the caves (even in the south the winters are often freezing cold). The middle classes rented caravans while the super-rich enjoyed the luxury of the Auberge des Seguins, right at the foot of the cliff with its routes *Le Bout du Monde*: *La Rose*, *Chouca* and *Le Minimum*. The most famous cave-dweller is still François Legrand who before becoming World Champion spent a whole winter squatting in a cave by *La Plage*.

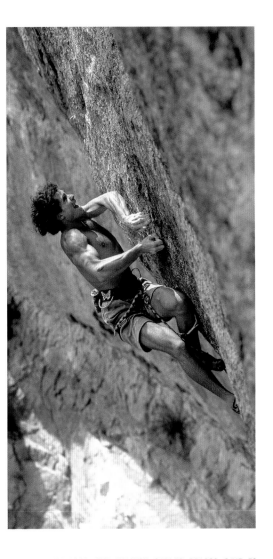

Today Buoux is a worked out rock face. It has been entirely explored and the untouched rock is forbidden, but its fame and relaxed way of life still attract numerous fans of vertical tourism.

The beautiful cliff face of Ceüse is perched majestically at an altitude of 2,000 metres above Gap, on a massif five kilometres of almost perfect convexity. It had long been explored by brave but anonymous climbers but it only became famous when Patrick Edlinger fell in love with it and spent some time there. Thanks to his 4x4 and his drill, he quickly bolted some bold routes which further contributed to the legend.

At the end of the 1980s, Jean-Christophe Lafaille had not yet joined the select circle of leading mountaineers. He soloed *Rêve de Gosse* (F8a+) on the nearby Roche des Arnauds and *Le Privilège du Serpent* (F7c+) on Ceüse while continuing to explore. It was he who bolted *Biographie,* a futuristic and completely natural route (something worth mentioning in this period of relentless interference) in 1990. It was subsequently freed by Arnaud Petit in 1996 with a grade of F8c+. Unable to reach the final boulder section Arnaud, with great perceptiveness, added an intermediate belay and left the project open until the young Chris Sharma made it his life project and the new hardest route in the world. Naturally there is more to Ceüse than this and, in spite of the long approach, hordes of people flock there every summer for the hundreds of routes of irreproachable quality. Here there are many events covered by the media, justifying its reputation. Unlike Buoux, it is still topical and the centre of numerous projects.

To many, Buoux is the most beautiful place in the world until the first Spanish competitions at La Riba when we found Siurna to be a serious rival. This hilltop village, built on a rocky promontory, has a superb view of the Sierra de Montsant, comparable to the deserts of New Mexico or the Atlas Mountains. With its kilometres of orange-coloured limestone rock faces, Siurna marked Spain's emergence into the world of modern climbing. It swiftly became a centre of top difficulty ascents with, for instance, *Odi Social*, an F8c opened by Carles Brascó in 1992 and upped to F8c+, which shows that, contrary to popular belief, Spanish ratings are not generous everywhere, especially not in Siurna! His *Biographie* was soon renamed *La Rambla*, showing that a few beautiful photographs, published in the right magazines, are sufficient to attract the crowds. After a few barren years, *La Rambla* benefited from the general popularity of Spain and the growing fame of the nearby village of Margalef. Today it is one of the regions in the world with the largest number of ninth grade routes and, thanks to legendary local bolters such as Toni Arbonès, it continues to grow because its rocky potential is so vast that the guidebook gets thicker with each edition.

Buoux, Ceüse and Siurana: these three sites have at least one point in common: as well as being outstanding cliffs, they are first and foremost magical places.

In France, growing numbers of enthusiasts were flocking to the climbing regions, the South-East naturally but also the Alps, the Pyrenees, Fontainebleau for bouldering and Alsace. The discipline was becoming more and more frantic and routes are bolted like mad. In other words, the sport became increasingly democratic, from novice to expert. A few characters stood out, such as the Nice-born Axel Franco who explored many new sectors, transforming the Alpes-Maritimes into a new top-level climbing Mecca: Gorges du Loup and Castillon to mention but two.

Jérôme Rochelle distinguished himself with a rare exploit: he free-climbed using an auto-belay device and solo the *Directe de la Concave* which he had already freed at F8a+ but, more notable than the difficulty was the unusual aspect of the climb. Imagine walking alone for over an hour through the Calanques of Marseilles, reaching an isolated cliff overhanging above the sea and aid-climbing an old 1950s route belayed with pitons whose bolter, Georges Livanos, admitted that even on the first ascent were already second-hand and incredibly old. Then halfway you free-climb an F8a+ pitch on medium rock, belayed by a DIY Gri-Gri which you secure to the belay with some elastic, to cope with the force of the shock. You fall several times hoping the system will work and, you have to continue, always alone, until you succeed.

Jean-Minh Trinh-Thieu is the archetype of the keen amateur. He was a primary school teacher in Alsace and, thanks to YouTube, the whole world can see his fall on *Gaia* in the Peak District in England. 'As a globe trotter' this could just as well have happened in Australia, Frankenjura, the Czech Republic or Canada. JMTT was one of those all-rounders (boulder, trad, sport, wall) who touched the top level without actually reaching it; nonetheless he climbed an F8c in 1995. Since those days, JMTT has been a route setter for competitions and he ran a rope-making company before setting up his own climbing hall.

Another native of Alsace is Pierre Bollinger who also stood out at the time. He was younger than JMMT but he approached the discipline in the same spirit. At first JMTT refused to coach him because he found him insufficiently motivated. Goaded by this, Bollinger spent his time training on climbing walls before conquering *L'Art*, the celebrated F8c route in the Kronthal which had only been climbed twice before, by JMTT and Loïc Fossard. Pierre Bollinger was just 16 at the time. Withdrawing from competitions and dropping his apprenticeship as a joiner, he concentrated exclusively on boulders and routes at the limit of his abilities. Long-limbed, with his blond hair gathered in a ponytail and a flowing, rather slow style, he looks extraordinarily like Patrick Edlinger two decades earlier. With very little money, he travelled around Europe and elsewhere to draw up an impressive tick-list of climbs with grades of F8c and more before conquering the 9th grade in 2001 with *Hugh*, mentioned above.

Two 'famous unknown' climbers are Cathy Wagner and Sébastien Hémery, who for over 20 years explored European rock faces without sponsors, travelling thousands of kilometres and conquering countless hard routes. In 2004, Sébastien celebrated his thousandth 'eight'. To celebrate this 'anniversary' he deliberately chose a route called *Fanatic* and he has now exceeded the bar of 2,000.

JEAN-MINH TRINH-THIEU IN THE PEAK DISTRICT, ON *THE BRAILLE TRAIL*, BURBAGE SOUTH, E7 6C, A JOHNNY DAWES CREATION.

–

PAGE 195:

YOUNG PIERRE BOLLINGER IN 2001 ON *HUGH*, F9A, EAUX-CLAIRES.

CHARISMATICALLY YOURS

In America, the new prodigy was Chris Sharma. He was runner-up in the World Championship in 1997 at the age of 16, having won the junior category two years in succession at Laval. It turned out that these would be the best competition results of his long career. In the same year he 'skipped' a number of events in the States in order to travel to Europe, including France where he explored some low-key but difficult routes in Orgon, not to mention the unmissable rock of Buoux and 'a few boulders near Paris', meaning Fontainebleau but, most importantly, he spent six weeks in Ceüse trying to conquer *Biographie*, which he eventually achieved after four years of repeated attempts.

SOMETIMES ROPED, FRED NICOLE, THE HIGH PRIEST OF BOULDERING.

In central Europe, in a brutal but charismatic way, several climbers were trying to apply bouldering techniques, 'the power of strength', to rock-climbing. Two of the climbers doing this were Fred Nicole and Klem Loskot. Loskot was an unusual figure who soon made a name for himself. Indeed, going from zero to F8c in a mere four years, he left many observers speechless, especially given his weight. Touring around his home town of Salzburg in Austria and in Switzerland, the narrowest notches and terrifying lunges became his speciality, as they were of his mentor, Fred Nicole (see box). Soon he had such a fine collection of F9s that some people began to question the validity of these ratings on unknown rock faces. Not interested in professional climbing and even less in competition, he came to prefer exotic trips which sometimes included surfing and deep water soloing, of which he was a pioneer. He then gave up climbing for several years, surfing, skiing and starting a family.

Today, at the age of nearly 40, he has returned to climbing, up to the 9th grade. His boulders are now revisited by top climbers such as Nalle Hukkataival and Dave Graham who are full of admiration for the level of difficulty achieved by the Austrian almost 20 years ago. Dave has said that: "Klem is the climber who inspires me most". *Nanuk*, V14, was opened by Nicole in 1997 and only repeated at the end of 2012 by Martin Schidlowski.

In 2014 Nalle Hukkataival added a sit start to *Bügeleisen*, created at the same time by Klem at V13 and described it as the hardest boulder he had ever encountered. Considering the Finn's level, this was quite something.

The Austrian was a visionary ahead of his time. He has written two books, *The 11th Grade* and *Emotional Landscape*, leading some to call him the 'climbing philosopher'. They include sayings such as: 'Being a visionary, that's in your head. But strength is in your guts!' Or again: 'To enchain a route: you need a will of iron while abandoning all expectations'.

THE AUSTRIAN KLEM LOSKOT ON THE ESCORIAL, SPAIN.

FRED NICOLE
GENTLE STRENGTH

———

The Swiss Fred Nicole is probably the climber who has most promoted bouldering over last 30 years.

He has developed a kind of 'soft' professionalism towards his discipline. He does not look for sponsors at any cost, he has an ecological, public-spirited view of the planet and he takes public transport rather than a car to go climbing. He discovered climbing and mountaineering early in life thanks to his brother François who was also a top-level climber. Jibé and I first met them both in 1984, on the plateau of the Aiguille du Midi during a snowstorm. We took refuge in their tent and the two adolescents surprised us by describing the beauty of the Swiss cliffs, then unknown to us.

Exceptionally muscular with the thickest forearms in the world of climbing, it was obvious that he would distinguish himself particularly where pure strength mattered most. Bouldering, not yet well-known in Switzerland, seemed to be made for him. But in the event it was *Le Toit d'Auguste*, not far from Nice, which made him famous. Although very short, this route was the peak of difficulty for its first ascensionist, Patrick Berhault. In 1987, Fred Nicole, just 17, repeated it for the first time, immediately followed by his brother and suggested a rating of F8b+. He remembers Philippe Steulet telephoning his parents at the time: "He asked my father how his son could say such a ridiculous thing. My father replied that he trusted us and anyway he could not care less about climbing." Although it was not his favourite discipline, he roped-up regularly at Saint Loup which he had been visiting since he first started climbing. This little known Swiss crag became famous in 1993 when Fred conquered *Bain de Sang*. Rated F9a, one of the first at the time, this grade was later regularly questioned, some climbers repeating it judging it too high.

Controversies over grades after first ascents often occurred with extreme boulders opened by Fred. As a result, he decided to announce a bracket of ratings. Admittedly it is a delicate matter for a first ascensionist to give a definitive grade when climbers of a similar level have not confirmed it. Criticism is easy but climbing is more difficult. In Branson (Switzerland) Nicole opened *La danse des Balrogs* (f8b, 1992) and *Radja* (f8b+, 1996, the first in the world) but his main claim to fame is as a pioneer opening up new areas.

In the 1990s, having become famous, he began travelling to the four corners of the world, from Australia to India. In Hueco, Texas – a major new climbing site in America – he repeated and opened legendary boulders which were then featured in magazines, attracting numerous climbers in spite of the distance. Examples were *Crown of Aragorn* (V13/f8b, 1996) and *Terremer* (V1/f8c, 2006). In Rocklands in South Africa, he opened *Oliphants Dawn* (V14/f8b, 2000), only repeated 12 years later by Nalle Hukkataival and *Black Eagle sit* (V15/f8c, 2002).

Nonetheless, it was in Switzerland that he was most prolific. His most famous masterpiece is still *Dreamtime*, first climbed in Cresciano in 2000 with a suggested rating making it the first f8c in the world. Again, the level of difficulty was subsequently downgraded but Fred retorted that the holds had been improved after his ascent. A fierce opponent of chipping, he believes that: "Chipping is a means of adapting the environment to one's own needs, while it is the reverse which should apply."

Nevertheless this boulder was the crowning of the long love affair between Fred and Ticino which holds treasures such as Cresciano and Magic Wood. Originally explored anonymously and largely ignored, this region has since then become a top-level Mecca of climbing, attracting climbers from all over the world.

Now over 40 years old, Fred is still an enthusiast seeking the ultimate move, while always respecting nature and other people.

FRED NICOLE, AT THE BEGINNING OF 2007, REPEATING *WITNESS THE FITNESS*, V15 ON OZARKS, ARKANSAS, ESTABLISHED 2005 BY CHRIS SHARMA.

ANDALUSIAN MISTS

Spain was an evolving country from a climbing point of view and it too experienced controversies, in a way comparable to those surrounding *Akira*. At the origin of the debate was the climber Bernabé Fernandez, rather isolated in his native Andalusia. He did not travel much, nor did he repeat other benchmark routes which would have enabled him to compare his level with what was happening elsewhere in the world. He was a disconcerting character who has always announced exceptional performances: the first Spanish F8c (*Hara Kiri* at the age of 17) and F8c+ (*Mojave*, 1994) for instance. Unfortunately, as Alexander Huber quickly pointed out, Bernabé Fernandez seldom operated away from his own doorstep and his results in international competitions bore no resemblance to his ratings. In 1996 he announced that he had conquered *Orujo*, a F9a overhang also near Malaga. It was 'the first Spanish F9 and one of the four hardest routes in the world.' It included several bolted-on artificial holds but two years later he removed three of them to raise the level to F9a+. From an ethical point of view his declarations were contradictory to say the least: "We do not choose the difficulties, it is the rock which decides", he told the journalist David Munilla but, later, his web site included the following about *Orujo*: "In my opinion, any bolter has the right to alter his routes at will, as long as they have not been repeated, so repeats would be forced to use the first ascensionist's methods." Dani Andrada went to have a look at *Orujo* and later reproached Fernandez with having broken natural holds next to artificial ones after his ascents.

Scepticism moved up a notch in July 2003: after three years of attempts at Vilanieva del Rosario, Fernandez announced the first ascent of a gigantic traverse under an arch, ending with an F8c boulder section some 82 metres long with over 400 moves. Excellent rest positions enable the route to be divided into 3 sections. This was *Chilam Balam* and its rating was fanciful for the time: F9b+. Like *Akira* eight years earlier, this would have made it by far the hardest route in the world. Once more fierce debates ensued. The belayer, a novice, is said to have disappeared in England and no one else had actually seen Fernandez complete it. That said, he soon returned with a photographer and proved that he had mastered the sections. Huber and Andrada were nonplussed, the latter wondering why there was no trace of chalk or rubber on the top crux. Others came to his defence, arguing on the contrary that no one could prove that he had lied and that he should therefore have the benefit of the doubt. Sceptical, the Spanish magazine, *Desnivel,* commented ironically: "Bernabé told us that after these controversies he has lost interest in climbing and that in any case, having conquered the first F9b+ in the world, he would stop top level climbing. No one forced him to announce this grade but as he did, yes, we shall ask him to prove it".

In 2006, Chris Sharma worked on the climb for three weeks without being able to join up the various sections. He did not want to give an opinion on whether Fernandez was telling the truth or not but he admitted that the route was 'visionary and futuristic'. The *Chilam Balam* myth then fell into oblivion, some believing the route to be impossible until April 2011, when the amazing Adam Ondra climbed it in a mere three days. He suggested a rating of an 'easy' F9b; he then redpointed his next project *La Planta de Shiva* (F9b).

THE YOUNG CZECH ADAM ONDRA FINDING A SPECTACULAR REST ON *CHILAM BALAM* IN 2011.

–

PAGE 201:

BERNABÉ FERNANDEZ ON *MOJAVE*, THE FIRST SPANISH F8C+ IN 1994, TORCAL DE ANTEQUERA, MALAGA, ANDALUCIA.

CITIUS, ALTIUS, FORTIUS
FREE CLIMBING TAKES OVER

'Faster, higher, stronger.' The Olympic motto proposed by Pierre de Coubertin applies perfectly to the development of the great climbing routes. Over the past 30 years, new difficulties have been developed on rock faces and even more so on boulders. The same approach has also been applied to ever-higher and more mountainous rock faces, with the development of multi-pitch climbs. Here are a few significant examples reflecting the frenzied activity of the time.

In 1954 Joe Brown set the standard with the Fissure Brown on the West Face of the Aiguille de Blaitière in the Mont Blanc massif; this was getting very close to today's F6c. In the 1980s several great historic routes, attempted over and over again, often with too many pitons, were freed: *Directe américaine* on the Drus (Benoît Grison, J. F. Peyroux 1980), *Voie Bonatti* on the Grand Capucin (Jibé Tribout, David Chambre, 1983), *Face sud du Fou* (Eric Escoffier, 1983) and later *Divine Providence* on the Pilier d'Angle (Thierry Renault and Alain Ghersen, 1990).

Meanwhile under the impetus of the indefatigable Geneva-born Michel Piola, dozens of new routes were created away from cracks using pegs and bolts, thus leading to the seventh grade above 3,000 metres. A Piola route should be savoured like a good wine, particularly those in the Envers des Aiguilles.
In 1982, the solo express ascent of *Directe Américaine* (F6c) by Christophe Profit in three hours ten minutes astonished everyone by its boldness and speed. Was the mountain about to become a giant rock face or even a vertical stadium?
Today the 8th grade has become a reality on Mont Blanc with *Digital Crack* (F8a) and *Voie Petit* on the Grand Capucin with an F8b pitch.

This trend continued to evolve at higher altitudes on the limestone cliff faces of the central Alps. In the Dolomites, after Jean-Claude Droyer had revealed the potential of the Tre Cime, Manolo and Heinz Mariacher were the pioneers. Manolo climbed in the spirit of maximum exposure while Mariacher climbed in the spirit of opening and popularisation, as for instance on the enormous South Face of the Marmolada with its classic routes *Abrakadabra* (1980) and *Temps Modernes* in 1982.

Not far away was the perfect example of these developments, *Attraverso il Pesce*, the famous route *The Fish* created

THE AUSTRIAN HEINZ MARIACHER, DOLOMITES FREE-CLIMBING PIONEER, ON HIS *TEMPI MODERNISSIMI*, F7C+, MARMOLADA, 1986

in 1981 by two unknown Slovak climbers, Igor Koller and Indrich Siustr, then freed in 1987 by Mariacher and Bruno Pederiva. Beyond the grade, F7b+, getting to the top was already a victory.

As Maurizio Oviglia explains, repeating 'old' routes free shows: "The desire to progress, to show that even an already existing route can be revived and gain in difficulty and status, while at the same time paying tribute to those who opened it in the past". The great Comici would have enjoyed this renewed interest in adventure and the unknown, after several rather disappointing decades marked by the excessive use of aid climbing equipment and pitons.

THE AUSTRIAN BEAT KAMMERLANDER ON HIS ICONIC *SILBERGEIER*, RÄTIKON, SWITZERLAND.

More recently, Pietro Dal Prà, Mauro 'Bubu' Bole and Rolando Larcher have pioneered these great 'modern' routes, bolted from the bottom. With the drill hanging from their shoulder and a lot of determination, they remove virtually all risk of a fatal accident but great exploits are not excluded. Some have become internationally famous, such as *Hotel Supramonte* (F8b max, F7c obligatory) in Sardinia, opened by Larcher in 1999, then conquered completely free by Pietro Dal Prà in the following year and by Martina Cufar in 2004.
Mentally, there has also been a complete change of approach. The initiator was Alexander Huber whose routes since the year 2000 have included the overhangs of the Tre Cime (*Bellavista* and *Pan Aroma*, F8c). He has made the most of his climbing potential with gear more suitable for an adventure playground. "The way in which the enormous roof of *Bellavista* was crossed was also important: climbing an F8c in the extreme cold and bleakness characteristic of a north-facing cliff and all without the safety of solid bolts!"

In Switzerland, the Rätikon and the Wendenstock have become very popular because of their beauty but also dreaded because of the seriousness and run-out nature of the routes. On the Rätikon, the Swiss Martin Scheel opened routes from the bottom which inspired climbers for decades: *Amarcord* (F7b+, 1984), *Acacia* (F7c+, 1988).
In the 1990s, the Austrian Beat Kammerlander did 'test-pieces' in Rätikon, routes climbed from the bottom up such as *Unendliche Geschichte*, followed by the illustrious *Silbergeier* which, together with *The End of Silence* by Thomas Huber and *Des Kaiser neue Kleider* by Stefan Glowacz, formed a challenging F8b/F8b+ trilogy which Glowacz was the first to achieve. Silbergeier would also see its first female ascent in 2012 by the Swiss Nina Caprez. who, after a competition career, made the transition on to longer hard routes such as *Hotel Supramonte, Ali Baba,* and *Orbayu* (attempt).

Since then, top-level climbers have taken to higher altitudes to develop the most extreme moves. For instance, the Spanish Pou brothers climbed the magnificent, misty Naranjo de Bulnes (Picos de Europa) with their multi-pitch *Orbayu*; at one time a contender for the title of 'the hardest long route in the world'. A 9th grade was proposed for it but it was soon downgraded to F8c by the Belgian Nicolas Favresse.

In a different style, Philippe Mussato has conquered numerous routes on the high cliffs of the French Pre-Alps. He has been climbing since the 1980s, leaving in his wake

aesthetic routes always including run-outs, a little in the spirit of the Rätikon: "Climbing really starts when you forget about the points. It is much more thrilling and a higher level of skill is required. What we must fight against are routes which are not memorable. We must cultivate rarity in climbing". An example is *Ali Baba*, opened in 2002 on the Paroi Dérobée d'Aiglun where routes all overhang with multiple 8th grade pitches. Today it is used as on-sight test for the best climbers, both men and women.

Africa, less visited than the other continents, is famous today for its now legendary route *Tough Enough*: 10 pitches on the extraordinarily smooth rock faces of the Tsaranoro massif in Madagascar opened by Daniel Gebel and Ari Steinel 2005. The route was subsequently explored by a series of famous climbers including Arnaud Petit, Sylvain Millet and François Legrand who freed the pitches one by one, each of a consistently high level there being seven pitches between F8a and F8b. Then at the age of 17, Adam Ondra, did better than anyone, although his only experience was indoor competition climbing. Accompanied by Pietro Dal Prà, he successfully climbed all the pitches on-sight, except two which he completed at the next attempt.

Bordering on mountaineering, the next challenge consisted of achieving the same technical level on higher, more distant rock faces such as the Himalaya and Patagonia. Such a one was *Riders in the Storm* opened in 1991 on the Torres del Paine in Patagonia by a legendary roped party including Wolfgang Güllich, Kurt Albert and Bernd Arnold: this was a steep F7c on nuts and with run-outs.

Even the sinister North Face of the Eiger has its free climbing fans such as the German Robert Jasper who free-climbed the 8th grade *Directe Japonaise*; this was an old route with aid points, opened at the time only after immense persistence, which clearly shows how things have evolved since then. And, on the same face, Ueli Steck, the celebrated Swiss Alpinist added *Pacienca* (F8a 2008). Last but not least, in 2009 the Huber brothers freed the F7c+ *Eternal Flame* on the Nameless Trango Tower at 6,000m, a route opened 20 years earlier by Wolfgang Güllich and Kurt Albert who, at the time, climbed about 80% of it free.

The freeing of the Cerro Torre in two stages in January 2012 by the historic *Compressor Route* is another excellent example of the free-climbing trend. At this time, many American climbers and mountaineers were active in this part of South America, staying in El Chaltén, the little town at the foot of Cerro FitzRoy and Cerro Torre. The Americans Jason Kruk and Hayden Kennedy had climbed Cerro Torre without freeing it and controversially on their descent they took the initiative to break Maestri's historic ladder of bolts. In their opinion, Maestri's action in 1970 had been a complete atrocity; his use of bolts and heavy machinery being an outrage, even at the time and in so doing he stole this ascent from the future. A few days later, after three years of relentless determination, the young Austrian David Lama finally reached the summit of the 'impossible mountain' without falling and without aid. The son of an Austrian mother and Nepalese father, he is one of the prodigies of recent years who has since made a successful transition to bold mountaineering.

PAGE 204:

EMERGING FROM THE PICOS DE EUROPA MIST, THE SWISS NINA CAPREZ FREED EACH PITCH ONE BY ONE OF *ORBAYU*, NARANJO DE BULNES, F8C MAX, IN 2014. BUT SHE COULDN'T LINK ALL OF THEM ALL IN ONE PUSH.

—

PAGE 205:

ARNAUD PETIT STRUGGLING WITH THE TINY CRIMPS ON THE 5TH PITCH OF *TOUGH ENOUGH*, F8A+, TSARANORO, MADAGASCAR.

PAGE 206:

THE AMERICAN STEPH DAVIS ON THE FAMOUS SALATHÉ *HEADWALL*, EL CAP, 5.13B/C, DURING THE FIRST FREE FEMALE ASCENT IN 2005.

—

PAGE 207:

EL CAPITAN AGAIN WITH THE FRENCH WOMAN STÉPHANIE BODET FREEING *FREERIDER* (VI, 5.12D) IN 2007.

In America, the adventure on the great cliffs was still centred mainly in Yosemite. There are few really new modern routes and these cliffs have been so frequently explored in the past that the challenge now is to ascend the legendary routes such as *The Nose* and *Salathé* free and to create connections (*Freerider*). The Huber brothers were particularly active on El Cap: *El Niño*, *Golden Gate* and *El Corazon* have become on-sight challenges with 8th grade pitches, sometimes protected by bolts and sometimes not.

All this heralded those extensive projects on all continents which were to attract the best sport climbers in search of vast open spaces and who would take the ninth grade to unprecedented heights.

THE TURN OF THE CENTURY

In the 1990s, the development of artificial climbing structures came to maturity. No longer exclusive to federations and clubs, they now took on a private and commercial dimensions which was a real revolution. Indoors or out, decorative or purely functional, from a local boulder to vast halls filled with ropes, their manufacture soon became an industry in itself, assisted by the fact that the discipline was now recognised in schools and universities.

The French, the British and then the Belgians led the way with pioneering companies such as Entre-Prises (6,000 walls built since 1987), The Foundry (Sheffield), Terre Neuve (Belgium), Espace Vertical (Grenoble) and the Grimper wall centre (Aix-en-Provence). Soon private indoor climbing centres spread like wildfire on both sides of the Atlantic.

For the present generation, more rivalry and frequent competitions require a degree of professionalism which is becoming harder to manage. To make a living from climbing, it is necessary be at the top of a pyramid whose base is growing constantly. Admittedly, with the increasing number of climbers and the growing popularity of climbing, the size and number of manufacturers catering for the sport has grown as well. This in turn has led to technical improvement in equipment: ever thinner and more supple ropes, lighter harnesses and quickdraws, safer and more dynamic belaying systems and better fitting climbing shoes with greater friction.

This was how things stood at the end of the 20th century and, finally, what is new after a century climbing?

What used to be a leisure activity for slightly eccentric gentlemen has become a top level athletic discipline. It is a discipline in which women have distinguished them-selves and have completely transformed the practice and perception of what was for a long time the preserve of men.

Competition was originally latent but it has become more official and publicised, sometimes turning an adventurous way of life into a simple sports activity. Thanks to technological progress, modern society, which disapproves of individual risk-taking, has made climbing as safe as possible. Free solo climbing has almost disappeared. Exploits are associated more with performance and the rules of the game have evolved while at the same time individual media exposure is becoming easier by the day.

But human behaviour has remained unchanged in its diversity. As Reinhold Messner wrote in his book *The 7th Grade* some 40 years ago: "The concepts of perfor-mance and success play a major part in the constant search for ever longer, more difficult ascents. 'Success' is partly responsible for the growing trend of sport climbing insofar as the desire to practise this discipline usually depends on how successful the climber is. Unsuccessful results usually discourage the climber. But which scales, which values will allow us to assess this success, since in climbing there is no 'productive' success?"

209

Non-productive success. This was probably what the Swiss-American Eric Talmadge felt in 2000 when he finally grabbed the last hold of the 15 metres of *Im Reich des Shogun* in the Basel Jura. Yet another hard route? No, much more, the route of a lifetime. A folly, an obsession which had lasted almost 15 years and over 500 attempts: "I tried everything to conquer this route, including trying in the worst conditions as far as the site, the weather and myself were concerned. I also practised on a climbing wall on which I had reproduced the cruxes. I tried different diets, numerous physical and mental exercises, I even hoped that levitation would help. And I succeeded. And now?"

THE SWISS ERIC TALMADGE ON *IM REICH DES SHOGUN*, JURA BÂLOIS, SWITZERLAND.

Indeed, what next? A fading desire for climbing, a budding interest for Buddhism and meditation. "What I felt more than anything, besides the satisfaction of having succeeded in conquering the route, was a feeling of liberation." Then, a lot of top-level climbers failed trying to repeat it until Adam Ondra succeeded in 2009 after five brief attempts

Passion. Possession. Fifteen years, 15 metres. Five attempts or 500. In the context of all this, does it really matter whether a grade is F9a or F9a+?

05

THE
WORLD
CONNECTS

AS THE WORLD ADJUSTED TO BOTH THE GOOD AND THE BAD OF SOCIETY AS THE NEW MILLENIUM DAWNED, THE CLIMBING WORLD HAD CAUSE TO CELEBRATE SOMETHING POSITIVE WITH THE IMPACT MADE BY THE YOUNG CHRIS SHARMA ON JULY 18TH 2001 WITH HIS DEVASTATING ASCENT OF CEÜSE'S *BIOGRAPHIE*; THE 'SHARMA ERA' AS SOME OF HIS FELLOW AMERICANS CALLED IT.

PAGE 210:

MAN OF THE NEW CENTURY: THE CALIFORNIAN CHRIS SHARMA ON *LA RAMBLA EXTENSION*, F9A+, SIURANA, ESPAGNE.

–

PAGE 212:

CHRIS SHARMA CLOSE TO HEAVEN ON THE CRUX OF *BIOGRAPHIE*, F9A+, CEÜSE, FRANCE.

Biographie, renamed *Realization* by Sharma, was the start of the Sharma era. Graded F9a+, the climb magically combined the legendary site of Ceüse, a brilliant climber and a route with a long history. It also marked the culmination of a new approach by a new generation. It was initially bolted in the late 1980s by Jean-Christophe Lafaille who named it *Biographie*. (Lafaille went missing in 2006 when attempting a winter solo climb of Makalu, the fifth highest peak in the world.) In 1996 Arnaud Petit climbed the first long section (F8c+) but he was unable to do the next section, which was shorter and more boulder-like. He fixed an intermediate anchor and left the project open.

Sharma became completely obsessed with the route and he tried many times to complete the connection to the final section. This was the first F9a+, unless one considers Ondra's earlier suggestion that *Open Air* had that grade. Equivalent to the American grade 5.15a, the fact that it was achieved by an American illustrates the growing strength of the wave of young climbers in that country who would revitalise climbing in the years to come.

CHRIS SHARMA MENTALLY REHEARSING THE MOVES.

The fact that Chris Sharma renamed the route caused some controversy, but characteristically he immediately clarified the situation: "I renamed this route *Realization* because the first part, *Biographie*, ended in the middle and I wanted to differentiate the two. The French were annoyed because I changed the name but, after discussing the matter with French friends, I understood the history of the route and the French tradition of letting the first ascensionist name his route. I told them I didn't mind if the route kept the name *Biographie*. Now most of the time, during my conferences, I use the name *Biographie* when I talk about the route. I believe the situation was unclear because of the intermediate belay and I did not want to discredit the first part or to use the same name. Personally I believe people can call the route whatever they like. Naming a route is just for pleasure. The perfection of the route speaks for itself. This bit of rock was there long before we were, so it's a bit silly to argue about it."

CHRIS SHARMA
THE FIRST ROCK STAR

—

Over the last 20 years, an increasing number of active climbers have been accumulating an impressive list of achievements, both in competition and on the rock face, but those who have developed a true vision are much rarer.

Among the select, Chris Sharma is the one who has completely transformed the approach to modern climbing. Each of his great achievements is unusual and inspired.

Es Pontàs is a good example. This is a rock arch off the coast of Mallorca, a deep water solo or 'psicobloc' route, as much 'psycho' as it is 'bouldering'. It is one of the hardest climbs in the world because of the difficulty of the moves and the linking together of them and because it can only be reached by swimming. Working solo, there is no opportunity to work the moves. Like *Jumbo Love*, deep in the Mojave mountains at an altitude of 2,500 metres, where the approach is incredibly long and difficult, taking several hours.

Sharma was already aware of the importance of achievement in life and in 2013 he said: "What matters is to leave something behind, something which will last. No one remembers who won the World Cup in 1997 but everyone knows who opened *Action Directe*."

His full name is revealing: Chris Omprakash Sharma. In Sanskrit, 'Omprakash' means 'light of creation' and 'Sharma' means 'joy' or 'good luck'. His parents belonged to the Flower Power generation and were disciples of the Indian yoga master Baba Hari Dass who was very influential in California in the 1970s. Born in 1981, Chris discovered climbing almost by accident at Berkeley when still very young. He took part in the first training courses organised by the couple Didier Raboutou and Robyn Erbesfield. Raboutou was not impressed by his foot technique, which was never his strong point, but he immediately recognised this young boy's incredible motivation and determination when it was a matter of conquering a route. He was evidently talented, but the degree of talent can only be measured by the test of time.

He dropped out of school to devote himself entirely to climbing, so it was fortunate that his competition debut was so impressive in the World Championship in 1995 at the tender age of 14, Senior runner-up at 16 and winner of the X-Games at 18. He described his first great climbing tour at the time, hitchhiking through France with Tommy Caldwell, as his true initiation into the world: "Travelling, meeting people and enjoying new experiences."

In fact, the passion for 'real' rock and the social life of an itinerant climber suited him better than the organised timetable of competitive events, an area in which he lacked the vital touch of aggression. Beating rivals was not what he was after. He enjoyed fighting, underlining each movement with a howl, but the fight was against the rock or against himself.

After a serious injury he had to stop climbing for a year, giving him the chance to reconsider his choices. But there was this project far away in Ceüse, in France, on which he had already worked so long. So beautiful, so high, so hard. He could not get the magical *Biographie* route out of his head. Having recovered, he discovered deep water soloing in the Balearic Islands and fell in love with it. Next he travelled to India to meditate and then he went on a Buddhist pilgrimage on the island of Shikoku in Japan, walking hundreds of kilometres and camping alone in its gloomy forests. Before conquering *Biographie*, the essence of the modern long route, he spent two years backpacking without ever putting on a harness, just bouldering. 'Try harder and be happy' was his mantra at the time.

Thanks to his low-key, open-minded approach, he retained the trust of his sponsors such as Beaver Theodosakis, the founder of the prAna clothing brand. His bold projects and his natural charisma were ideal for both movie and still photography. Sharma appealed to people's imagination, whether in magazines or in the films of which he soon became the star. *King Lines* (2007), *Progression* (2009) and *The Scene* (2011) are not just a series of beautiful images but, like the best Hollywood scenarios, they also tell the story of a quest filled with ambushes.

Each generation has its icons. *Midnight Lightning* in Yosemite was *the* boulder of the 1970s, while that of the start of the new millennium it was *The Mandala*, also in California on the other side of the Sierra. When Sharma climbed this magnificent outcrop he did not give it a grade though it was thought to range between V12 to V14, depending on the number of broken holds and whether the start was direct or sitting but, in any event, the attraction of the route is as strong as it has ever been. Pure Sharma: he who created a legend becomes a legend himself.

It is interesting that today the most repeated F8c in the world is one Sharma's creations: *Fish Eye* in Oliana, Catalonia. His other first ascents, also much repeated, include *Mind Control* (F8c+), also in Oliana, *Era Vella* (F9a) in Margalef and the F9a+ *Biographie*.

In 2007, he decided he wanted to settle down somewhere after more than 10 years of nomadic life during which he had slept mainly in airports. Being in a relationship at the time with the Spanish climber Daila Ojeda, he chose Catalonia and bought a house not far from Santa Linya, whose giant caves boast the largest number of grade F9 routes in the world, many of them done by him. It was unexpected to see this young nomad with a house, a partner, a dog and a car. Normal life was beckoning.

Almost 20 years have passed since he created his first important route, *Necessary Evil* (Virgin River Gorge), in 1996. As a 5.14c or F8c+, this was the hardest route opened by an American at the time, and he was still only 14 years old. Now, his list of achievements includes 36 9th grade routes, most of which were also first ascents.

For the same reason that he has no scorecard on the climbing web site www.8a.nu, he dislikes grading his exploits; he also disapproves of the concept of a list of achievements. He is not interested in collecting high grades and adding to statistics but, he is always in search of his next dream line. Beyond the figures, whether on boulders or on cliffs, his aim has always been to tackle climbs that are at his limit – *king lines* as he calls them; a powerful alchemy of size, difficulty and aesthetics. "It is all about the level of difficulty of a first ascent: never being quite certain that it will be possible. But one must confident enough to take on the challenge. Every time I try to set the standard as high as possible so that the next generation can benefit from it. That is how climbing evolves."

It was in this spirit that *Dreamcatcher* in Squamish, *Papichulo*, *Pachamama* and *Fight or Flight* in Oliana, *Neanderthal* in Santa Linya and *Golpe de Estado* in Siurana were born. In an article about him, the sports newspaper *L'Équipe* described him as the 'coolest sportsman in the world'. But sometimes even a wise man (a description he dislikes and which rather irritates him) can be a little irritated. In 2010, for instance, other top climbers such as the Finn Nalle Hukkataival tried their hand at his project *First round, first minute* in Margalef which was causing him problems. After some prevarication, being the great champion that he is, he admitted that it was a good thing that the project should be open to others. In the end he received his just reward since he was the one who climbed it first. And when Adam Ondra preceded him by one month on the F9b+ *La Dura Dura* route, currently the hardest route in the world, he was a good sport about it.

Today, this cool-looking sportsman is also an accomplished businessman, one of those rare climbers who make a more than comfortable living from their sport and their sponsors. Entering the next stage in his life, he still climbs but gradually he has been changing the focus of his activities: he runs his own indoor-climbing centre Sender One in Santa Ana, California, he organises psicobloc competitions, and he travels the world to propagate his dreams. His name has become a benchmark in the history of climbing.

But this does not prevent him from still being involved in extreme projects, including ones in his beloved Catalonia. Age has not diminished his passion in any way: "I now realise the importance of climbing for me, it is a way of life, of expressing myself, of existing in this world. I now understand that new routes have always been evolving. And there will always be omething harder to climb."

In any case, for all those who love climbing and are interested in the history of this sport, there will always a pre-Sharma era and a post-Sharma one.

PAGE 215: CHRIS SHARMA. PAGE 216: ON *LA RAMBLA EXTENSION*, F9A+, SIURANA.

Since then, *Biographie* has become a top-level milestone, a must for the best climbers, 12 of whom have added it to their own list. The first to repeat it, in 2004, was as local as could be, Sylvain Millet, born in Gap. He had made it a lifetime project and eventually succeeded after countless attempts. After 2010 and a broken hold, the start became harder (about F8a boulder). In 2012 Adam Ondra made a memorable flash (that is, at the first attempt but knowing the moves) before falling after succeeding on the first part.

In 2014 the young German prodigy Alexander Megos, who had already repeated *Action Directe*, checked the route, without having seen it previously on the Internet. He then worked and climbed it on the same day on just his third attempt. This clearly shows how much matters had progressed in the 13 years since Sharma's first ascent. To achieve this, Megos believed 'that is more important to be 100% on top mentally than physically'.

No doubt the first on-sights by women will be equally memorable. The fact that today a woman conquering *Biographie* has become a possibility is probably thanks to the efforts of the Basque climber Josune Bereziartu, the first woman to cross the magical bar of the 9th grade, 11 years after Wolfgang Güllich had done so.

With the best list of achievement in the history of women's competition in France, Liv Sansoz transferred her skills to the rock face. In 2000, with *Hasta La Vista* on Mount Charleston, a much tampered-with top-level site, she secured the second women's F8c+ in all categories, after Josune Bereziartu who at the time was the only woman to have exceeded F8c. Since then, some Spanish benchmark routes such as *Fish Eye* (F8c) and *Mind Control* (F8c+) in Oliana, have been repeated many times (by Daila Ojeda, Nina Caprez, Caroline Ciavaldini, Sasha DiGiulian, Barbara Raudner, Florence Pinet among others). But few women have conquered the 9th grade since Josune did so during the years 2002-2005; only Charlotte Durif, Alizée Dufraisse, Sasha DiGiulian, Muriel Sarkany, Jenny Lavarda, Angela Eiter, Mar Alvarez, Ashima Shiraishi and finally Anak Verhoeven have done so, and then not until 2011 or later.
This indicates how much ahead of her time Josune Bereziartu was. When she joined the club of the 9th grade, no more than 20 men had done so (today there are estimated to be about 300).

Another advanced performance was that of Marietta Uhden, the only woman to have made an F8c+ first ascent (a German 11) when she climbed *Sonne Im Herzen* at Kochel in 2001. Sadly she died in 2014.

CAROLINE CIAVALDINI TRAD-CLIMBING

IN ROCKLANDS, *THE DOUBLE CRACK*.

JOSUNE BEREZIARTU
THE FEMALE 9TH DEGREE

It was thanks to Josune Bereziartu that women's climbing finally reached the 9th grade. This was no surprise in view of the consistent, sound progress she had made in the 1990s. In the past, most top women climbers had opted for recognition in competition and only a handful, led by Lynn Hill, had chosen high-level difficulty.

Basque through and through, as her name indicates, she met her future companion Rikardo Otegui after making her debut in the mountains. While he was already climbing F8b routes, she had only reached F6c. But by relentless training and extreme determination she caught up with him. She soon lost interest in Spanish and international competitions where she could not develop her full potential and began to concentrate on the local cliffs. A professional through and through, she blossomed at this high level and soon reached the eighth grade. In 1996 she was the first Spanish woman to ascend an F8b+, *Kampezu*, and in 1998 she became the first woman in the world to climb an F8c, *Honky Tonky*. She regularly tackled on-sight F8a routes. "My aim was not to contribute to the development of women's climbing but simply to make progress myself. What interests me most is a challenging route which motivates me to train and push myself to the limit."

She secured her second and third F8c grades (*White Zombie* and *Ras* in Baltoza, also in the Basque country). These were followed by *Les Spécialistes Direct* (Verdon, F8c), *Macumba Club* Orgon, F8c), *Last Soul Sacrifice* (Gorges du Loup, F8c), and then the F8c+ routes *Honky Tonk Mix* (2000) and *Noïa* (Italy, 2001). Then she trained for a whole year with a single objective in mind: to reach the 9th grade. The small holds of Saint-Loup in Switzerland suited her style and her strong points perfectly.

There was some controversy over the grading of her first 9th grade ascent, *Bain de Sang* (F9a) in 2002, so she made another in Japan in 2004 and notably in 2005 with *Bimbaluna*, again in Saint-Loup, F9a+. Encouraged by her ability to overcome extreme difficulties, in 2006 she secured the first female F8b+ on-sight ever (*Hydrophobia* in Montsant, Catalonia).

She had also reached the highest bouldering level with *E la nave va* in Switzerland, a V13 traverse, 2003.
No doubt aware of having reached her peak in this quest, she extended her activities to include adventurous projects with her partner of many years, Rikardo Otegui, such as opening long routes in Ordesa in the Spanish Pyrenees in a bold 'trad' style: *Divina Comedia* (2006), *El Ojo Critico* (2007) and *El Castillo de los Sacristanes* (2009).

DAVE GRAHAM THE ARTIST

At the start of the new millennium, it was another young American who caused a sensation. Born on the East Coast, Dave Graham was of the same generation and culture as Chris Sharma and Tommy Caldwell. Although he does not have Chris Sharma's physique and muscles, the fact that he started climbing in Rumney, New Hampshire, explains the incredible strength of his fingers. After opening *The Fly* (F9a) in Rumney and repeating Sharma's already legendary boulder *The Mandala*, he came to Europe. He collected plus signs on both boulders and cliffs, where even *Action Directe* and *Biographie* succumbed to his brilliance. A nomadic climber by nature, he was a sort of Jack Kerouac of climbing. As his fellow-countryman Paul Robinson put it: "I would say that Dave Graham is an anomaly, he is the only person who manages to live off climbing without ever having taken part in competitions."

A colourful, complex figure, Dave has thought a lot about his relationship with climbing: "Making progress is a constantly moving thought which is subjective. The art of improving as a climber is closely linked to everything else in my life; it is just one piece of a giant puzzle. These pieces fit together thanks to climbing, and making progress depends as much on my past as on the future... I learnt early on that people tended to think of me as an artist and more recently as an athlete, even though I'm not one. My parents saw me first as an artist, then they started saying I was an athlete. But now I would consider myself an artist above all."

Two years after *Biographie*, a second route claimed the title of F9a+: Alex Huber's *La Rambla* in Siurana, but in its complete *Extension* version which had been created by Dani Andrada: he made a clever traverse which enabled an ascent, not to the top of that wall but by the exit of the neighbouring line, *La Reina Mora*. Unfortunately for Dani, in spite of over 100 attempts and several falls below the belay, he never succeeded in conquering *La Rambla* itself. He still oscillates between success and failure, between frustration and fulfilment, the moods which punctuate life and are experienced by all top-level climbers. It was his young fellow-countryman Ramón Julián who had the pleasure of conquering *La Rambla Extension* (also after many attempts), followed by the equally young Edu Marín. There was some disagreement between them regarding an unused hold, but development continued: Chris Sharma repeated it more quickly and Adam Ondra did even better, but eventually Alex Megos climbed it on just his second attempt in 2014. The route was the same: climbers were simply becoming stronger.

Since then, *La Rambla* has been among the pantheon of those few pitches which symbolise modern extreme climbing. The first 9th grades were short routes with specialised boulder moves and most experts could only envisage the future as an evolution of this style of pure strength. But history has proved them wrong, since the latest routes are the opposite, pitches several metres long (almost 100 moves for *La Rambla Extension*) which also include intense boulder passages.

THE AMERICAN, DAVE GRAHAM, IN ROCKLANDS AREA, SOUTH AFRICA.

SOLO

Solo. 'Supreme climbing,' as Patrick Edlinger famously put it in his film *Life at your Fingertips*. The two syllables of the word still retain all their aura and magic. 'One man, one cliff' is another timeless expression of the idea.

Solo climbing first arose with mountaineering, but its practice is immemorial and universal. Bouldering is itself an initial, limited, form of mountaineering created by the hazards of geology, and when it exceeds a few metres and so becomes a highball where a fall could be serious, it is no different from solo climbing.

There is a distinction between free solo (unroped) and self-belayed solo, the latter being more like a 'climbing journey' because of its increased duration and the safety provided the rope (Bonatti on the Dru was a typical example). Free solo brings with it a brief realisation of the uncertainty of survival.

Solo climbers have included Paul Preuss at the beginning of the 20th century, Comici, and, 25 years later, Claudio Barbier at the Tre Cime, and the young Reinhold Messner scouring the Dolomites. More recently these climbers have been succeeded by Patrick Berhault and Patrick Edlinger in the Verdon and at Buoux, John Bachar and Peter Croft in Yosemite, Jerry Moffatt on the *Great Wall* at Cloggy, Antoine Le Menestrel with *Revelations* on Raven Tor, and the urban climber Alain Robert with his skyscraper ascents.

More than the grading itself, it is the boldness of the project which singles it out and makes an impression. Examples are the Spanish climber Carlos Garcia, suspended from the interminable overhang of *La Fiesta del biceps* at Mallos de Riglos, and Alexander Huber on the direct lines of the *Brandler-Hasse* on the Tre Cime. In 2005 Michael Reardon, a Hollywood film producer, climbed completely on-sight *Romantic Warrior*, a route consisting of nine 5.12 pitches in the Californian Needles. Of this John Bachar, another adept on-sight solo climber, said: "This is way beyond what I could have done." Only Alex Honnold has dared to repeat this solo climb, in 2014. Reardon was killed two years later on the Irish coast, swept away by a wave having just down-climbed a cliff.

Another solo climber was Jim Erickson, a beatnik of the hippy years, who cycled round Colorado in search of rock faces, before mountain bikes were invented. His approach to climbing was very simple; opening new routes solo without any reconnaissance abseiling: a first attempt, possibly followed by down-climbing if he did not feel up to it. Then he would return later and persevere until he had succeeded. All he needed was a bag of chalk, a pair of climbing shoes and some quickdraws. Thus equipped, he conquered about 30 F6a and F6b lines until his peak, *Cassandra*, a treacherous F6c whose crux was 70 metres from the ground. Later a fall on a minor route in which he broke both ankles and a wrist put an end to his career, and as he put it, saved him from a worse fate. "I used to think that if I was killed climbing, it would not be so bad, but after my accident I realised that life had become much more precious to me."

THE SPANIARD, CARLOS GARCIA FREE-SOLOING THE HEART BREAKING *LA FIESTA DEL BICEPS*, MALLOS DE RIGLOS.

Nowadays the number of solo climbers is definitely decreasing. By contrast, 30 years ago most top-level climbers were tempted by solo climbing at times. Admittedly their reasons for doing so were often dictated by their need for media coverage. In the absence of the hierarchy which was later created by competitions, the most ambitious, but not necessarily the most talented as far as pure difficulty was concerned, found a way to stay in the public eye.

Having said this, 'solo' implies an absolute command of the discipline, both in one's own eyes and in those of the world. Today the same results can be achieved without taking the far from negligible risks by winning a competition. Some sponsors even cancelled their contracts with well-known climbers such as Alex Honnold because they no longer wanted to be associated with solo climbing on rock faces. Some of the media have been somewhat hypocritical: the web site 8a.nu has decided not to mention 'any climbing event with a potential danger of death', ignoring the fact that solo climbing is inseparable from the history of the sport. It is impossible to get away from the fact that there are risks in solo-climbing, where the phrase 'life hangs from your fingertips' is not just a sensational expression but a simple statement of the truth.

It is true that, when soloing, one lives more intensely than with a rope between your legs. As Alexander Huber put it: "Solo climbing brings out the best in me and it is a way of achieving well-being. It creates the most intense memories. Nothing has made my life as intensely felt as my solo climbs."

Perhaps this is why an endemic culture of solo climbing has survived in a few rare places in the world. An example is the gritstone area in England where the lead climber often has to leave his rope at the bottom of the cliff because the route has no runners. This may seem exaggerated but, while drills are found everywhere else, could one possibly imagine elsewhere a piece of solid rock on a major site which has been opened solo and thus 'transformed' into a route, then preserved permanently in its original condition? This may be the case with the new highballs, boulders over five metres high which are often closer to a solo climb since falling is not permitted even with countless crash-pads.

THE AUSTRIAN, HANSJÖRG AUER ALONE ON *THE FISH*, MARMOLADA. CHECK THE EAGLE.

LEFT: HIS FELLOW COUNTRYMAN ALEX HUBER LETTING IN ALL HANG OUT ON THE *BRANDLER — HASSE*, CIMA GRANDE, DOLOMITES.

RIGHT: THE FRENCHMAN, ALAIN ROBERT AKA *SPIDERMAN*.

Nevertheless a few climbers have revived the tradition. Before Alain Robert was climbing buildings like Spiderman, he had made a lasting impression with his daring solo ascents, from the F8b at Omblèze to *La Nuit du lézard* (F8a+) at Buoux and *Polpot* (F7c+) in the Verdon: 'a brief experience of death'. Spiderman climbing in the city is good for television but the risk taken on a 100-metre high building is as great as or even more so than on a good old rock face.

Solo climbing is still largely a male preserve but it has also appealed to some women. Catherine Destivelle was the first top-level climber to be attracted by solo climbing, displaying her skills on the North Face of the Eiger. More recently, Steph Davis combined solo and BASE jumping when climbing the *Diamond* on Long's Peak, the red sandstone of Indian Creek and the towers of Canyonlands. She had been the first woman the climb the *Salathé Wall* free, an achievement comparable to that of Lynn Hill on *The Nose*. With her then husband, Dean Potter, they formed a fearless couple.

In April 2007, the Austrian Hansjörg Auer went down in history by ascending *The Fish (or Il Pesce)* on the Marmolada climbing the 37 pitches of this legendary route with a very delicate F7b+ crux in less than three hours. Having only climbed the route roped once before, he abseiled solo to work on the key passages. This was a solo without anyone else present, which was not always the case for others as for instance Dean Potter was always followed and filmed, as more recently is Alex Honnold (see boxes). From this moment, when the solo climber literally turned into an actor, that is, when he accepted or organised the media coverage of his climb, inviting a photographer, a film cameraman and witnesses, he turned his performance into a show. Climbing is often associated with a sincere, quasi-mystical message of the search for excellence but, this rejection of the conventional rules of society, is now recorded and publicised on glossy paper and YouTube. We have become the 'Society of Spectacle'.

Every time one tries to attach ideas to actions such as solo climbing, it becomes apparent that it is useless to try and to draw certainties or ready-made truths from it. Above all, the climber 'lives' a solo. Perhaps it gains in authenticity when it is combined with solitude?

In the end, the most beautiful solos are those we shall never hear about, which we shall not be able to monopolise and which will escape our relentless need to classify everything.

ALEX HONNOLD
FACING THE WALL

—

A young kid, living in a converted van, moving from cliff to cliff, usually climbing free solo, entrusting his life to his fingetips. Alex Honnold is reminiscent of Patrick Edlinger, except that he is a tall brown-haired young man, not a tall blond one.

Since Patrick Edlinger and Patrick Berhault, only a few lone climbers have left their mark, such as Hansjörg Auer on *The Fish* on the Marmolada or, in a very different style, the tireless Alain Robert on the skyscrapers of the world. The solo climber is now an endangered species. There are many ways of expressing oneself and acquiring recognition in the world of climbing, and most of them are less dangerous. Yet in recent years the name of Alex Honnold has appeared regularly in magazines for his exploits which are beyond all comprehension, such daredevil deeds seeming to be incompatible with a normal psychological and emotional state.

A true Californian, he was a normal teenage climber until the age of 18. Then he dropped out of Berkeley where he was studying engineering in order to devote himself entirely to climbing. Naturally he chose to perfect his climbing skills in the nearby Yosemite Valley. Although not ignoring short pitches, his size, his talent at climbing cracks and his natural endurance over prolonged periods of effort led him towards long multi-pitch routes.

He really began to make a name for himself in Yosemite in 2007. On El Cap, he free-climbed (roped) the 37 pitches of *Freerider* in one day. Then as a tribute to the legendary Peter Croft (one of his mentors, the other being John Bachar), he soloed (no ropes) *Astroman* and *Rostrum* in one day; two cult routes in the Valley. It was like landing on the Moon which had been done but nobody thought would be repeated.

Alex does not only climb solo but he trains on climbing walls and has his own cliff scorecard on 8a.nu (Profile: 'lives in a white van, reads long books, sleeps and leads the simple life') where his excellent level (F8a on-sight, F8c after several attempts) prompts him to even more larger-than-life adventures.

The following year, he tackled Zion where he achieved his technically most daring solo of the 400-metre *Moonlight Buttress*, an aid-climb which was later freed at around F7c. Only by climbing it can one understand the sustained level of commitment when climbing with just bare hands which is needed when climbing such a route unroped. Having soloed quite successfully myself a long time ago, I sometimes found myself on the crux pitch, barely managing to hook onto an undercling, feet flat on the smooth sandstone, saying to myself: 'This guy is mad!' He also soloed the world-famous *North West Face* of Half Dome several times, clocking a time of one hour 22 minutes in 2012.

If there is one place in the climbing world which is perfectly in tune with Alex's boldness and his ability to disconnect mentally, it is the Peak District in England. There, even when roped, one feels as if one is soloing. In a few days and between rain showers, he on-sighted the 'classic' routes of the 1980s, immortalised in the film *Hard Grit*: *Gaïa*, *Parthian Shot*, *New Statesman*, *Meshuga* (solo), *Master's Edge*, *Gaïa* again solo and even *London Wall* solo on-sight.

His new fame attracted the media and sponsors. His simplicity, not to say shyness, his schoolboy looks and his smile made him the darling of American television networks. The National Geographic produced a video devoted to him, as did the famous programme *60 Minutes* on CBS, filming him in Yosemite as he climbed the solos of Sentinel North Face (done

before) and of *Phoenix* 5.13a (a first solo). He was awarded the 'Golden Piton' while The North Face brand made him one of its ambassadors which enabled him to travel all over the world.

In 2012 his craziest projects came to fruition, still in his fast and nimble style. In May, roped with another legend of the Yosemite, Tommy Caldwell, he tackled the Triple Crown, the enchaînement of the three most famous big walls of the Valley: Mount Watkins, El Capitan (by *Freerider*) and Half Dome. In other words, they climbed almost 80 pitches most of the time free and simul-climbing, no one stopped at belays and the two men climbed at the same time, simply belayed by the runners between them. Falling was absolutely forbidden. This involved a little running between routes as well as a short car ride, not to mention climbing a whole night with a headtorch. The result of the challenge was a total time of just over 21 hours.

It was an amazing performance but for Alex it had only been a reconnaissance, a sort of trial run for the same pro-gramme free solo. Although it had poured with rain the previous day, three weeks later he was at the foot of Mount Watkins again. A short, now legendary video posted on the Internet shows him aid-climbing as he negotiates a key passage, one foot slipping just as he was about to clip a karabiner. For once, he lost his legendary cool for a moment. Then it was *The Nose* at night and Half Dome in the morning, finishing at the top in less than 19 hours in front of bemused and admiring 'tourists'. By his own admission, this time he had reached his limit.

But taking advantage of this supersonic form and after he and ultra-specialist Hans Florine had just missed *The Nose* speed record by 45 seconds, the two friends then shattered the record of this vertical marathon of 900 metres by completing it in two hours 23 minutes and 51 seconds, in other words an average of four minutes per pitch.

A real marathon of the peaks took place with Tommy Caldwell in February 2014 in Patagonia with the first complete traverse of FitzRoy and its satellites: almost a kilometre of roller coaster in five days, covering highly technical elevation changes of over 4,000 metres in the Patagonian mountains, which had by now become the Chamonix for the North Americans.

Then he moved from the granite cliffs and their reassu-ring cracks to the limestone slabs of *El Sendero Luminoso* on El Potrero Chico in Mexico, which were much less safe to solo. He covered the 15 pitches, 11 of them 5.12, in less than three hours. Finally, he celebrated his 29th birthday with 290 pitches in a single day on Squamish's University Wall. His boldness appears to know no limits but he always used as few climbing aids as possible, following a strict ethic in the tradition of Reinhold Messner in the 1960s.

He still has this crazy dream of being the first man to climb El Capitan solo free, probably by *Freerider*, the most suitable (or to be precise, the least impossible) route in spite of the *Teflon Corner*, so called because it looks so slippery. Today only he would dare to envisage such a project.

CLIMBING, A CHILD'S GAME?

The average age of top-level climbers is gradually going down. Adam Ondra, Chris Sharma and to a lesser extent David Lama were all child prodigies in their time. Nowadays seeing children under 10 achieving the eighth grade is no longer a surprise. Some less successful climbers looking for excuses will say that at this age, lactic acid has not yet developed, that all the holds are very large, and having started from a tender age, they do not know the fear of falling.

Some countries have systems which recruit and coach promising youngsters for competition. Often the parents are climbers themselves who coach their children in the hope that they will have a brilliant future, often for the best and sometimes for the worst.

There are also climbing families where several of the children are involved. When their careers ended, Didier Raboutou turned away from climbing and focused on other interests such as cycling, while Robyn Erbesfield wrote about her career as a climber in *Sport Climbing with Robyn Erbesfield*. She remained involved in climbing, organising discovery and coaching workshops for children three to seven years old: ABC for Kids. Their own children were among the first to benefit. Shawn, born in 1998, reached F8b+ at the age of 12, and perhaps even more impressive, his sister Brooke, born in 2001, climbed an F8b at Red River at the age of nine. There has been a lot of progress since the 1980s when Marc le Ménestrel was considered a child prodigy and nicknamed 'Bébé 7a' at the age of 12.

Still highly motivated, Robyn has reached that level again at the age of almost 45. "Many people look at me and wonder when Shawn and Brooke belay me, but I reassure them, saying that they do it better than most of my adult friends. We fill my climbing bag with stones and attach it to Brooke so that she is not pulled into the air too high." Apart from performance, it is the family spirit sharing the same passion that keeps the world of climbing young.

Ashima Shiraishi was born in New York in 2001 and is the perfect embodiment of this phenomenon as her precocious performance shows. She bouldered V10 (f7c+) at the age of eight, V11 when nine, and climbed *Crown of Aragorn*, the famous V13 (f8b) boulder in Hueco opened by Fred Nicole, at the age of 10, an unprecedented series of achievements. In 2014, she was the second woman after Tomoko Ogawa to achieve a V14 (f8b+), and this at the age of 13.

She is equally impressive on cliffs, having already reached F8c+ (*Southern Smoke*, Red River Gorge) at the age of 11, and since then she has confirmed her potential in a most convincing manner. In March 2015, still only 13, she made history again by becoming the first woman to achieve a F9a+: *Open your mind direct* on Santa Linya in Catalonia. This was an already existing F9a where one of the key holds had broken, after which she was the first climber to repeat it. With this latest exploit,

SHAWN AND BROOKE RABOUTOU-ERBESFIELD.

THE YOUNG NEW-YORKER ASHIMA SHIRAISHI.

she has further reduced the gap between the sexes at the top level, and one wonders how high her limits will be in view of her precocity and enormous potential. Given this, what will she be doing at the age of 20 or 25, assuming she is still climbing? It is impossible to say, not least because gifted children sometimes lose interest in their original passion, while others end up becoming Mozart or Maradona.

Now aged 15, Kai Lightner discovered climbing in an indoor climbing centre in North Carolina. He has already reached 5.14 and always does well in junior competitions, becoming World Champion in his category in 2014. This would be considered almost normal nowadays, were it not for his Afro-American origins which make him a pioneer in that respect. Will he become an example, followed by other young people from ethnic minorities or from developing countries (such as Africa and India) who will be taking part in the growing universality of climbing hitherto ignored by whole sectors of society?

At the other end of the age spectrum, people are climbing until they are much older, doing 7th, even 8th grades at the age of over 50 has become quite common, and some 'old' climbers even make a gallant last stand with a F9a. We can already anticipate seeing the first 70 and 80-year olds who, having climbed all their life and followed a healthy lifestyle, with a little luck will still be climbing until the day they die.

This rejuvenation of climbers is linked to the exponential spread of indoor climbing centres and artificial climbing structures. Originally rather home-made until the mid-1990s, these have subsequently become a real social phenomenon which in turn has generated its own industry. The geographic spread of indoor centres in many cities has enabled traditional climbers to train more often, away from the wind and the rain, excessive cold or heat, and darkness – in other words, all the things which make up the charm of outdoor life. But, at the same time, they have also attracted a new public, many of them women, between the ages of 25 and 40, who go to them as they would to fitness centres. They also appeal to young people, still studying, who will be the foundation of future generations of climbers.

FOR OLDIES TOO

On the opposite side of those prime athletic years is a modern increase of longevity which can be seen with even 50-year olds freeing hard routes becoming quite common. Some crazy old addicts even reach the French 9th grade or compete in the senior category; notably some talented former professional athletes such Manolo, Ben Moon and Beat Kammerlander for example.

Manolo for instance, the Italian star from the 80s, waited until recent years to achieve his hardest redpoints : *Bain de sang* and *Bimbaluna* at Saint-Loup, Switzerland, *Eternit* at Vettre Feltrine in his beloved Dolomites which also hosts his famous *Solo per vecchi guerrieri*, (Only for the old warriors); four horrific slab pitches, the last one being F8c and mandatory F7c between the bolts. Despite his now whitened red-haired mane, the Austrian, Beat Kammerlander, (born 1959), stays very active, especially in trad climbing, most remembered for his already mentioned and legendary *Prinzip Hoffnung*. The same motivation also goes for Ben Moon, now close to his 50s but meeting the French 9th grade in 2015 thanks to the very sustained *Rainshadow* at Malham.

Not less passionate but unknown, stand non pro-climbers, such the Frenchman François Tournois, who has achieved an impressive tick-list of hundreds of hard routes up to F8c; most of them climbed after reaching 50.

Sometimes it is parenthood which creates the longevity: Robyn Erbesfield, maybe motivated by her children or the Spanish Novato Marin. His son Edu is one of the strongest Iberian sport climbers and often pairs with Novato, 63 years old, for his boldest projects on such repetitions as *Pan Aroma* on the Cima Ovest de Lavaredo in July 2014, then in 2015, *Orbayu* on the Naranjo de Bulnes, *Digital Crack* and the Grand Capucin's *Petit Route* in the Mont Blanc range.

The famous Italian novelist Erri de Luca, author of *Poids du papillon,* discovered climbing late succeeding on *La Teoria dell* F8a, (Aeronaute grotta in Sperlonga) in 2002 at the age of 52: "I succeeded, feeling good and strong. This stamina route suited me well and I spent three to four months there because I enjoyed it, not for the grade but for the line, straight and natural. It's just a nice game climbers play."

More astonishing is Marcel Remy, father of the prolific swiss climbers Claude and Yves Remy. Despite being more than 90 years old, he's still on the rocks, leading 5.10. He reminds us of Riccardo Cassin's spirit, climbing one more time 'his' Piz Badile *North Face* aged 78.

In the future, we can easily imagine the first 70 or 80-year olds still passionate after a lifetime of climbing. Thanks to good health, a proper and continuous training (in climbing gyms for instance) and a slice of luck, they will go for it till their last day.

LEFT: MANOLO, 52 YEARS OLD, ON *ETERNIT*, F9A,
VETTRE FELTRINE, DOLOMITES.
RIGHT: BEAT KAMMERLANDER, 55 YEARS OLD, ON
DREI SIEBE, F8B, BÜRSERWÄNDLE, AUSTRIA.

I WOULDN'T TRUST HIM FURTHER THAN I COULD 'SPIT'

The past few years have seen the emergence of new approaches which sometimes seem like a return to basics after all the 'plastic' years. First of all there has been a revival of 'trad' climbing. In search of new thrills, top-level climbers have opened extreme sport routes using only nuts in Germany, Italy, Switzerland and Austria, where veteran Beat Kammerlander made a clean ascent of *Prinzip Hoffnung* in Bürs, Vorarlberg: 40 metres of a harrowing slab on bad runners for a grade of 10/10+ or F8b/F8b+.

Harder still, others repeat already bolted routes which are climbable with natural protection. This practice, known as greenpointing, is perfectly illustrated by *Black Bean*, in Ceüse, a 'classic' F8b, repeated 'ecologically' by Arnaud Petit: "I see this as a step forward in that, even outside Britain, climbers realise that they are not forced to use bolts." (Or 'spits' as the French call them.)

Some have even proposed the 'greying' of holds: that is, once it has been demonstrated that a section can be climbed without the hated hold, it is filled in and painted the colour of the rock. Nevertheless this raises a problem in that it involves modifying recognised existing routes after the event. Interestingly enough, those who promote this new philosophy are often the ones who chipped these holds 20 or 30 years ago.

Sometimes these 'inventors' go as far as to question the very definition of free-climbing. For instance, how should one categorise 'dry tooling', derived from ice-climbing, where ice-axes and crampons are used, which are after all artificial tools? Sometimes climbing shoes even replace crampons, as was the case with Will Mayo in *The Existensionalist* (summer 2014).

The British are in the lead in hazardous 'trad' climbing, with colourful characters bringing a fresh perspective to a discipline which is often too standardised. They are tackling problems on gritstone approaching E10 7a (or around the French F8b/F8b+),

ARNAUD PETIT GREENPOINTING *BLACK BEAN*, F8B IN CEÜSE, FRANCE.

—

PAGE 237:

THE BRITISH LEO HOULDING ON HIS OWN *THE PROPHET*, E9 7A OR 5.13D, EL CAPITAN

at first top-roping, then making headpoint ascents: Neil Bentley (*Equilibrium* on Burbage), James Pearson (*The Promise*), John Arran (*Doctor Doolittle* on Curbar). Then there is *Meshuga* ('only' E9 6c), immortalised by Seb Grieve in the excellent film *Hard Grit*. Many climbers there have ended up falling down a grassy slope, ripping out some miserable protections seemingly still amused by it all, gritstone offering suicide risk for both the falling climber and the belayers stood beneath.

Further north, the Scot, Dave MacLeod announced an E11 7a in 2006. At the time *Rhapsody* was the hardest trad route in the world, the equivalent of an F8c/F8c+ on nuts with a potential fall of 70m at the end of it all; well illustrated in the film *E11*. Since then, repeat ascensionists (the Canadian Sonnie Trotter, then Steve McClure and finally James Pearson in 2014) have been arguing about what number to add to the 'E' and the way the route had been opened (eliminating exit, nuts placed in advance, down-climbing to ground level).
Since then, MacLeod has continued to hunt on his home territory, searching for an improbable and even more dangerous route on Ben Nevis, better known for its ice and mixed climbing. *Echo Wall*, not graded this time, required many hours of work to expose the route by removing the snow with a spade.

As well as being an excellent trad climber, Steve McClure was for a long time the best sport climber in Britain. He opened the two top-level overhanging limestone routes on Raven Tor and Malham, *Mutations* (F9a, 1998) and *Overshadow* (the first English F9a+, 2007). The latter has only been repeated by Adam Ondra who confirmed the grade (the young Czech has become a standard authority on grading).

MODERN GRISTONE HEADPOINTING.
LEFT: *BIGGER BARON*, E10 7A, FIRST ASCENT BY PETE WHITTAKER.
CENTRE: SONNIE TROTTER IN HIS OWN BACK YARD IN CANADA, HEADPOINTING *FAMILY MAN*, F8C OR 5.14B R, SKAHA BLUFFS.
RIGHT: THE YOUNG BRIT, KATY WHITTAKER ON *BRAILLE TRAIL*, E7 6C, BURBAGE SOUTH, PEAK DISTRICT. PLEASE NOTE THE FUNNY GEAR USED (A DOORKNOB FOR INSTANCE...).

LEFT: TRICKY PROTECTIONS FOR THE CANADIAN SARAH HART ON *MAN FROM DELMONTE*, 5.12D, SQUAMISH, CANADA.

CENTRE: THE AMERICAN, MADALEINE SORKIN ON *RUBY'S CAFE*, 5.13A, INDIAN CREEK, USA.

RIGHT: PETE WHITTAKER, AGAIN, FINGER JAMMING ON THE FAMOUS *COBRA CRACK* IN SQUAMISH, CANADA.

In June 2014, James McHaffie claimed a typically British challenge when in just over 19 hours, he soloed 100 'Extreme' routes in the Lake District, in other words, those with the legendary 'E' in their grading: "Some were long, others short, sometimes the rock was great, sometimes less so but the landscape was always fantastic."
The following month, the young Pete Whittaker did even better in the Peak District: 150 'Es' in one day. This type of feat had first been achieved by Ron Fawcett almost 30 years earlier, when he did 100 in one day.

Leo Houlding and Tim Emmett, on the other hand, are all-terrain adventurers. Leo travelled all over the world, from Antarctica to Baffin Island and to the slopes of Everest (even wearing a replica of George Mallory's outfit in 1924), while Tim dry-tooled the hardest routes in the world, as well as BASE jumping. Leo Houlding also had a love affair with El Capitan: having been the first British climber to free it (at the age of 18), after a 10-year effort, he completed another project in 2010, a very austere challenge nearby: *The Prophet*. Such perseverance was comparable to the seven years Tommy Caldwell spent freeing *Dawn Wall*.

As for Tim Emmett, he climbed one of the most terrifying trad routes of recent years: *Muy Caliente* E10 in Pembrokeshire, Wales. This time it involved climbing an F8b with run-outs which offered potential ground falls. Later James Pearson bravely flashed the route, climbing it from the bottom without practising the moves, an even 'hotter' exploit than Tim Emmet's: "When headpointing, it is not enough to be a brilliant climber, what you need above all is self-knowledge in an objectively dangerous situation."

Two British climbers, Tom Randall and Pete Whittaker, devised another climbing style to snatch the first of the longest and most difficult off-width cracks in the world from the Americans. (An off-width crack is one wide enough to squeeze part of your body.) Known as *Century Crack*, 5.14b, it is a wide horizontal crack 50 metres long on a rocky plateau in the middle of the Utah desert. Through the Internet, they were able to assess the exact width of the crack and reproduce it faithfully at home in Sheffield. Tom built a replica in his cellar with jams of the right size and trained there six days a week for two years. Working on placing the gigantic Friends, they 'climbed' the equivalent of thousands of metres, as well as doing 250,000 ab exercises and 40,000 pull-ups. When they arrived on site in 2011, the two men, known as the Wide Boyz, made a few trial runs before facing the beast. This kind of walking with your feet on the ceiling (known as the *leavittation* technique after its inventor Randy Leavitt) involves exposed, painful climbing (the ground is never very far below) in an out-of-the-ordinary style which Tom describes as being as psychological as it is physical in its approach. After numerous attempts, the climbers took over an hour and a half to complete the pitch.

The girls were not to be outdone. Hazel Findlay, Emma Twyford and Katy Whittaker (Pete Whittaker's sister) could climb F8c grades in Spain but they were also experts in bold trad climbing in the Peak District and on sea cliffs. Hazel was the first woman to secure an E9, on the cliffs of Devon.

Cobra Crack in Squamish, Canada, is also a contender for the title of the world's hardest crack climb and Didier Berthod has made numerous attempts on it. Introduced to climbing by his parents when young, Berthod was an outstanding Swiss climber very much in the tradition of Fred Nicole and Elie Chevieux. At 16 he was climbing F8b+ but, it was in the United States that he discovered his true passion of trad cracks. He opened *Greenspit* in Val d'Orco in trad style in 2003, but *Cobra Crack* escaped him because of an injury. It was finally opened by Sonnie Trotter in 2006. Since then Didier Berthod has discovered another route, the way to God, and has joined a religious community in Switzerland.

As to freebase climbing, represented by Dean Potter, being a fringe discipline, it is not likely to become very popular...

The sport of DWS (Deep Water Solo) or psico-bloc is more convivial and fun which came into being in Majorca in the Balearic Islands in the late 1970s, where it was introduced by Miguel Riera. It gradually spread throughout the world, especially along European and Asian coasts. What could be more fun than climbing above the water without constraints? The only problem is that things become tougher with extra height, and above 15 metres, any fall is strongly inadvisable.

THE PERFECT OVERHANGING ARCH OF ES PONTAS, MALLORCA ISLAND.

Chris Sharma made a major step forward when he climber the underside of *Es Pontàs* in 2007. This natural arch, just off the south-east coast of Majorca, is almost perfectly symmetrical. Sharma, a shrewd media star, decided to tackle this 'impossible' leap with his usual determination, as can be seen in one of the best climbing films of recent years: *King Lines*.

Does the final grading, F9a+, really take the particular nature of this route into account? As a psicobloc and one of the most difficult routes in the world, some still see it as the hardest to repeat solo, even in the age of F9b+. The magical arch is still waiting for someone to repeat Sharma's feat.

DEAN POTTER
THE MAN WHO WANTED TO FLY

"I am caught up in a whirlwind. The heavens around me are collapsing. I am losing consciousness, I am falling into limbo while my body is becoming like a bird's wing. I feel a void behind me, like my father tugging at my shirt. Tears are welling up in my eyes and I have a lump in my throat. The ground is rushing towards me. I turn round and take off."

This is how Dean Potter described his earliest childhood memory, a recurring dream which haunted him until he could make it come true; flying instead of dying.
From a childhood in New Hampshire to the big walls of Yosemite and Patagonia, not to mention the North Face of the Eiger, he always saw himself as a modern Icarus, involved in a subtle game with the rocks, the risk of death and the heavens.

Arriving in Yosemite, he became one of its emblematic 'Stone Monkeys'. These half-hobo, half-climber characters who had little money but tried to stay as long as possible in the Valley. Perpetuating the legend of Camp 4, they played cat-and-mouse with the park wardens, especially when they were suddenly tempted to make a forbidden leap, BASE jumping from the top of El Capitan. The Stone Monkeys saw themselves as the humble but worthy heirs of the Stone Masters of the 1970s.

In less than a decade, thanks to some very daring speed solos which were widely covered by the media, Dean Potter became a cult figure in the same way as Chris Sharma, Dave Graham and Tony Caldwell had done. Admittedly, he did not tackle 9th grades like them, but he had the guts (or foolishness) to tackle an unroped 7th grade on-sight.
Solo ascents of *The Nose*, *Half Dome* and *Astroman*, sometimes running, highballs (very high boulders) or cratering which seemed likely to lead at best to life in wheelchair, the legendary

highline traverse (that is, a slackline across a void of several hundred metres) of *Lost Arrow* without belay, these were all extremely high-risk activities he undertook.

He was a very colourful character. When we met him in the Yosemite, he had half a beard and half a moustache, like two faces in one! He had met his ideal woman, Steph Davis, a crack climber and also a top level BASE jumper who became his female alter-ego and probably the only woman who made as many bold solos finished off by jumps. They separated but she still climbs in the same spirit.

A climber through and through, Dean gave free rein to his creativity by combining climbing, mountaineering, slack line, BASE jumping and wing-suit flying to create new activities of which he was virtually the only person in the world to indulge. For instance he invented the concept of FreeBASE: making an unroped ascent of a steep rock face with an overhang with only a 2.5 kg parachute on his back as life insurance. This was how he climbed the *Rostrum* in the Yosemite (without falling) and cut a swathe when he conquered *Deep Blue Sea* in the same way again, some 300 metres culminating at F7c, on the right edge of the famous North Face of the Eiger. To prepare himself for this project, he spent a month in the Oberland training to fall, camping for days at an altitude of over 3,000 metres like a Tibetan monk in his cave, on the edge of the rock face. He stumbled once on the hard edge and down-climbed in a panic through the thick fog – the perfect conditions for building a legend. It must said that FreeBASE does not have many followers.

Dean was also a successful pure solo mountaineer climbing in Patagonia, the area that is so popular with American climbers. In 2002, taking advantage of a window of opportunity in the weather, he flashed the *Super Couloir* on FitzRoy in record time (first solo ascent), opened yet another new route

on FitzRoy and finished off with Cerro Torre. He returned to the Cerro Torre four years later in order to jump from it but in the end he decided against it – a wise decision.

For a short time he held the speed record for an ascent of *The Nose* on El Capitan in two hours 36 minutes 45 seconds. Unlike previous contenders, (the Huber brothers, Yuji Hirayama and Hans Florine) Dean and his climbing partner Sean Leary never stopped, both climbing uninterruptedly with always two or three points of protection between them; a single pitch 900 metres long. It was much more dangerous but much more efficient. What their achievement showed was that the limit today is dictated by a climber's cardiac health and that with even more basic training, the legendary two-hour barrier could be broken.

In his 40s, Dean Potter continued to lead his itinerant life, travelling in a van provided by one of his sponsors. He appeared regularly at evenings where climbing documentaries and slide shows were presented. With his calm voice and quasi-guru appearance, he continued to inspire fans.

He was a legendary climber but he was not always successful in conquering the hardest routes or reaching the top step of the podium. Instead he acted as a beacon for the future, following his own unique, original path without worrying about conventions. He died in May 2015 in his beloved Yosemite when he made a fatal BASE jump. A few days earlier, he wrote his last words: 'In my dreams I'm flying, black wings spread. I listen to the world around me, fully aware, open to the call'.

PAGE 242: DEAN POTTER (1972–2015) AND WHISPER. PAGE 243: WHISPER ENCOURAGES DEAN ON *ZEN CRACK*, MOAB, UTAH, AN UNGRADED HIGHBALL, 2008. PAGE 244: THE SLACKLINE, ONE OF DEAN POTTER'S OTHER PASSIONS. PICTURED HERE IN THE MAGNIFICENT SETTING OF TAFT POINT, YOSEMITE. PAGE 245: AS A TRIBUTE TO THE LATE WOLFGANG GÜLLICH, DEAN FREE SPACE SOLOING ON *SEPARATE REALITY*, YOSEMITE.

WHAT FUTURE FOR COMPETITIONS?

Prompted by Sharma again, the first psicobloc competitions in natural water or swimming pools proved to be spectacular events, both live and on television. This could point to a future other than the Olympic dream. The recognition of climbing as an Olympic discipline is too dependent on uncontrollable economic, and even political factors, rather than on the intrinsic interest of the competitions or their representation of the Olympic ideal.

While the standard in the major championships has increased significantly, reflecting the rising level of achievement, the organisation of the events has changed very little over the past 25 years. Only when the temperaments of the climbers clash is the necessary dramatic intensity produced. Unfortunately, these events usually take place with bland background music which does nothing to enhance the atmosphere. Perhaps it would be better to follow the examples of athletics and tennis, where tension and drama are magnified by the silence, punctuated by loud outbursts of public applause.

Nevertheless, one of the major benefits of the organised competition system is that the best climbers are now recognised as top-level sportsmen and women, as they are in other disciplines. As a result, climbing now benefits from advances in scientific research applied to the sport, in particular in the field of training.

Today, Udo Neumann is team manager of the German bouldering team. In 1993 he and the American climber Dale Goddard wrote the modern training bible, entitled *Performance Rock Climbing*. Influenced by John Gill, Neumann has since concentrated on the concept of kinesthesis or proprioception which, according to the dictionary, is the conscious perception of the position and moves of the various parts of the body: "What is important is generating energy through the moves. You can develop as much strength as possible but above all the *momentum* must be preserved, in other words the dynamism of the moves. What is difficult is not so much reaching a hold, as hanging on to it while controlling the balance."

Although some people still believe that climbing is all about pure strength, it has been shown that a climber should learn to control the body in motion, a concept applied in gymnastics and in the past by Jacky Godoffe in bouldering. Recently, opening the World Championships of bouldering, he remarked on the evolution of athletes: "In the past, 20 years ago, competition was very stressful for climbers who were only used to rock faces where they could take weeks, months or even years to conquer a boulder or a route. Suddenly to be faced with only a few minutes to prepare themselves felt strange to them. Now, athletes training in indoor centres are used to resin and competitions and they are less stressed because they have grown up with them."

Today top level climbing has also become a discipline in which speed matters. In competition but also bouldering and on the rock face, speed is synonymous with success. This becomes apparent when watching Adam Ondra climbing – often it is like watching a speeded-up film.

Meanwhile other coaches have decided to take a holistic approach. For instance, the Spanish climber David Macià, who also trained Ramonet and Edu Marin, has developed an original alternative method called *Or9anic*. This is an acronym standing for optionality, respect, globalisation, adaptation, nature, imagination and creativity, and it enables you to reach top level by listening to yourself: "It is a method which sees every individual as a unique and irreplaceable being. It is therefore necessary to know the characteristics of each person in order to adapt it to their way of being. Training methods must be adapted to the climber and not the other way round."

As in all sports, doping has often been mentioned in climbing but nothing positive has ever been revealed. Admittedly some people have tested positive, like Chris Sharma for cannabis in 2001 after winning a victory in the bouldering World Championship in Munich. But, a Californian climber who does not smoke joints is like an Englishman or a German who does not drink beer. It is more likely that his happy state was the result of conquering *Biographie*.

More recently, Charlotte Durif, clearly disillusioned, did not beat about the bush when she said that anorexia was a kind of doping which had spread to most women's world championship podiums: 'From a sports point of view, this kind of doping disgusts me. Although no drugs are involved, it is an artificial physical process in the same way as blood transfusion. Today athletes no longer compete on an equal footing and sporting fairness no longer exists.'

Certainly the fight against anorexia as a disease is a noble cause and it should be encouraged but it is also true that weight, like height, can play a major part in fighting against gravity. Nevertheless, athletes of both sexes who have a 'heavier' morphology or who are short have still managed to win or to perform. This is one of the differences between climbing and commoner sports: the perfect body does not exist, whether in bouldering or rock-climbing.

PODIUMS AND PEOPLE

Until Romain Desgranges won the European Champion's title in 2013, Sandrine Levet and Alex Chabot had been the last great French champions before the country lost its supremacy. Sandrine Levet was extremely versatile and successful in her speciality at bouldering events, winning three Cups and one World Championship between 2003 and 2005. She also did well in competitions, winning Arco 2006 and several international podium positions. As for Alex Chabot, he won the gold medal in the World Championship three times between 2001 and 2003, the European Championship title twice, plus three Rock Masters in Arco and several other titles. A native of Rheims, he had travelled south and settled in Nice. There he was a frequent visitor to the Gorges du Loup where he reached the 9th grade, climbing *Kinematix* and *PuntX*.

ALEX CHABOT, FRENCH KING OF THE EARLY 2000s LEAD COMPETITIONS.

Chabot was also one of the first athletes to dare to rebel against the official authorities. In 2006 he refused to wear a strip with the colours of a federal sponsor whose values he did not share. His refusal to promote the sponsor resulted in his immediate expulsion. Thoroughly disillusioned, at the age of 25 he decided to give up competitions. Since then he has gradually extended his universe, travelling round the world and into the high mountains.

Succeeding these men on the podiums were representatives of the most dynamic country in recent years — Spain.

The Czech Tomas Mrazek has also combined a fine career on climbing walls (World Champion in 2003 and 2005) and on rock faces, being the second climber to ascend an F8c on-sight (*Pata Negra*, Rodellar) in 2005. Since then he has since achieved 10 or more 9th grades.

Some small countries such as Slovenia, with two million inhabitants, stand out. It has been involved for decades in mountaineering in the Alps and the Himalaya and there is a national tradition of being involved in climbing sports. In 2001 Martina Cufar won the World Championship and in the last round in 2014 Slovenia was the first to have three athletes in the first five places, Mina Markovic, Maja Vidmar and Domen Skofic.

Before that, Belgium had also distinguished itself thanks to Muriel Sarkany who dominated the scene in the early years of the new millennium (five Cups and a World Championship title among others). In 2013, at the age of 39, happy to have left the world of competitions, she conquered *Punt X* in the Gorges

du Loup, a confirmed and athletic F9a. By becoming one of those rare women to reach the 9th grade, she confirmed her versatility and showed that it is always possible to advance even after reaching the top level.

Between 2003 and 2011, the Austrian Angela Eiter's achievements were the most impressive in the history of women's competition with four championships and three World Cups as well as seven Arco titles. Today this young woman lives and climbs in the mountains (with two F9a ascents in autumn 2014 followed by a third one the next spring) and she clearly sees how competitions are different: "There is a strict order in competition because you are told where and when to climb." She now coaches promising young climbers: "I feel it is very important that children's specialisation in competition should be balanced by open-air outings so that they also discover the original spirit of climbing."

ABOVE FROM LEFT TO RIGHT:

THE CZECH TOMAS MRAZEK IN SERRE-CHEVALIER, 2005 AND THE AUSTRIAN ATHLETE JAKOB SCHUBERT.

BELOW FROM LEFT TO RIGHT:

THE CANADIAN SEAN MCCOLL STEALS THE SHOW IN 2015 IN MARSEILLE, FRANCE.

THE BELGIAN MURIEL SARKANY AND THE AUSTRIAN ANGELA EITER; QUEENS OF THE WALLS.

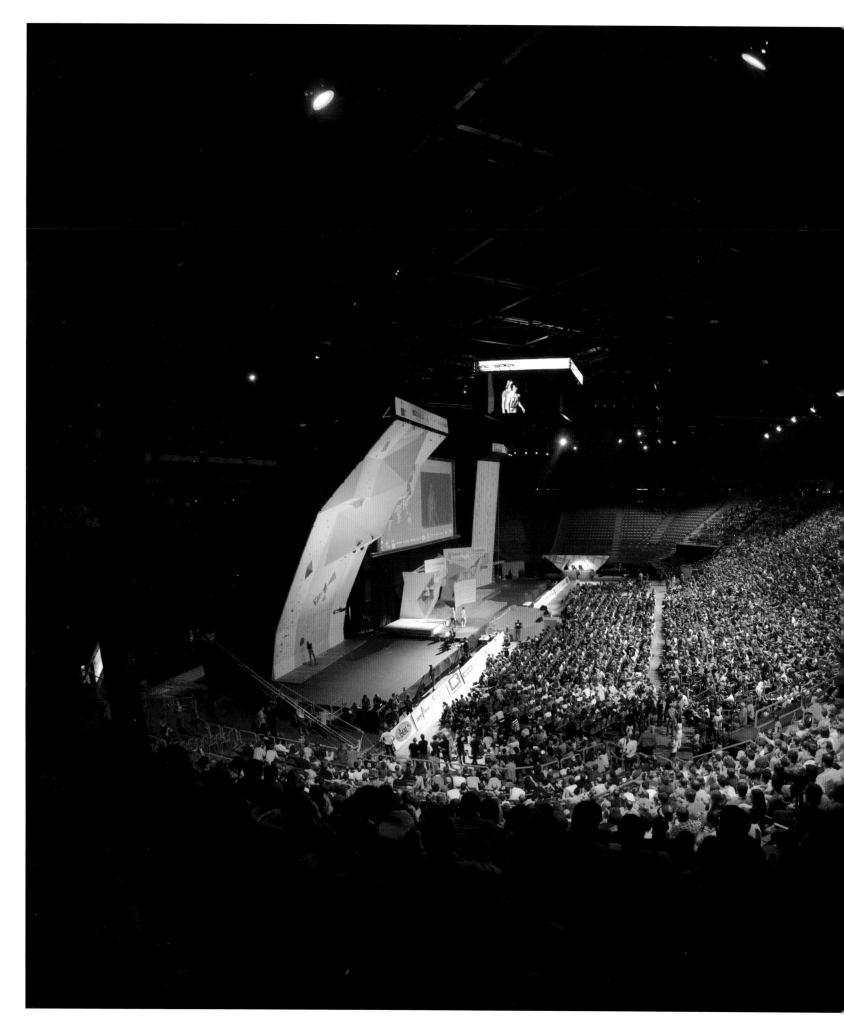

Austria has probably been the most successful country in the last 10 years with a particularly effective coaching structure, entirely dedicated to training new champions. This 'factory of champions' has produced the Stöhr-Fischhuber couple who will be mentioned later and, Jakob Schubert, who appeared on the scene in 2011 and immediately won the World Cup, then the Championships in the following year and the Cup again in 2014. He ended that year with a flourish, joining the very select F9b club by conquering *Fight or Flight* in Oliana.

The main surprise and disappointment has been North America, even though it has a highly structured programme, a dense network of training staff and many professional athletes. The Canadian Sean McColl and the young American climbers Alex Puccio and Sasha DiGiulian, are often well-placed but its last international champion was Robyn Erbesfield in 1995.

Asia is the continent which now threatens the supremacy of Europe. Less structured but extremely effective, Asian climbing has continued to develop after the emergence of the celebrated Yuji Hirayama. Aesthetic, supple and nimble but also

PAGES 250-251:

8,000 ENTHUSIASTIC SPECTATORS IN PARIS-BERCY DURING THE 2012 WORLD CHAMPIONSHIPS.

—

PAGE 251:

ROMAIN DESGRANGES, THE BEST CURRENT FRENCH LEAD-COMPETITOR.

PAGE 252:

THE JAPANESE SACHI AMMA WHO WON THE LEAD
WORLD CUP SERIES IN 2012 AND 2013.

—

PAGE 253:

AND, HIS FELLOW COUNTRY WOMAN ALTER-EGO FOR
BOULDERING COMPS, AKIYO NOGUCHI.

very light, the Japanese and Koreans are formidable opponents. The Japanese Sachi Amma dominated the last two World Cups while also building up an amazing list of achievements with seven F9a and F9b climbs on the Catalan cliffs in less than three weeks. Together with Adam Ondra, he marks a return to a lighter, leaner physique. His compatriot Akiyo Noguchi already has three bouldering world titles to her credit. As for the Korean Jain Kim, she has been dominating top-level climbing for five years. Her performance in the final of the 2014 World Championships at Gijon was truly dazzling for its self-control and relaxation. Finally, on the competition podiums as well as on the crags, are shining the representatives of the most dynamic country of climbers and climbing in recent years: Spain.

THE SPANISH WAVE

Spain did not come from nowhere to dominate sport climbing as it does today. Its potential was already obvious in the 1960s and 1970s when aid-climbing was in vogue. At the time Mallos de Riglos, Montserrat (almost 4,000 routes on conglomerate rock) and the great rock faces of Terradets were well-known destinations. In 1985 their development became exponential through the systematic use of bolts, resulting in the discovery of gems such as Siurana. Dozens of new destinations appeared on the map in Catalonia, Andalusia, the Basque country and as far away as the Balearic Islands. A few foreign visitors such as John Redhead, Martin Scheel (the first Spanish F8b, *Vuelo a Ciegas*) and Marc Le Menestrel came to explore the possibilities and motivate the local climbers.

Montgrony and its colonnettes, Margalef and Raco de la Misa, the flagship sector of the Sierra de Montsant, Oliana and the vast cave of Santa Linya, La Pedriza

PAGE 254: RODELLAR.

–

PAGE 255:

ABOVE LEFT: 'RAMONET' PUIGBLANQUE ON THE LAST MOVES OF LA RAMBLA EXTENSION, F9A+, SIURANA, SPAIN.

ABOVE RIGHT: ANNA IBAÑEZ AND MONTSE PASCUEL, THE FIRST OUTSTANDING SPANISH FEMALE CLIMBERS.

BELOW: PATXI USOBIAGA ON PAMINTZA (F8B/8B+), CUEVA DE BALTZOLA, BASQUE COUNTRY.

and its granite slabs not far from Madrid, Cienca, Chulilla, Montañejos, El Chorro and Andalusia, Albarracin and its thousands of boulders, the Basque Country with the Baltzola cave and Onate; the best known rock-climbing today whilst the remaining potential is enormous.

The climbing areas of Spain are now easy to get to but the other side of the coin is that they can sometimes be overcrowded. Today, some rock faces have become the victims of their popularity and many climbers visit specially to add well-known routes to their list of achievements. "In Spain it is no longer a matter of just climbing or the beauty of the routes. It is a race for grades," Cedric Lachat commented but the first people to become interested in Spanish rock faces were the Spanish themselves and for a good reason. Since there were plenty of rock faces to climb near home, there was an ever-increasing number of skilful climbers and this created a lively social life around the crags.

In the Pantheon of climbers, Rafaele Comino was the child prodigy of the 1980s. At 16 he had already reached F8b+ (*El Prisoniero*) after several attempts and a solo F7c. In 1988 he was filmed climbing solo in a documentary for Spanish national television: with his long blond hair, headband and nimble moves he was a perfect clone of Edlinger in *Life at the Fingertips*. At the time, few climbers anywhere had reached that level.

In 1992 Carles Brasco opened *Odi Social* in Siurana (F8c, then F8c+ after a hold was broken) and repeated Patxi Arocena's *El Sicario*, which he downgraded to F8b+.

There are some unforgettable images, of Carlos Garcia hanging solo on the conglomerate lumps on Riglos in the last overhangs of the *Fiesta del biceps* in 1989, Alexander Huber tackling *La Rambla* in the mid-1990s and, the appearance of the fanatical Dani Andrada who has been climbing since he was 12 and is still doing so at 40.

In 1992, when just 16, Andrada had already chalked up 57 8th grade routes and by the year 2000, this figure reached the symbolic figure of 1,000. It has more than doubled since. Very methodical, he keeps detailed records of all his ascents.

A competitor in his early years, he is also the climber with the largest number of 9th grades, nearly 50, and all of them in Spain. His peak was reached when he announced a F9b, *Ali Hulk Sit Start Extension* in Rodellar, a sitting-start boulder problem at the bottom of an *Akira*-like cave, involving over 80 moves. But beyond the numbers and statistics, this all-rounder is also a brilliant bolt climber and the archetype of successful Catalan climbing. His motto has always been *A muerte* ('To the death') which is now so famous that it is a cry used throughout the world to encourage a climber.

Thanks to the decision of the Spanish federation in the late 1990s to create training centres for promising young climbers, a new generation emerged at the start of the new millennium which has more than proved itself since then.

RAMON PUIGBLANQUE AKA RAMONET, SERRE-CHEVALIER FINAL 2005.

In the tradition of Didier Raboutou and Robert Cortijo, Ramón Julián Puigblanque has clearly shown that a lack of height (1.59 metres) is no obstacle to excellence. An ambitious 20-year old in 2001, Ramonet soon distinguished himself in competition and on the rock faces of Europe where his list of cruxes soon became outrageously long as on a trip to the Gorges du Loup when he chalked up 10 routes between F8c and F9a in 10 days.

In 2003, after over 40 attempts, he conquered *La Rambla*, *Extension* 'invented' by Andrada, completing this Spanish story.
Since then, in addition to two World Championship titles (2007 and 2011), he has won the Arco Rock Master eight times between 2005 and 2013, a record which will be hard to beat. Thanks to fanatical training ('where I use pure strength to compensate for my small size'), he has secured the most impressive list of achievements in Spanish rock climbing. He is also the climber with the largest number of 9th grade routes (over 50) and this seems likely to increase even when he retires from competitions.

Just behind him comes the young Basque climber, Patxi Usobiaga, the only other World Champion (2009) and Arco Master during the period of Ramón's supremacy. Between 2006 and 2011, their mastery of difficulty events was truly overwhelming. Usobiaga was another competitor who trained hard at indoor climbing centres. This enabled him to conquer the most famous 9th grade routes, such as *La Rambla*, *Action Directe*, *Biographie*, *Escalatamaster* and *Kinematix*. Unfortunately, injuries in a car crash ended his climbing career in 2011 and after that he concentrated on his other passion, surfing. He has now returned to the field of climbing, running personalised training plans. One of the climbers he has coached is Adam Ondra who became double World Champion in 2014.

PATXI USOBIAGA, LEAD WORLD CHAMPION IN 2009.

When he started, Ramonet climbed with Edu Marin who at 16 had already reached the grade of F8b on-sight and would soon be the first to repeat *La Rambla intégrale*. But Marin was never as successful in competition as Ramón.

Although less brilliant on artificial climbing walls, Iker Pou's repeat of *Action Directe* in 2000 at the age of 22, together with his success on the crag and on the major European routes have made him one of the prolific crux hunters. He made several trips from the Basque Country to the Frankenjura just for the sake of 15 moves, a true example of passion.

Iker Pou perfectly symbolises the state of mind which prevailed at the time in the Basque Country with climbers such as Josune Bereziartu, Rikardo Otegui, Patxi Arocena, Patxi Usobiaga and Leire Aguirre: "The fanatical attitude of the Basques towards climbing is unique in the world and many of them climb every day without making a living from it."

Like many top climbers at the start of the new millennium, Iker Pou was soon convinced that climbers in the 1980s and 1990s had been much harsher in grading

climbs than the new generation, who are mainly interested in improving their scorecard on the climbing web site 8a.nu: "This is a radical change in climbing as I see it. I have a feeling that what matters to climbers today are the grades, ignoring what has made climbing a real philosophy of life."

Spanish women too have distinguished themselves. After Montse Pascual 20 years ago, then Anna Ibáñez (first Iberian female to free a F7b in 1987) and Ana León (the first Spanish woman to conquer an 8th grade in 1991 with *Musas Inquietantes* on El Chorro), Helena Aleman made several F8c ascents in 2010. Daila Ojeda, Dani Andrada's partner and then Chris Sharma's, has ascended some of the finest routes in the world, from *Tom… et je ris* in the Verdon to the F8c+ *Mind Control* in Oliana. Then in 2014 the Catalan Mar Alvarez, a firefighter by profession, at the age of 34 became the second Spanish woman (and the first non-professional) to reach the 9th grade with *Era Vella* in Margalef. Opened by Chris Sharma in 2009, this route has become the most repeated F9a in the world with some 30 ascents already.

Spain is the country with by far the largest number of 9th grade routes in the world, mainly in Catalonia and the Basque Country. At the last count there were more than 130 but the number continues to grow.

This is also a place where any climber looking for routes of all grades in an exotic setting with safe fixed-gear could spend the rest of his life without being bored.

DANI ANDRADA ON THE UNROPED FIRST PART OF HIS
ALI-HULK SIT START EXTENSION, F9B, RODELLAR, 2007.

BOULDERING TOO (WITH A SMALL F GRADE)

Essentially, an outdoor activity such as bouldering competitions and indoor events have been well-established since the late 1990s with their own calendars and they are now on a par with roped climbing events. So as not sacrifice everything to pure physical strength and also to improve the show, climbing styles have gradually become more dynamic and often disconcerting, with the holds usually spherical or triangular, requiring jumping for holds or 'dynos' as they are fondly known. It is often said that, above all, one must be a gymnast with strong fingers. These competitions take place with a musical background which creates a carnival atmosphere and reduces the seriousness of the event.

At the start of the new millennium, the discipline was still dominated by the French. In 2001, Myriam Motteau became the first World Champion in the history of the discipline, followed by Sandrine Levet three times, then Juliette Danion who won the 2007 Cup. Jérôme Meyer, won the World Cup in 2001 and 2003, challenged mainly by the Italians Mauro Calibani and Christian Core who also became international champions.

Since then the Austrian couple Anna Stöhr and Kilian Fischhuber, having won 11 world titles between them, have dominated the bouldering scene for so long and so regularly as to depress their rivals until Fischhuber's retirement at the end of 2014.

ABOVE: THE ITALIAN CHRISTIAN CORE WON THE BOULDERING WORLD CHAMPIONSHIPS IN 2003.
BELOW: THE MAGICAL DUO OF THE BOULDERING COMPS, AUSTRIANS ANNA STÖHR AND KILIAN FISCHHUBER.

Jan Hojer is the most successful German climber in this discipline and he won the World Cup in 2014. He is equally at ease on real rock, even in a roped party, and has made a fast repeat of *Action Directe*. He says: "You must be sure of being strong enough to overcome the problems in less than four minutes which is why I think no one should take part in the final unless they are capable of climbing f8b/f8b+ on natural boulders. Natural boulders keep me motivated." Conversely, Adam Ondra believes that: "Without the motivation of competition, I would not train as hard as I do." He then reaps the benefits outdoors. He was bouldering World Champion in 2014 but he remains clear-headed: "Bouldering competitions are more a lottery than roped ones. I honestly think that the latter are harder to win."

Surprisingly, an almost unknown 31-year old Iranian, Mohammad Jafari Mahmodabadi, won the 2015 National Bouldering Championship in the United States, ahead of all the American climbers.

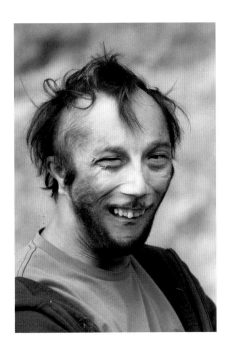

LEFT: THE FRENCHMAN PHILIPPE RIBIÈRE, HANDIGRIMPE FOUNDER.
RIGHT: THE SPANISH URKO CARMONA.

Competition climbing now also includes paraclimbing for the disabled with their own events. These have been made popular by charismatic figures such as the founder of Handigrimpe, Philippe Ribière, and the Spaniard Urko Carmona, who succeeded flashing in F8a with only one leg, proving yet again that willpower and passion are stronger than anything.

THE BOULDER
AND FOR A FEW EXTRA MOVES

In the past 30 years, bouldering has changed so significantly that a whole book could be written about it. Having been a rather discreet activity, it has become extremely popular with many climbers, and the level of difficulty has risen rapidly.

But assessing the level of difficulty in bouldering is even more subjective than in other types of climbing. Purists consider that the 'real' boulder is the quest for the ultimate movement and that beyond four or five moves, it becomes something else. Others include everything which is not too far from the ground and which does not involve a rope: traverses, linking boulder problems and so on. Physique also plays a vital part: if you are short or tall, some holds will never be within reach while if you are tall, some mantels will be impossible without your mouth and knees meeting.

In short, in bouldering more than elsewhere the accuracy of the grading must be taken with a pinch of salt. Even top climbers who sometimes refuse to give a grading agree with this. In 2004, Fred Nicole summed it up as follows: "Bouldering has become extremely popular in the past few years and it has spread almost everywhere in the world. In such conditions, it is difficult to establish a common language."

Since Fontainebleau and its long heritage and John Gill's revolutionary theories, the quest for the perfect movement has continued. During the 1970s and 1980s, the free-climbing movement also spread to Bleau and the 7th grade was soon reached. Jérôme Jean-Charles, a brilliant and eccentric character who was also France's first Rubik Cube champion, climbed *Carnage*, the first 7b, in 1977. Then in 1983 Pierre Richard reached 7c with *L'Abbé*.

In March 1987, I reported in the magazine *Vertical* that 'Alain Ghersen has done everything there is to do in Bleau, he has climbed all the boulders'. This was an amazing achievement. The only climbers on a par with him were Marc Le Menestrel and Jacky Godoffe.

Godoffe was undoubtedly the most prolific 'bleausard' of the 1980s. Thanks to his previous training as a gymnast and his extraordinary muscular strength, this eternally young-looking redhead introduced a new athletic, dynamic dimension to the discipline. He opened some of the most famous routes in the Forest: *C'était demain*, *Big Boss* and later the world-famous *Fat Man* roof (f8b). Roped, Jacky played a major part in the success of the first competitions 30 years ago when his speed caused a real sensation.

In the early 1990s, an innovative accessory appeared which revolutionised bouldering. These were the crash-pads, first seen in Hueco, Texas and originally

THE FRENCHMAN JACKY GODOFFE, MAJOR 'BLEAU' CHARACTER, HERE PICTURED ON *PARTENAIRE PARTICULIER*, f8A+, ÉLÉPHANT, 1986.

sold by small manufacturers in car parks at bouldering sites. At first, used only by top climbers, today they are part of every climber's basic equipment and they have increased the possibilities regarding difficulty and exposure by transforming the most fearsome high boulders conquered solo into less dangerous highballs. As a result of this improvement in safety and the increased sharing of information within the climbing community and media, bouldering has developed beyond recognition. It is often thought more practical and convivial than roped climbing on cliffs.

The 'Bleausard' scene now consists of a mixture of ages. There are 'veterans' such as Jean-Pierre Bouvier, known for his terrifying traverses skimming the rock on holds which only he seems able to see, Christophe Laumône and Philippe Le Denmat. There is also a new wave: Olivier Le Breton, Julien Nadiras, Seb Frigault, Antoine Vandeputte, Kevin Lopata, Vincent Pochon, and more recently, Guillaume Glairon-Mondet, the best French competition climber today.

JERRY MOFFATT ON *THE DOMINATOR*, FIRST V13 (OR f8B) IN YOSEMITE, 1993.

While Catherine Miquel became the first woman to conquer the 8th grade in 1999 with *Duel*, Marc Le Menestrel made a comeback in Bleau with a long-term project, *L'Alchimiste*: "I tried to reach an absolute in *L'Alchimiste*, the impression that at a certain point in your life, you have given the of your best." Thissymbolic boulder was later anonymously vandalised when the crux holds were broken and it was only reopened in 2015 by Nalle Hukkataival, using a new solution.

Interviewed by Patrick Edlinger, Marc Le Menestrel summed up his philosophy as follows: "In Bleau, you have three essential things: nature, performance and the people." That could also be a good reason for the growing success of bouldering, breaking down the difficulty into a few moves, and this in pleasant surroundings with a spirit of sharing.

LEFT: ALAIN GHERSEN WEARING TYPICAL 1980s LEGGINGS ON THE FIRST ASCENT OF *ENVIE D'AILES*, f7C, ÉLÉPHANT, FONTAINEBLEAU.

–

PAGE 265 :

ABOVE LEFT: MARC LE MENESTREL ON HIS 1997 VERSION OF *L'ALCHIMISTE*.

BELOW LEFT: THE FRENCHWOMAN CATHERINE MIQUEL ON *DUEL*, f8A, FRANCHARD CUISINIÈRE, FONTAINEBLEAU, 1999.

RIGHT: MAURO CALIBANI, FIRST BOULDERING WORLD CHAMPION IN THE HISTORY IN 2001, HERE PICTURED ON HIS OWN *TONINO 78*, f8C OR V15, MESCHIA, ITALY.

Since then, the Fontainebleau sandstone rocks have retained their status as a major destination. New, less centrally located zones have been discovered and new legendary f8c routes have been opened such as *Trip Hop* and *Satan i Helvete* (Seb Frigault) and *The Island* (Dave Graham, 2008).

Meanwhile, Fred Nicole and Klem Loskot have been travelling the world, pushing up the grades everywhere. Top cliff climbers such as Fred Rouhling and Tonio Lamiche in Ailefroide have been equally enthusiastic about short passages.

Besides the already existing sites revisited and revived such as Bleau, Yosemite, the Peak District and Frankenjura, climbers suddenly discovered a number of new destinations. It had become obvious that boulders existed in every continent. In America there were Hueco Tanks in Texas, Buttermilks and Happy Boulder near Bishop in California, the Triple Crown boulders, and others in Tennessee, Alabama and Georgia. In Africa, Rocklands, in Australia the Grampians and the Blue Mountains, in India at Hampi in northern Karnataka, in Japan and in New Zealand (Castle Hill).

There are even boulders deep in Himalaya or on the South American plateau at an altitude of over 4,500 metres, such as Las Rocas in Bolivia; everything is possible.

In Europe, climbers are spoilt for choice depending on the type of season and the rock. In France there are Chaos of Targassone, Annot and Ailefroide; in Spain, Albarracin, El Escorial and Castillo de Bayuela near Madrid, where Nacho Sanchez opened the first Iberian f8c boulder, *Entropia,* in 2011, in Switzerland, Magic Wood and the Ticino (Cresciano, Chironico) and in Italy Meschia, the Val di Mello, where Mellobloco is probably the most popular climbing event in the world, attracting some 4,000 climbers in the spring each year.

Naturally, these new climbing areas also mean that there are new generations of enthusiasts keen to leave their mark. The Italian Mauro Calibani was the first bouldering World Champion in 2001. Thickset with the body of a gymnast, he originally climbed on natural rock but more importantly he popularised Meschia, a fantastic bouldering area close to Rome and the Adriatic with Fontainebleau-style sandstone. It was actually a legendary 'bleuasard' figure, Bertrand Lemaire, living in Rome, who first explored it and took part in its development from 1996. Unfortunately it is on private property and there are problems with owners which has caused some difficulties; a recurrent problem which is likely to get worse. In 2004, to celebrate his 30th birthday, Calibani discovered his perfect boulder there, *Tonino 78*, with a lot of dynos and for which he suggested the first V16 or f8c+ which was unheard of at the time. This masterpiece would be repeated by his 'bleuasard' friends Julien Nadiras, after a month's hard work, and by Antoine Vandeputte. Like Ben Moon, Mauro Calibani has also created his own brand of clothes E9 made in Italy. Today he looks at the evolution of grades more objectively: "When I opened *Tonino*, it seemed to me harder than *Dreamtime*, the reference at the time for f8c, and it was subsequently downgraded. Ten years later, with hindsight, I believe *Tonino 78* should be considered a solid, historic f8c."

In 2003, his successor in the World Championship record books was also Italian: Christian Core. But it was in Liguria that he really reached his peak. By opening *Gioia* (V16 or f8c+) on the sandstone rocks in Varazze, he set the ultimate bouldering benchmark which combined extreme difficulty with the elegant aesthetics of the line and the moves.

The Basque climber Iker Arroitajauregi travels around Europe in his camper van in pursuit of boulders, far from the limelight. He does not baulk at travelling thousands of kilometres to improve a particular movement, thus reflecting the founding spirit of the discipline. The same is true of Bernd Zangerl, an Austrian who is not well-known but who is nevertheless one of those restless top level climbers. He made the first repeat of *Dreamtime* in its original version before new holds made their appearance while others disappeared. In 2003 he added two more f8c grades to his collection, *Viva la evolucion* in Magic Wood and *Newine*. But he too is not obsessed by numbers: "People should not think that the grade is the most important thing. It is not good for climbing."

John Gaskins is probably the English climber who has pushed extreme movement to the maximum in his country. In the early part of the millennium, after a second repeat (roped) of *Hubble* in 1994, he opened three f8c problems: *Walk away assis*, *Il Pirata* and *Shadowplay*, a route where some climbers are still unable to detect the holds.

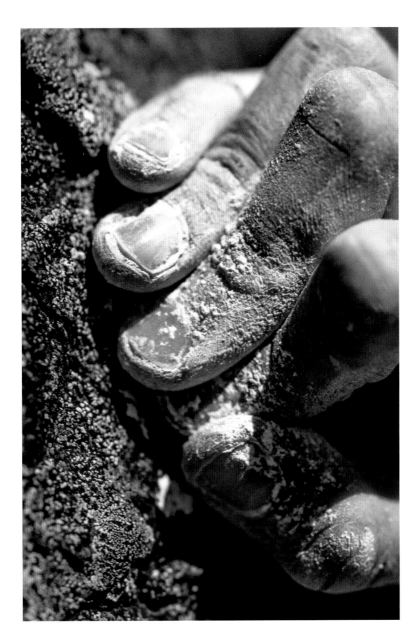

Another typically English story concerns *Violent new breed* on the Yorkshire limestone crag at Giggleswick; two bolts, six metres and F9a+. Gaskins had wanted to do it much earlier but an essential hold was loose and he glued it back on. When he came back to try again he found that the hold had been chipped off and in its place were the words 'Tut, tut' written in chalk. Much later, in 2004, he overcame this problem without the hold.

In the United States a new generation of near 30-year olds took over from Sharma and Graham, who were still active in the field. This new wave of climbers completely revitalised bouldering, opening passages 'ever closer to the limits of human possibilities' (f8c+ or present-day V16). They also explored new areas, particularly in the Rocky Mountains, and more recently they have been travelling the world looking for new challenges.

A Bohemian outsider is Jason Kehl, who, in the tradition of John Redhead, is as much an artist as a climber. He sees climbing as an artistic outlet, a means of self-expression. His first ascents include the gigantic *Evilution* (V12 in Bishop) and he was the first to reach the bouldering grade of f9a with *The Fly* in Rumney, tackling its eight metres without a rope in 2003.

His fellow-countryman Kevin Jorgeson is also a fan of highballs. In 2009, he climbed *Ambrosia* in the Buttermilks: a V11 problem, followed by a good 5.13 according to American standards. It starts with a boulder and finishes 15 metres higher up as a free solo.

At the age of 28, Paul Robinson admits that his competition experience has helped him but, like Dave Graham, he has chosen to explore new natural rock in his long trips in South Africa, Switzerland, Australia and the Rocky Mountain National Park in Colorado: "As I'm really no longer a competitor, I think that the best way of maintaining my lifestyle as a professional climber is to push the limits in bouldering. Opening challenging routes, not always V15, but routes which will remembered such as *Midnight Lighting*, *The Mandala*, *Spectre* and *Karma* in the past. My main objective today is to find new sites and to discover gems which will be appreciated by generations to come."

All muscle, the squat Daniel Woods is quite the opposite of the skinny Robinson. But he goes on the same natural crags without deserting the competitions. In 2014, he conquered one of the very few routes carrying today's maximum grade of V16 or f8c+, *The Process* in Bishop. He climbed it in the depths of winter at night with plenty of lighting, taking advantage of the lower temperatures. He has also climbed on the steep slopes of Mount Kinabalu in Indonesia, roped up with Yuji Hirayama.

Then there is Jimmy Webb, from Tennessee, who is like a survivor from the 1970s with his woodcutter's beard but his achievements are definitely at the 21st century level such as in 2014 completing *The Understanding*, an f8c at Magic Wood, in one day, not to mention many F8b flashes.

Nalle Hukkataival is 29 years old and comes from Finland, an unlikely country for a climber. He made his debut on resin climbing walls where, with his hand-ball player's physique, he won the Arco Masters in his early years. After repeating many of the most challenging routes (he is one of the rare repeaters of *Gioia*), he is now a compulsive explorer with a special affection for the sandstone rocks of South Africa and Australia and for opening routes on high, bold boulders such as *Livin' Large* (Rocklands, V15).

THE ITALIAN CHRISTIAN CORE LEVITATING ON HIS OWN *GIOIA*, f8C+ OR V16, VARAZZE, ITALY.

THE PROLIFIC AMERICAN TRAVELLER PAUL ROBINSON ON *GOURMANDISE*, f8B, CUVIER-REMPART, FONTAINE-BLEAU.

Sometimes, this little world of climbers gets over-excited about grades and occasionally a perverse pleasure is taken in downgrading a new problem done by a colleague but the general atmosphere is one of healthy rivalry. Everyone climbs together and tackles problems together, filming each other and often travelling together.

As on the rock face, it is through new achievements that the progress made can be assessed and although there is not yet a 9th grade in bouldering, it will soon happen because after a period of inflation, grades seem to have stabilised. At the moment there are just a handful of f8c/V16 grades, the most famous of which is *Gioia* in Varazze. Interestingly, the only climber to have conquered two V16s is the same one who has also achieved the roped 9th grade, Adam Ondra.

Originally an exclusively male activity, with its convivial atmosphere, bouldering now attracts women climbers, starting with the ascent of *The Mandala* by American Lisa Rands in 2008. Today all the most famous boulders are within reach of the best and youngest fingers, such as those of 14-year old Ashima Shiraishi and her fellow American Alex Puccio who in 2014 linked several f8b and f8b+ problems. Because of its atmosphere of sharing and simplicity, bouldering combines the fundamental values of free climbing advocated in the 19th century with those of the future: the quest for the perfect movement.

A CONNECTED NETWORK

Whilst traditional specialist magazines continue to survive (*Climbing* and *Rock and Ice* in the US, *Klettern* in Germany, *Desnivel* and *Escalar* in Spain, *Up* in Italy and *Grimper* in France, to mention but a few), today, climbing throughout the world is linked together by the social networks. The best-known example is the website 8a.nu which acts as the Facebook of climbing. It was created in 1999 by the Swede Jens Larssen who was then coaching young Swedish climbers. His objective was to list and publicise their achievements. With the emergence of new means of communication such as mobile phones, smart phones and tablets, the site has become the crossroads of news and videos of the climbing world. Journalists are not involved because everyone is free to write what they want and to announce their achievements. Today 8a.nu is a sharing platform for young climbers, disparaged but essential. It gathers together details of routes and achievements, displaying and categorising them. In a way, it turns its users into consumers but, at the same time, it is an invaluable monitoring platform. Through it, the exponential growth of the discipline in all its forms, as a sport, as media events, as a tourist attraction and as a social force, can be followed. New trends are revealed through commentaries which 'demythologise' the values of the past while at the same revealing a fascination for that 'golden age', thus contributing to its revival.

Hence the brilliant but slightly perverse idea of the scorecard, attributing points for each performance and placing climbers in a classification enabling them to dream of exploits to improve their position. Admittedly, since the appearance of Pierre Allain's book *Alpinisme et compétition* in 1949, it has been apparent that any rock face can become an arena where performances are assessed, thus leading to classifications. But is the climber with the most points necessarily the best climber in the world? Many competitors, such as Adam Ondra, Ramon Julian, Sasha DiGiulian, Alex Puccio and Daniel Woods, play the game, but others, such as Chris Sharma, Alex Megos and Paul Robinson, do not. As Paul Robinson remarked: "Nowadays, information is immediate. Within 24 hours, it is already old news, regardless of its importance. Personally I do not climb only for grades but mainly to improve my climbing, to make it more universal."

The classifications in 8a.nu are somewhat bizarre, since stars rub shoulders with unknowns (according to the website, 50,000 are registered) whose performances cannot be verified.

Inevitably there are liars or jokers in such a forum. Philippe Moser announced an f8c boulder in Provence which in the end turned out to be a f7b, and Jeremy Thoman's fanciful scorecard is always available to look at. As the philosopher Günther Anders long ago observed, 'lying becomes superfluous in a world where a lie has become a truth'.

Today inventing a 'virtual' climb has become a popular pastime, known as 'trolling' because its followers create fictional characters as elusive as trolls. At the start of the 21st century, for instance, a certain Sven Lavransen appeared on one of the first American social networks. Supposedly he had recently arrived in the US from Norway and he soon modestly announced that he had flashed all the classic challenges in Colorado with disconcerting ease, but he remained desperately untraceable. Initially suspecting each other, local experts who were also trollers in their spare time made enquiries in Norwegian climbing circles and it turned out that no Sven Lavransen had ever climbed anything. Having failed to discover his actual identity, they realised they in turn had been well and truly trolled.

More generally, when specialist media or well-known climbers cast serious doubt on the achievements of other top climbers, who are often followed by the media, one enters troubled waters. For instance the Englishman Richard Simpson who conquered *Action Directe* also claimed to be a boxer who had never lost a match, to have run a marathon in under two hours 30 minutes, and a mile in under four minutes, but all without any proof.

Who or what should be condemned, the mendacious rumour, or the person who claims too many things they are unable to prove? Charlotte Durif, the second woman to climb a F9a (with *PPP* in the Verdon in 2011) has recently been challenged by third party media over several of her major achievements, including what would officially be the first female on-sight F8c, *Les rois du pétrole* on the Pic Saint Loup in 2010. Does her success in competition prove her credibility and so clear her name? This could be an effective way of assessing the true level of each climber but there are too many examples to the contrary. Wolfgang Güllich, for example, was an outstanding all-rounder, but he was less impressive at on-sight climbing or in climbing wall competitions.

The German Markus Bock, 'master' of the Frankenjura with his numerous firsts, has strongly denounced those who cannot prove their achievements. As a professional athlete, the Swiss Cédric Lachat observed that 'today no one can take part in the race for the best performance without supporting evidence'. Others like Jacky Godoffe prefer to believe that 'When you invest yourself in an extreme project, it is because you love climbing. I do not believe that you could tackle tough boulders if you were telling lies'. Nonetheless, the need for supporting evidence (such as unedited videos and reliable witnesses) for an important achievement has become imperative.

While leisure climbing is what most climbers are seeking, for others it is a way of pushing back their limits. And nothing has changed since the 1930s or earlier and competition does not only exist in official championships organised by the federations. Competition is also there on the boulders and cliffs all over the world for those enthusiasts who, whatever their level, try not only to improve their performance but also to position themselves in relation to others and even possibly to attract the attention of the largest number of people.

MEANWHILE, ON THE CLIFFS...

In September 2008, Chris Sharma travelled to the very heart of the Mojave Desert in California, not far from the border with Nevada. His destination was an enormous limestone cave in Clark Mountain, hard to get to at an altitude of over 2,000 metres. There, Randy Leavitt had bolted a futuristic route almost 80 metres long with an exposed overhang. After over 100 attempts, spread over several periods because of the logistical (and psychological) problems which are inevitable with such an isolated project, *Jumbo Love* was freed by the blond Californian. He proposed a 5.15b, the equivalent of a European F9b. This grade had been applied earlier to *Akira* and *Chilam Balam*, and in 2007 Dani Andrada gave the same grade to his long boulder problem *Ali Hulk Sit Start Extension* in Rodellar. The conquest of this extraordinary route *Jumbo Love*, which is so difficult that it has not been repeated, truly confirmed Sharma's top-level status. Two months later, back in Spain, he confirmed his position by climbing *Golpe de Estado* in Siurana.

In 2011, as Sharma turned 30, a newcomer appeared on the climbing scene: Adam Ondra. After an impeccably progressive climbing career in his own country, the Czech Republic, he now felt ready to explore new territories.

A performer but also an explorer, it was in one of the new top-level Meccas, the enormous Flatanger cave on the Norwegian coast, that he found the long overhang he was searching for. This granite overhang consisted of challenging bouldering moves alternating with long dynos and it had the advantage of being pleasantly cool in the summer months. He completed the project in October 2012, and proposed an evocative name for it, *Change*, perfectly suited to the F9b+ he had given it.

It also reflected an evolution, geologically speaking, because for the first time in many years, the most extreme route opened was on granite, not limestone.

Admittedly, at the time granite with its fractal geometry seemed less suitable for the new trends in sport climbing than limestone overhangs with a wider range of holds but, this trend has been completely reversed in recent years. In addition to the awesome challenges of Flatanger, Tommy Caldwell's first free ascent of *Dawn Wall* on El Capitan caused a sensation and, from the United States to Europe, recently the most challenging boulders have been granite.

The following winter, Ondra joined Sharma in Spain for an open project planned by Sharma on the new rock face of Oliana, less steep but more treacherous. There too, the name chosen by Chris Sharma, *La dura dura*, clearly reflects the level of technical difficulty (F9b+ again) but also the commitment involved in progressing from 'that'll do' to a cry of triumph. It was a magnificent example of sportsmanship as the still young Sharma watched the even younger Czech prodigy precede him, on his own project at that. He may have been disappointed to have missed the first ascent

IN MARCH 2013, CHRIS SHARMA CLAIMING THE SECOND ASCENT OF HIS OWN PROJECT *LA DURA DURA*, F9B+, OLIANA, SPAIN.

MOMENTS OF COMPLICITY BETWEEN CHRIS SHARMA AND ADAM ONDRA AT THE FOOT OF *LA DURA DURA*, A SHARED SUCCESS.

but, positive as always, he saw it as a motivation to surpass himself. Having come so close to the goal, Sharma persevered and in the following month he too succeeded: "I thought about my own evolution on routes like *Biographie* where I was lucky that someone who did not feel up to climbing it had had the foresight to bolt it, giving me the opportunity years later to progress as a climber. With *La dura dura*, I thought I could do the same; bolt it and leave it open for some top-level climber to climb it. And this is what happened. I did not think I could do it but seeing Adam has been a thrilling experience and motivated me again. I started thinking that, although it seemed inhuman, I still had a chance to succeed. And that too has happened!' The symbol of more than a century of evolution, this new 'hardest route' is situated on a 'little' ridge 40 metres below much larger, less steep rock faces which a few decades ago would have been the first to attract the climbers' attention.

In December 2013, not far from his home in the Czech Republic, Ondra completed a project five years long which he had bolted, *Vasil, Vasil*. Admittedly it was not the most aesthetic route but, the succession of bouldering-like moves enabled him to announce a F9b+ for the third time.

In March 2015 Sharma the King of Kings made a spectacular return to the limelight, thus proving that his motivation and level are still intact. Not far from Barcelona, at Cova de Ocell, he opened the hardest granite route in the world, *El Bon Combat*, announcing a F9b+ grade. It is an uncharacteristic succession of boulder problems on a type of rock which promises thrills while encouraging creative moves, in other words a new *King Line*. "With this new project, I realised that I no longer felt any pressure, that I had nothing to prove any more and that what I really enjoyed was to attempt hard routes of exceptional quality, to climb just for myself. In a way, it is a like a return to basics. As for the future, I want to continue climbing hard and go on enjoying it."

ADAM ONDRA
THE BEST OF THREE WORLDS

—

What can one still wish for at the age of 22 when one has already reached all the peaks in one's field? That is Adam Ondra's situation.

He is the only man to have climbed well over 100 9th grade routes, followed by Ramón Julián who has only climbed half that number and that is without taking into account all the 9th grades he has downgraded. At the same time, he is also the climber who has concentrated most on exploring new levels of difficulty. Until recently, Chris Sharma has accompanied him in the quest for F9b and then F9b+, but now it seems that the future is more in the hands of the young Czech, whose motivation and thirst for constant progress never seems to run dry.

Until recently, his only weak point had been in that other world of competitions where, in spite of excellent results and supreme versatility in bouldering, he had failed to win the biggest titles to which he could legitimately aspire but in the late summer of 2014, in less than three weeks, he became the first climber to secure the perfect double: the bouldering World Championship and the lead climbing World Championship. To achieve this he had trained specifically for four months at indoor climbing centres, 30 hours a week, six days out of seven: "I must say that I really enjoyed it; the sacrifice, the pain. In the end, you must just climb a LOT. Isn't that great? Compared to working on an outdoor project, you simply carry out many more moves on a daily basis and it really pays off."

Adam Ondra was one of the many child prodigies one finds in the world today. Encouraged by his parents, themselves enthusiastic climbers, he touched his first holds at the age of six. Two years later he was already doing F7b+ on-sight and, in the following year, he achieved his first F8a after several attempts and so it continued. By 11, he was already tackling F8c routes and the media were becoming seriously interested in him, all the more so because he was equally strong in all styles. In 2006, at the age of 12, on holiday on the Côte d'Azur, he conquered *Alien Carnage*, an F8c+, in Castillon, with the

greatest of ease, watched by some bemused locals. At the time he was already doing some F8b on-sights. Soon afterwards he conquered his first F9a, *Martin Krpan* in Misca Pec in Slovenia, which made him the youngest 9th grade climber in history (13 years nine months). Eight years later, he celebrated his hundredth 9th grade in Poland.

Ondra went on to win the junior world titles in 2007 and 2008. The following year he competed in the senior championships, winning the World Cup in lead climbing and taking second place in the World Championships behind Patxi Usobiaga, then at the height of his career. In 2010, he won the bouldering World Cup, becoming the first climber to win the titles in both the main disciplines. This was followed by his double in 2014.

Meanwhile, until he had his driving licence, his father would drive him several hundred kilometres each weekend to the German Frankenjura, the nearest site with the densest network of sport climbs. Very sensibly, Ondra did not concentrate exclusively on competition climbing. While his rivals competed for podium positions living between training walls and isolation rooms, he travelled the world in search of legendary boulders and cliffs.

While still studying, Ondra managed to reach the top in all the sport climbing disciplines: cliffs, on-sight, long routes and boulder. There is a film of him climbing *La Rambla intégrale*, watched by Andrada, who is at first incredulous and then irritated because in numerous attempts he had never managed to conquer it. Spain soon became Ondra's second home where the country's enormous network of extreme routes led to his numerous exploits between 2010 and 2014, gradually leading to the conquest of the 'true' F9a on-sight (three to date) and the first three F9b+ grades in history.

In 2013, to take one example among many, he enchained three F9a routes in the Frankenjura in one day. He has also

conquered most F9b routes in the world, whether his own creations such as *Move* at Flatanger in Norway and one of his new favourite destinations, or those opened by others such as *First Round*, *First Minute*, *Fight or Flight* and *Golpe de Estado* opened by his friend Chris Sharma.

As regards natural boulders, doing better than the experts in the field, he is the only climber to have twice achieved V16 (or f8c+) with the first repeat of *Gioia* and the opening of the traverse *Terranova* in 2011 near Brno in the Czech Republic, as well as flashing a V14 (f8b+) in Fontainebleau (*Gecko assis*).

As far as long routes are concerned, Ondra has already astonished the world of climbing in 2008 with his ascent on-sight, the first, of *Hotel Supramonte* in Sardinia and *WoGü* in the Rätikon. This was followed in 2010 by a trip to Madagascar with the bemusing first free ascents of *Tough Enough* and *Mora Mora*. The extreme solo, in the style of Alex Honnold, is perhaps the only discipline he has not tackled but it does not attract many young climbers today except in the more entertaining, less dangerous form of Deep Water Soloing.

In other words, Adam Ondra has achieved more at his young age than 99% of other top level climbers achieve in their entire life. But these head-spinning statistics do little to help understand the climber as a person.

Ondra is also a man of style which, compared to that of his young contemporaries, could be defined as 'classic'; technique, footwork and incredible body moves, associated with amazing speed when he needs to accelerate. Tall, he benefits from an exceptional weight-height ratio, over minus 20 (that is the number of centimetres above the metre minus the number of kilos). Watching him climb, one sometimes has the impression that the film has been speeded up. His slim, long-limbed appearance with his incredibly long neck is out of tune with the current trend of body-building – although recently he has filled out a little.

During the summer of 2014, then coached by Patxi Usobiaga in the Basque Country, the video recording of his exploits shows him climbing a 9th grade on-sight with perfect command. His moves on *Il Domani* in the famous Baltzola

cave where Josune B often distinguished herself, seem to flow with incredible ease and it becomes obvious that he is the best because he climbs better. In other words, he is better than anyone else at making the most of his physical and psychological strengths, while also anticipating, always being a step ahead.

In contrast with the past, when overgradings were made, Ondra is very cautious and reserved on the subject of this evolution: 'Everything depends on the gap you want between grades. But for my part, it would prefer it to be sizeable. Because the more you approach the limits, the more the difficulty becomes specific and therefore less objective'. He has also thought a lot about the tactics to adopt in relation to the effort required: 'It is always controlling one's effectiveness which makes an ascent on-sight much harder. You must climb more slowly because it is difficult to know whether you can lunge or not and what the next hold will look like. I take numerous very brief breaks to reflect on the next step. They are only few tenths of a second each time but multiplied by 20, it takes a lot of energy. The only way to climb a F9a on-sight is to increase your redpoint level so as to completely master this difficulty. Some people use up a lot of energy climbing on-sight, but I think you can reduce the gap between on-sight and redpointing to a minimum'. Thanks to all this, he has become a kind of master-standard of grades, in particular for the 'monuments' of the past decades.

Cliffs, boulders, competitions, he is the perfect convergence point of these three worlds which are sometimes opposed to each other. The past, the present and the future. If one was to sum up Ondra in one sentence, it might be as follows: 'A complete athlete who is still writing history while always respecting his mantra: 'Honesty above all''.

PAGE 277: ADAM ONDRA. PAGE 278: F9B+, THE NEXT LIMIT, LA DURA DURA FIRST ASCENT, OLIANA, FEBRUARY 2013. PAGE 279: ONE F8C ON-SIGHTED AMONGST SO MANY OTHERS FOR ADAM: *EL CALVARIO DEL SICARIO* IN CUENCA, SPAIN.

If Adam Ondra could be described as squaring the circle of modern climbing, the list of 'strong' female and male climbers has become so long and international that it approaches the size of a telephone directory. Vincent Albrand, one of the keenest observers in recent years, summed up the change: "If you had to queue on an 8th grade route 20 years ago, it was really bad luck, but nowadays it has become quite common in some fashionable sites. Like the offside rule in football, climbing grades will always be the subject of debate and probably also part its charm. It must be said that grades are much more blurred and easier to change than results in athletics. For instance, pole vaulters cannot measure their performance themselves and even less can they decide how long a metre is."

The French scene today is extremely active. It includes former competition climbers who have reconverted to rock-climbing, such as Daniel Du Lac (winner of the bouldering World Cup in 2004), Mike Fuselier and Caroline Ciavaldini, (several times Junior World Champion and since then placed in many competitions), veteran trad climbers such as Yann 'Diego' Ghesquiers, still at the top after over 25 years, and all the young climbers who have grown up on training and competition and who are now taking a liking to 'real' rock.

Gérôme Pouvreau made a sensational debut, becoming a surprise World Champion in 2001 at the age of 17. Was this too quick, too soon? In any case, he soon decided to focus on the crags all over the world, from India to the United States, in search of the most beautiful 'cruxes', always accompanied by Florence Pinet. In the south of France, he specialised in secu-

GÉRÔME POUVREAU ON *DIRECTE DES SPÉCIALISTES*, F8C, VERDON.

–

PAGE 281:

FLORENCE PINET GRABS PERFECT TUFAS ON *WEDDING PRESENT*, F8A+, CIDTIBI, TURKEY.

ring first ascents of difficult projects which had hitherto defeated the attempts of the best climbers: *Aubade directe* on Montagne Sainte Victoire, *La Madone* in Lourmarin, both F9a+, as well as *Sachidananda*, the legendary project in Orgon, and *Moksha* on Pic Saint-Loup. He is still among the most active French climbers at the top difficulty level with his friends Enzo Oddo and Seb Bouin, all of whom have bravely chosen this narrow and difficult path, with the need to attract sponsors so as make a living doing it.

In 2011 when Enzo Oddo dropped out of school aged only 15, he had already repeated F9a+ standards such as *Biographie* and *Aubade*. Reflecting on his future, he explained: "I don't really know where I'm going, but if any job in the future was to depend on my results at school, I would be rejected in advance, not to say dead." Berhault, Edlinger and Sharma were all drop-outs too, and they have done pretty well…

Less well-known, Seb Bouin did not drop out of school but at the same time he was already collecting F9s, so that today he has the most of any French climber

(over 20, slightly ahead of Enzo Oddo). In spring 2015, exactly 20 years after the attempt on *Akira* by Fred Rouhling, he even joined the F9b royalty thanks to *Chilam Balam*, the Andalusian pearl already mentioned, thus confirming his remarkable potential.

Alizée Dufraisse, a former pole vaulting champion who spends her winters in Catalonia, is one of the rare women to have reached the 9th grade (*La Reina Mora* in Siurana in 2012). Since then she has focused on emblematic projects, including routes hitherto the preserve of male climbers such as *La Rambla Extension* and *Biographie* but beyond the grades themselves, she is truly determined to become the first woman to conquer them, bringing down the psychological barriers between the sexes.

In the same spirit, in 2012, the New Zealand female climber Mayan Smith-Gobat repeated the legendary *Punks in the Gym* in the Arapiles in Australia, 'only' an F8b+ but much more 'traditional' than the Catalan overhangs. The same was true of the American Paige Claassen in 2014 with *Just do it* at Smith Rocks. As for her compatriot, Beth Rodden, following in Lynn Hill's footsteps, in 2008 she signed the toughest American pitch in 'trad' style with *Meltdown* (5.14c or F8c+) in Yosemite. A dark overhanging crack which she climbed in style, she delicately inserted nuts which she were stuck to her harness with tape so that she could reach them more easily.

ABOVE LEFT: THE AMERICAN JONATHAN SIEGRIST CRUISING *LUCY WIDE*, F7C+, VORALPSEE, SWITZERLAND.
ABOVE RIGHT: THE GERMAN JULIUS WESTPHAL CLAIMING THE FIRST ALSACIAN F9A IN 2007 WITH *ALOHA* ON KRONTHAL.
BELOW: THE YOUNG FRENCHMAN SEB BOUIN ALWAYS TRIES TO POCKET AS MANY AS POSSIBLE GRADE 9, HERE PICTURED ON *PPP*, F9A, GALETAS CAVE, VERDON.

Jonathan Siegrist and Sasha DiGiulian in the United States, Julius Westphal, Daniel Jung and Felix Neumärker in Germany, Cédric Lachat and Nina Caprez in Switzerland, Magnus Mitboe in Norway, Pablo Barbero in Spain, Jorg Verhoeven in the Netherlands, Klemen Becan and Domen Skofic in Slovenia, Jenny Lavarda, Fabio

THE YOUNG GERMAN PRODIGY ALEX MEGOS.

Crespi, Stefano Ghisolfi and Gabriele Moroni in Italy, together with many others, are all representatives of this international revival, regularly climbing the 9th grade.

One of those new young talents, the German Alexander Megos, has already left his mark on the record books.

When on 24 March 2013, at the age of 19, he successfully on-sighted *Estado Critico* (F9a) in Siurana, it was the first time that a 9th grade route had been climbed this way. It was no coincidence because in the same week he climbed the neighbouring *La Rambla intégrale* after two attempts, only just missing it in the flash version.

Adam Ondra had previously twice been credited with such a performance. But like Yuji Hirayama in the past, he believed that *Golden Ticket* and *Pure imagination*, both in Red River Gorge, did not deserve so high a grade.

Alexander Megos discovered climbing at the age of six and he made his debut in competition with the help of qualified coaches. After winning the German Championship and becoming European runner-up, his interests changed from competition to rock-climbing. Perpetuating the traditions of the great travelling cliff climbers, he now travels the world climbing interesting sites, famous or not. His progress between 2010 and 2014 was as dazzling as the speed with which he completed his projects. For instance, in one trip to Australia he conquered both the first F9a on that continent (*R.E.D.*, for *Retired Extremely Dangerous*, an old project bolted by Garth Miller in Blue Mountains) and a new extreme boulder (*Wheelchair*, 36 or f9a+).

His almost classic physique, his youthful looks, his calm, down-to-earth ambition and his potential whose limit is still unknown, put him in the same category as Adam Ondra. According to those close to him, half his training consists in a holistic approach with exercises unconnected with climbing: "The most important thing is to enjoy climbing. It is not worth training hard to win competitions or to conquer hard routes if it spoils your pleasure in climbing. And if in the meantime you turn to some other sport, sooner or later you will come back to climbing because it is the best sport in world."

TOMMY CALDWELL AND DAWN WALL
MAKING HISTORY

—

It was in Yosemite that Tommy Cadwell conceived the most ambitious project of recent years with *Dawn Wall*; the whitest and smoothest part of the monolith, explored 40 years earlier by Warren Harding, during his *Wall of Early Morning Light* mentioned earlier. Probably no one has ever worked so long on a big wall. Every autumn since 2008, he has gone and set up camp with his portaledge, defying snow storms, wet conditions, and injuries and attracted top level climbers such as Jonathan Siegrist, Kevin Jorgeson and Chris Sharma.

Tommy Caldwell is undoubtedly one of the most important climbers of the last 15 years. In his youth, he was one the first climbers to introduce the French 9th grade to the United States with *Kryptonite* and then *Flex Luthor*. In spite of missing an index finger, lost when closing a camping table, he took up mountaineering in Patagonia but it was really in Yosemite that he revealed his true potential. There he made a rare free ascent of *The Nose*, followed by a succession of enchainments such as freeing *The Nose* and *Freerider* in less than 24 hours.

The *Dawn Wall* project was even more ambitious. Taking in the *Mescalito* aid-climb*, Dawn Wall* has no fewer than 32 pitches several hundred metres above the ground, almost half of them 8th and 9th grades. Also, there are three consecutive 5.14d (F9a), a long traverse with non-existent footholds and an enormous lateral lunge to top it all. There is a fascinating video showing how Tommy Caldwell screwed a few holds on the wall of his chalet aiming to replicate this famous movement of the *Dyno Pitch*. That is the beauty of modern climbing: training in your sitting room to defy the largest monolith in the world.

Between the autumns 2013 and 2014, Tommy succeeded in freeing the hardest pitches, one after the other, on the way to conquering Yosemite's first F9a grades. Now that he had ascended each pitch separately, the project of the 'hardest route in the world' remains open. As Adam Ondra admitted when climbing *Tough Enough*: "It will always be more difficult to link several F9a pitches consecutively than doing a F9c close to the ground."

On 27 December 2014, accompanied by Kevin Jorgeson, who initially specialised more in bouldering, he set off to connect all the pitches in a single ascent, the Push. That day the dry cold atmosphere had created the perfect conditions for optimum adhesion. It was freezing but the climbers were comfortable with three double portaledges. The main problem was keeping the skin of their fingers in good conditions and avoiding ice falling on their suspended camp site.

While Jorgeson was struggling to keep his fingers in good condition, Tommy regularly eliminated difficulties, finally opting for an easier version (even so an F8b+) of *Dyno Pitch*. Soon afterward Jorgeson conquered this in its hardest, F9a version. Finally on the 19th day, 14 January 2015, they made history when the roped party reached the summit of El Capitan. For Tommy this was the successful conclusion of the project of a lifetime and a long love affair with Yosemite: "I love dreaming big and finding new routes to explore. I cannot count the number of times that I thought of abandoning this crazy project which consumed my life but something always brought me back to it because it was such an inspiring project. The real reward is the process, what it teaches you and the kind of person it helps you to become. Everyone loves the idea of pushing oneself to the limit and flirting with what we think is impossible. In this world of ours so full of restrictions, some people feel the need to break the mould and rediscover this inner spark capable of rekindling our imagination."

As well as being one of the most significant performances in recent years, *Dawn Wall* has also become one of the routes most covered by the media. Thanks to Facebook and Twitter, its authors can be watched commenting live on each new development, constantly in the limelight.
It was the first time that it had been possible to follow so much live, and even major daily newspapers such as the *New York Times* reported on this major ascent which also attracted the congratulations of President Obama.
As Kevin Jorgeson said on reaching the summit: "I hope that this will inspire people to find their own *Dawn Wall*. I believe that everyone will conquer their own one day."

There is no doubt that this long-haul success is far from being the end of the story of the Yosemite Valley. Perhaps even one day someone will set foot on the summit of El Capitan, after climbing *Dawn Wall* on-sight without ever falling.

PAGE 284: TOMMY CALDWELL. PAGE 285: *THE DAWN WALL* TOPO BY KEVIN JORGESON. PAGES 286-287: ON THE 19TH PITCH (5.13D), TOMMY CALDWELL BEGINS TO LEAVE THE MAJOR DIFFICULTIES BEHIND ON DAWN WALL, YOSEMITE.

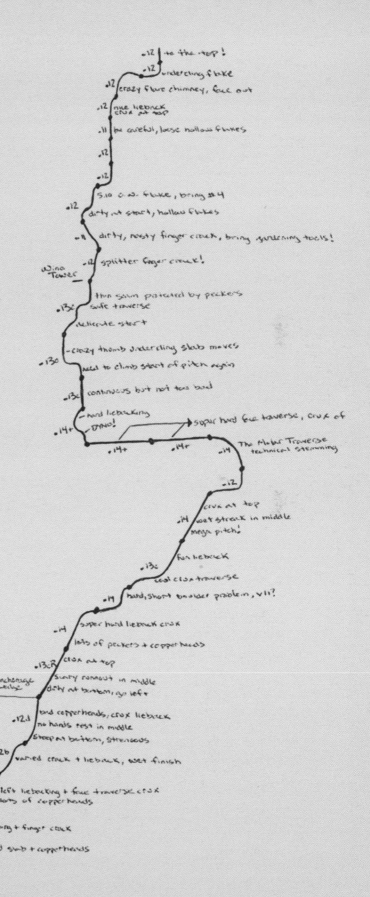

IT'S ALWAYS BETTER AS A COUPLE

Appealing to the media and providing performance, climbing couples are commoner than they were. In the past there were Robyn Erbesfield and Didier Raboutou, then Stéphanie Bodet and Arnaud Petit, Beth Rodden and Tommy Caldwell, Daila Ojeda and Chris Sharma, Anna Stöhr and Kilian Fischhuber. These have been followed by Caroline Ciavaldini and James Pearson, Nina Caprez and Cédric Lachat, Florence Pinet and Gérôme Pouvreau, to name but a few of the better known. Love combined with performance in exotic locations often produces beautiful, dream-like images, a glamorous cocktail which is bound to please both sponsors and the public.

The list of countries where it is exciting to climb is now much wider than the traditional European and American destinations: Mexico, Venezuela, Cuba, Brazil, Argentina, Mali, Morocco, Madagascar, Sicily, Turkey, Jordan, Oman, Reunion, India, Vietnam, Malaysia, Australia and Japan all have much to offer. This is to say nothing of China, whose economic development and increasingly open approach to tourism is bound to reveal vast unexplored regions with exciting challenges.

PAGE 288:

ABOVE LEFT: CHRIS SHARMA IN SPAIN IN 2007 WITH DAILA OJEDA AND MIGUEL RIERA.

BELOW LEFT: STÉPHANIE BODET AND ARNAUD PETIT.

RIGHT: ROBYN ERBESFIELD AND DIDIER RABOUTOU.

—

PAGE 289:

ABOVE: ARNAUD PETIT ON *SNAKE ON A TRAIN*, 32 OR F8B+ ON THE FAMOUS TAIPAN WALL, GRAMPIANS, AUSTRALIA.

BELOW: STÉPHANIE BODET ON THE 4TH PITCH OF LOST IN TRANSLATION, F8A, GETU, CHINA.

KALYMNOS, SUN, SEA AND ROCK

Kalymnos perfectly symbolises the new trend in vertical tourism to new exotic destinations. This fashion was started in Thailand at the beautiful location of Krabi some 20 years ago and it is recognised that the presence of climbers is often economically beneficial, especially in the seasons when 'traditional' tourism is less prevalent.

This Greek island in the Dodecanese archipelago has long been the capital of sponge fishing, ignored by mass tourism. But there were some Greek climbers, impressed by the potential of the limestone rock on the west coast, and they were followed by Italian climbers, including Andrea Di Bari and Andrea Gallo who in 1996 and 1997 started bolting the first routes.

The island soon became extremely popular as a result of articles which appeared in specialist magazines and the annual Climbing Festival which invited top level climbers which could also be followed on the Web. As was the case with Buoux some 20 years ago, a few spectacular images have encouraged people to travel thousands of miles to climb there. Its popularity is also the result of the excellent standard of route equipment provided by the authorities, offering a wide range of difficulties and cliffs. Aris Theodoropoulos, in particular, has worked very hard to promote climbing on the island, creating equipment plans, a multi-lingual website and a guidebook whose first edition was offered free to visitors to encourage them to come back and, though longer free, it now helps finance the development of new sectors and the renewal of holds damaged by sea erosion. Kalymnos is well-known for the comfort and quality of its equipment. People go there to indulge themselves.

ABOVE: THE VERY CONVENIENT KALYMNOS SCOOTERS.
BELOW: SOPHIE ADMIRING THE MAJESTUOUS KALYMNOS PANORAMA WITH TELENDOS ISLAND ON THE RIGHT.

At the start of the new millennium, thousands of European climbers were attracted by the 'sun, sea, and rock' lifestyle, hotels with panoramic views at affordable prices, night life, easy transport by motor scooter, swimming in the Aegean Sea, and numerous easily accessible, well-bolted cliffs, in particular around the village of Masouri. The exceptional quality of the rock has played a major part in this it being a pure, compact limestone whose colour ranges from grey to red with a lot of calcite. Kalymnos became legendary for the profusion and size of the stalactites and stalagmites in its caves (Grande Grotta and Sikati Cave).

Climbing in the area has expanded into the neighbouring island of Telendos. Though relatively isolated, having been separated from Kalymnos

THE HUGE TUFAS OF THE *GRANDE GROTTA* SOMETIMES OFFER SOME UNEXPECTED RESTS.

by an earthquake in the 6th century, it has some challenging rock faces as well as several long routes.

Today there are about 70 cliffs and 2,000 pitches from the easiest level to the 9th grade, the first one conquered by Adam Ondra (*Los Revolucionarios*, 2007).
In this increasingly globalised world, there is no doubt that new places like Kalymnos will be discovered and thrive on all the continents. These new exotic sites will benefit economically from the visits of climbing tourists.

THE CRAFTSMEN OF THE FUTURE

People who place bolt anchors play a fundamental part in rock-climbing, either within an official system with set safety standards or independently, establishing routes in new climbing areas.

There will always be some climbers who at their own expense bolt their own 'secret spots' which seldom remain secret for very long. So thanks are due to Laurent Triay, Antonin Rhodes, Pascal Faudou and those other anonymous bolters who have given their time and money to create new climbs which will delight future generations. As for Bruno Clément, nicknamed 'Graou', he is a solitary devotee of climbing who has made the Verdon his temple. He admits that he only bolts for himself and not for posterity. He is well-known but not a star, far away from the hustle and bustle of towns, of fashionable cliffs and even more importantly competitions he embodies another, almost retrograde, vision, closer to nature and far removed from the world at large: "In general all the futilities of modern times do not interest me and they pass me by."

He is a free addict. He sees aid climbing as 'designed for frustrated climbers who were never able to do what they wanted in climbing'. Among the hundreds of unregulated routes he has made and graciously bequeathed to the community, some such as *Tom et je ris* have become a compulsory rite of passage in the Verdon for top climbers and one of the most photographed climbs in the world.

THE FRENCHMAN BRUNO CLÉMENT AKA GRAOU ON *L'ALAMBIC SPATIO-TEMPOREL*, 60 METERS OF VERY BOLD F8C, LA CASTAPIAGNE, VERDON GORGE, FRANCE.

—

PAGE 293:

GRAOU IN TEILLON ON *ARQUESTRE PHILARMONIQUE*, F8B.

GRADUAL SHIFTS IN ETHICS

In 2015, do ethics still exist as a concept in climbing? The answer is probably yes, if the word is used in the plural. A single absolute rule does not exist. Nowadays the world of climbing is no longer dominated by intransigent censors who see the rules of the game as a mystical quest defined and interpreted by themselves. No one ethic is necessarily better than another, but it is important for climbers to report honestly the way these routes are climbed. One could say, like Sonnie Trotter, that 'the perfect style is on-sight from the ground, barefoot, free solo and without chalk. Apart from that everything is subjective, so no one has the right to criticise what anyone may do or adopt a particular ethic as being the rule'. On the other hand, it is difficult to see free climbing as a sport if there are no rules for comparing performances. If everyone had their own requirements and laws, it would be difficult to impose them on others. Admittedly, there are still some last historical bastions such as the former East Germany and some regions in the United Kingdom which have maintained their individual rules and even inspired a certain revival in some countries, as illustrated by greenpointing and headpointing, mentioned earlier. But the norm since then has been the 'French' model, developed in the 1980s, based on pure sport difficulty on fixed points and the avoidance of physical risk. Today, 'leisure' climbing, as illustrated by Kalymnos, is what appeals to most climbers. But this does not necessarily mean that the essential appeal of climbing has been diminished by the safety and other standards which are normal today.

Some climbers now try to make the best of both worlds, such as the Italians Rolando Larcher and Piero Dal Pra who climb high rock faces, starting from the ground towards the unknown but carrying a drill just in case. Nevertheless, the integrity of the raw material, the rock, has become the centre of attention again. Chipping holds is no longer fashionable and it is even disapproved of, the rock now being seen as a legacy to be bequeathed undamaged to future generations in the same way as any other precious heritage.

The American Henry Barber, an innovative pioneer who travelled the world in search of climbing thrills, was certain that: "The best experiences in life are doing more with less. Deliberately limiting one's equipment and accessories, and relying on one's good sense will enable you to move faster and broaden your climbing experience. By being less versatile and using more equipment, you limit your sensations, and this is true in life as well as in climbing. Climbing in a 'lean' style should be a metaphor of life. What you learn in climbing can give the confidence you need to face the challenges of everyday life."

ROCK-CLIMBING HAS ALWAYS BEEN A RELIGION IN THE UK. ORIGINALLY IN MANCHESTER'S PLATT CHAPEL (AND NOW MOVED TO THE OUTWARD BOUND TRUST'S CENTRE IN ESKDALE), THIS WINDOW COMMEMORATES SIEGFRIED HERFORD, ALREADY MENTIONED IN PART 1.
—
PAGE 295:
PURE MAGIC BETWEEN THE AUDIENCE AND THE SPANISH PARACLIMBER URKO CARMONA DURING THE 2012 WORLD CHAMPIONSHIPS.

ABOUT THE ROCK AND MEN

Today the 10th grade is getting closer. Within a few years it may be within reach of the best climbers and there is no doubt that its story will be written one day. It is interesting to note that it only took about 10 years to advance from the 8th to the 9th grade, but since the first F9a, almost 25 years have elapsed and F9b+ has only just been confirmed. Looking back 30 years, climbing a 7th grade route was already the mark of a very good climber. Then 20 years ago, climbing 8th grades was no longer considered top level and today several thousand climbing enthusiasts are able to do so.

On the other hand, although every day new names are added to the list of climbers who have conquered the 'lower' 9th grade, those who can achieve F9b can be counted on the fingers of one hand (in 2014, for instance, only three F9b ascents were recorded), and in the case of F9b+, only two climbers can claim it. It is a classic pyramid, extremely tapered at the top.

Beyond the subjectivity of these figures, it is clear that this top-level sport is reaching maturity. Also, it is a fact that most members of the elite (many of whom train for competition) choose not to concentrate entirely on getting beyond a particular grade on cliffs or boulders because, tackling a single route at the limit at one's capability is more a vocation than a pleasure. But, of course, there are a few people like Adam Ondra who enjoy both worlds to the full.

It is important to put these grades into perspective. In this book we have usually used the French grading system which is an accepted standard, but for an American, 5.15a (F9a+) is a more legendary barrier than the French 9th grade and, objectively, there is no more difference between F9b and F9b+ than there was between F7b and F7b+ almost 40 years ago.

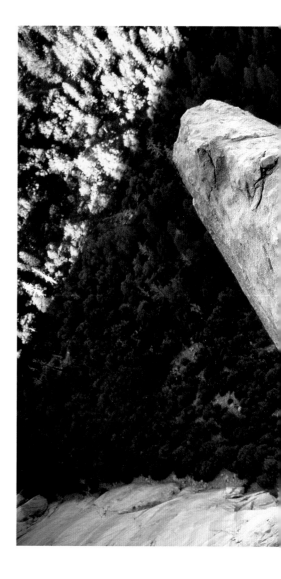

There is therefore no sense in limiting the history of climbing just to these excessively simplified classifications and tables. The first F8, the first F9? What was the style of climbing and which cliff was it? There are fierce debates which can arouse passions and inflate egos. It is surely better to focus on the moments when energies are concentrated on creating new perspectives, *The Crystal Horizon*, to quote the title of an important book by Reinhold Messner which has inspired so many climbers.

The idols of tomorrow will be found among the children of today, who are growing up with organised rock faces, climbing walls sold in kits, competitions with categories ranging from 'microbes' to 'veterans', and a top level of climbing which is increasingly standardised.

Will there be a new John Gill or Wolfgang Güllich among these future climbers? Those two men never followed anyone after their initiation phase. They ploughed their own furrows, ignoring the reactions of the climbing community and aiming to

achieve their own personal vision. It is not only their performances which inspire others but also the abstract quality created and transmitted by the climber. Conquering a F9b is nothing compared to the charisma that will give a child the desire to climb. Paradoxically, the often clumsy desire for systematic media coverage can often nip in the bud the inexpressible mystery necessary to achieve this aura.

Besides the performances which speak for themselves, it would appear that the need for charismatic examples requires a rationalisation which is at once authentic, coherent and innovative.

But, this not only true in the sport of climbing. How many brave athletes with impressive lists of achievements have fallen into oblivion, while some names, such as Ayrton Senna, Johann Cruyff, Roger Federer and Mohammed Ali, still inspire. In climbing there are many examples, such as the legendary names of Emilio Comici, Patrick Edlinger, Lynn Hill and Chris Sharma.

Is climbing a sport, a hobby, a passion, a lifestyle, an approach to something else? It can be all of these at the same time because of its universal values. To be greater than oneself just for a day, the time it takes to climb a route or boulder, such transcendence is like a promise of eternity.

HIGH ON EL CAPITAN, EYES ARE TURNED UPWARD

–

PAGES 298-299:

ALEX HONNOLD, LONELY SPOT LOST ON THE NW FACE OF HALF DOME, YOSEMITE.

When I asked my friend Marc Le Menestrel what a whole life dedicated to climbing meant for him, looking back over the last 30 years, he explained: "I am still often amazed at my passionate approach to climbing. I still sometimes shed tears of joy after climbing. Some time ago I feared that age, maturity and time might reduce my emotional awareness and passion but — no. I can share my energy, enthusiasm and passion, and I am thrilled to do so and I see it as an invitation to let go and live to the full the one life we have been given, our own."

ROCK AND MAN.
IN THE END IT IS ALWAYS
THE ROCK WHICH WILL HAVE
THE LAST WORD.

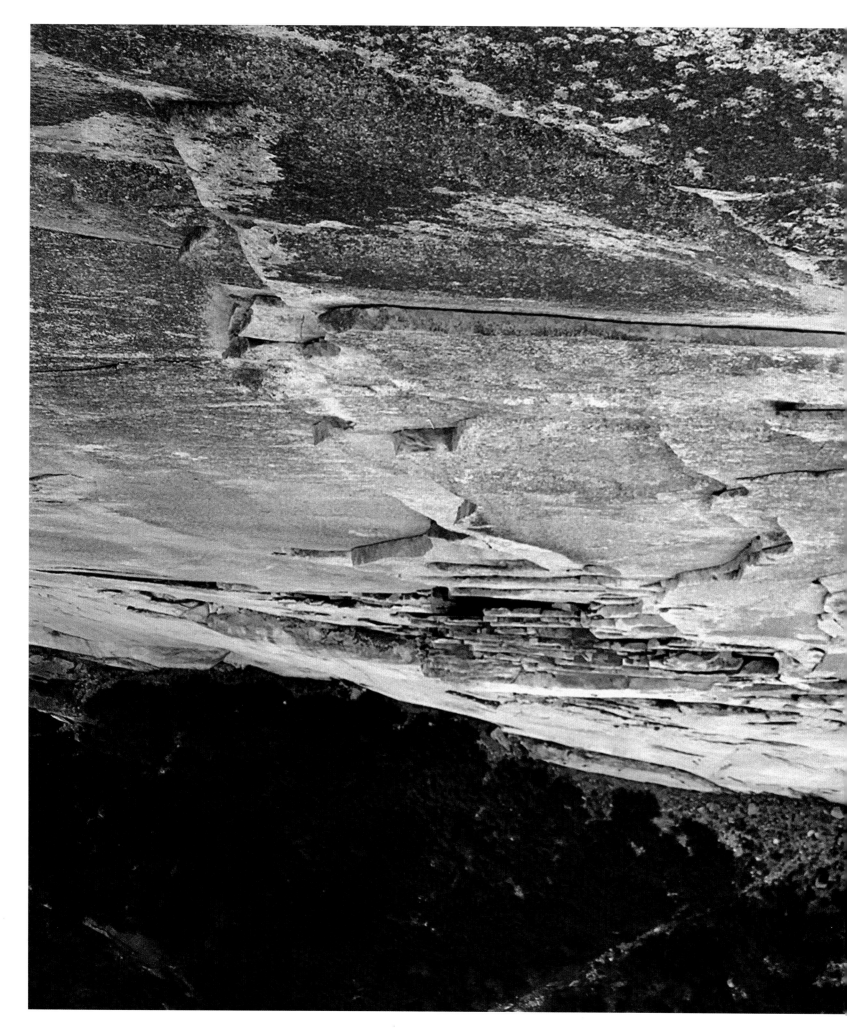

BIBLIOGRAPHY

A SMALL SELECTION OF INSPIRED AND INSPIRING WORKS

———

GEORGE D.ABRAHAM, The complete mountaineer, Methuen, 1923.

PAT AMENT, *John Gill, Master of rock*, Stackpole Books, 1998.

PAT AMENT, *Wizards of Rock: A History of Free Climbing in America*, Wilderness Press, Berkeley, 2002.

DAVID BELDEN, *Verdon sans frontières*, Denoël, 1983.

JOE BROWN, *The Hard Years, Phœnix,* 1967.

SEVERINO CASARA, *L'arte di arrampicare di Emilio Comici*, Hoepli, 1957.

SEVERINO CASARA, *Preuss, l'Alpinista leggendario,* Longanesi & C., 1970.

GLENN DENNY, Yose*mites in the sixties,* Patagonia Books, 2007.

ALAN HANKINSON, *The first tigers*, J.M Dent & Sons LTD, 1972.

PUBBLICAZIONI ISTREVI, *Gino Soldà e il suo tempo*, Cierre Edizioni, 2008

GEORGES LIVANOS, *Au-delà de la verticale*, Arthaud 1958

GEORGES LIVANOS, *Cassin, Il était une fois le sixième degré*, Arthaud, 1983.

MAZENOD, *Les alpinistes célèbres*, Mazenod, 1956.

REINHOLD MESSNER, *Le 7ème degré*, Arthaud, 1975, republished in 1987.

GEORGE MEYERS, *Yosemite climber*, Diadem Books, 1979.

JERRY MOFFATT, *Revelations*, Vertebrate Graphics, 2009.

Udo Neumann, Dale Goddard, *Performance Rock Climbing*, Stackpole Books, 1993.

JIM PERRIN, *The villain,* Arrow books*, 2006.

STEVE ROPER, *Yosemite Camp 4*, Guérin, 1996.

SIMON THOMPSON, *Unjustifiable Risk? : The Story of British Climbing*, Cicerone Press, 2010

KEITH TREACHER, *Siegfried Herford*, An Edwardian Rock Climber, 2000.

JEAN-BAPTISTE TRIBOUT ET DAVID CHAMBRE, *Le 8e degré*, Denoël, 1987.

BERNARD VAUCHER, *Des rochers et des hommes*, Éditions de l'Envol, 2001.

BERNARD VAUCHER, *Les fous du Verdon*, Guérin, 2008.

HEINZ ZAK, *Rockstars*, Cordee, 1996.

HEINZ ZAK, *Yosemite,* München, 2002.

TABLE
MAIN DIFFICULTY GRADES

—

ROCK

USA (YDS)	FRANCE	UIAA (GERMANY)	UK		AUSTRALIA
5.0	1	I	1	M	1
					2/3
5.1	2	II	2		4/5
5.2				D	6/7
5.3	3	III	3		8/9
5.4	4a	IV		VD	10/11
5.5	4b	IV+	4a	S	11/12
5.6	4c	V	4b	HS	13
5.7	5a	V+	4c	VS	14/15
5.8	5b	VI-		HVS	15/16
5.9	5c	VI	5a		17
5.10a	6a	VI+		E1	18
5.10b	6a+	VII-	5b		19
5.10c	6b	VII		E2	20
5.10d	6b+	VII+	5c		
5.11a	6c			E3	21
5.11b	6c+	VIII-			22
5.11c	6c/7a		6a	E4	23
5.11d	7a	VIII			24
5.12a	7a+	VIII+		E5	25
5.12b	7b				26
5.12c	7b+	IX-	6b	E6	27
5.12d	7c	IX			28
5.13a	7c+	IX+		E7	29
5.13b	8a		6c		
5.13c	8a+	X-		E8	30
5.13d	8b	X		E9	31
5.14a	8b+	X+	7a	E10	32
5.14b	8c				33
5.14c	8c+	XI-	7b	E11	34
5.14d	9a	XI			35
5.15a	9a+	XI+			36
5.15b	9b	XI+/XII-			37
5.15c	9b+	XII-			38

BOULDERING

USA (HUECO)	FRANCE (FONTAINEBLEAU)
V0	4
V0+	4+
V1	5
V2	5+
V3	6A
	6A+
V4	6B
	6B+
V5	6C
	6C+
V6	6C+
	7A
V7	7A+
V8	7B
	7B+
V9	7B+
	7C
V10	7C+
V11	8A
V12	8A+
V13	8B
V14	8B+
V15	8C
V16	8C+

ACKNOWLEDGEMENTS

A SPECIAL THANKS TO THE AUTHOR

To Sophie for her patience. To Jibé and Marc and Antoine for their unwavering friendship. To Catherine Destivelle for her faith and support throughout and to Geoff Birtles, gratitude for his invaluable help and all the precious advice.

THANKS TO THE AUTHOR AND PUBLISHER

The Team Altissimo Marseille, Vincent Albrand and the Team Grimper, David Atchinson-Jones, Yves Ballu, Thomas Ballenberger, Laurent Belluard, Sam Bié, Geoff Birtles, Stéphanie Bodet, Joe Brown, Tommy Caldwell, Mauro Calibani, Nina Caprez, Michel Charles, Caroline Ciavaldini, John Cleare, Joël Coqueugniot, Yann Corby, Christian Core, Pietro Crivellaro, Johnny Dawes, Didier Demeter, Leo Dickinson, John Dune, Bruno Dupety, Rainer Eder, Bibliothèque de l'ENSA, Robert Exertier, Dean Fidelman, Neil Foster, Tom Frost, Andrea Gallo, John Gill, Colin Haley, Sarah Hart, Lynn Hill, Alex Honnold, Anne Lauwaert, Leo Houlding, Alexander Huber, Luisa Iovane, Cathy Jolibert, Michel Jullien, Beat Kammerlander, Fred Labreveux, François Legrand, Hélène Le Menestrel, Robert Nicod, Françoise Lepron, François Lombard, Heinz Mariacher, Lothar Mauch, Gérard Merlin, Jerry Moffatt, Jo Montchaussé, Ben Moon, Fred Nicole, Gary Neptune, Robert Paragot, James Pearson, Eleanor Perry-Smith, Arnaud Petit, Florence Pinet, Gérôme Pouvreau, Rénald Quatrehomme, Alain Robert, Darío Rodríguez, Philippe Royer, Frank Scherrer, Christian Semm, Chris Sharma, Jonathan Siegrist, Ian Smith, Pascal Tournaire, Marco Troussier, Nicolas Tubador, Fred Tuscan, Valoo Tribout, Barney Vaucher, François Viroulet, Beth Wald, Rich Weather, Kathy Whittaker, Uli Wiesmeier, Florent Wolff, Michi Wyser, Heinz Zak, Maurizio Zanolla.

PHOTO CREDITS

Abraham, p.16 left, p.19 above left / **Rick Accamozzo**, p.82 below / **Kurt Albert**, p.263 / **Pat Ament**, p.50, p.90 centre, p.90 below / **David Atchisin-Jones**, p.157 / **John Bachar**, p.162, / **Thomas Ballenberger**, rear jacket below right, p.104 right, p.105, p.106, p.107 left, p.136, p.147, p.148, p.150 left, p.150 right, p. 283 / **Yves Ballu**, p.131 / **Sam Bié**, jacket front cover, p.204, p.210, p.216 / **Laurent Belluard,** p.184 / **Geoff Birtles**, p.31 below, p.73 left, p.73 right, p.74 left / **Dave Burleson**, p.232 above / **Andrew Burr**, p.228 / **Davide Carrari**, p.235 right / **Severino Casara**, p.34, p.35, p.36, p.37 / **David Chambre**, p.46, p.56 above left, p.67 above, p.69 right, p.72, p.107 right, p.123, p.125, p.126, p.128 centre, p.128 below, p.136 centre, p.159, p.192, p.239 centre, p.241, p.290-291 / **Sylvie Chappaz**, p.118 / **Jocelyn Chavy**, p.289 below / **Jimmy Chin**, p.206 / **Jai Critchley**, p.289 above / **John Cleare**, p.55 right / **Joel Coqueugniot**, p.68 / **Yann Corby**, p.194, p.195, p.248, p.256, p.282 above right / **Patrick Cordier**, p.153 / **Glenn Denny**, p.48, p.49 below right, p.51, p.52, p.53 / **Stephan Denys**, p.196, p.262, p.264b, p.265 above left, p.265 below left, p.266b, p.267 below, p.271 / **Leo Dickinson**, p.56 right, p.57 above / **Philippe Echaroux**, rabat / **Rainer Eder**, p.209 / **Greg Epperson**, p.82 above, p.83 / **Al Evans**, p.74 right / **Robert Exertier**, p.91, p.99, p.100, p.108, p.109, p.134 centre, p.135, p.138, p.145 above right / **Dean Fidelman**, back cover of hard back and rear jacket below left, p.44, p.85, p.242, p.243, p.244, p.245 / **Mary Gabrieli**, p.198 / **A. Gallo**, p.265 right / **Neil Foster**, p.141 / **Tom Frost**, p.47, p.49 above / **D. Gohin**, p.103 left / **Walter Hahn**, couverture, p.14, p.23 below, p.76 above, p.77 above / **Fried Henning**, p.29 below right / **Mike Hutton**, p.238 left / **John Houlahan**, p.142 right / **M. Houska**, p.170 / **Luisa Iovane**, p.202 / **Dave Kendal**, p.142 centre / **John Kirk**, p.113 above right / **Gérard Kosicki**, p.121 / **Fred Labreveux**, p.212, p.282 below right, p.292, p.293 / **Alastair Lee**, p.237 / **Françoise Lepron**, p.97 centre, p.115, p.126 below, p.129, p.132 left, p.134 above, p.151 / **Sean Leary**, p.207 / **James Linehan**, p.90 above / **Cameron Maier**, p.223 / **Stella Marchisio**, p.260 above, p.270 / **Eva Martos**, p.200 / **Peter Mathis**, p.185 left et right / **Gérard Merlin**, p.96 left, p.110, p.111 / **Françoise Montchaussé**, p.264 right / **Robert Nicod**, p.94, p.102, p.112 left, p.119 / **Arnaud Petit**, p.190 / **Marco Prezelj**, p.182 below / **Paul Relly**, p.29 above right / **Rey**, p.27 / **Corey Rich**, p.286-287 / **Tom Riley**, p.80 / **René Robert**, p.120 / **Darío Rodríguez**, p.132 right, p.165, p.168, p.176, p.177 above, p.179, p.181, p.193, p.197, p.203, p.213, p.215, p.220, p.221, p.225, p.233, p.247 above, p.247 below, p.249 above left, p.249 below centre, p.249 below right, p.249 above right, p.250, p.251, p.252, p.253, p.254, p.255, p.257, p.258, p.260 left, p.260 below right, p.261 right, p.274, p.275, p.277, p.278, p.279, p.288 above left, p.295 / **J. Roth**, p.232 below / **Gallen Rowell**, p.49 / **Philippe Royer**, p.96 right, p.144 left / **G.S. Sanson**, p.20 above left, p.20 above right / **Christian Semm**, p.282 left / **W. Schmidkunz**, p.29 left / **Jo Stadden**, p.238 right / **Pascal Tournaire**, p.66, p.145 below, p.177 below, p.182 above, p.183, p.187, p.189, p.191 above, p.261 left, p.266 above, p.269, p.288 below left, p.290 above, p.291 above, p.303 / **L. Triay**, p.205 / **Marco Troussier**, p.69 left centre, p.71 below / **Thomas Vialletet**, p.236 / **Beth Wald**, p.112 right, p.136 right, p.169 left, p.169 right, p.288 / **Rich Wheater**, p.239 left, p.239 right / **Uli Wiesmeier**, p.88 above, p.133, p.134 below, p.172, p.173 above, p.173 below, p.174, p.296-297 / **Heiko Wihelm**, p.226 left / **Geoffrey Winthrop Young**, p.20 below left / **Mike White**, p.86 / **Wills Young**, p.267 above / **John Woodhouse**, p.73 centre / **Heinz Zak**, rear jacket above right, p.89, p.116, p.149, p.154, p.158, p.160, p.161, p.164, p.166, p.167.

FROM PHOTO COLLECTIONS OF:

Coll. Paul Allain, p.40 above, p.40 below, p.41, p.42 above, p.42 below left, p.42 below right / **Coll. Bernd Arnold**, p.76 below, p.77 below, p.78, p.79 / **Coll. Jean-Pierre Bouvier**, p.103 right / **Coll. Tommy Caldwell**, p.284 / **Coll. Martin Boysen**, p.56 below left / **Coll. Barbier-Lauwaert**, p.58, p.59 / **Coll. Joe Brown**, p.54, p.55 left / **Coll. Nina Caprez**, p.210, rear jacket below centre / **Coll. C. Ciavaldini**, rear jacket above centre, p.180, p.219, p.240 / **Coll. Pietro Crivellaro**, p.26, p.27 left, p.31 above, p.32 left, p.32 right, p.33 above, p.33 below, p.39 above right, p.39 below right / **Coll. Beat Kammerlander**, p.203, p.235 left / **Coll. John Gill**, p.64, p.65 / **Coll. Grison**, p.97 above / **Coll. Alex Honnold**, p.230 / **Coll. Luisa Iovane**, p.130 above / **Coll. Ray Jardine**, p.88 / **Coll. Livanos**, p.57 below / **Coll. Sean Mc**, p.249 below left / **Coll. Cesare Maestri**, p.62 right, p.63 / **Coll. Reinhold Messner**, p.62, p.63, p.93 above / **Coll. Jerry Moffatt**, p.114, p.156 / **Coll. Ben Moon**, p.142 left / **Coll. Robert Paragot**, p.60 left / **Coll. Bepi Pellegrinon**, p.27 / **Coll. E. Perry-Smith**, p.22 above, p.23 above right, p.24, p.25, p.300, rear jacket above left / **Coll. Florence Pinet**, p.280, p.281 / **Coll. Frank Richter**, p.23 centre / **Coll. Alain Robert**, p.227 / **Coll. Sender**, p.229 above, p.229 below, p.298-299 / **Coll. Sonnie Trotter**, p.238 centre / **Coll. Varale**, p.39 below right / **Coll. Maurizio Zanolla**, p.97 below / **Coll. Jibe Tribout**, p.71 above, p.122, p.124, p.128 above right, p.130 below, p.144 right, p.191 below.

INSTITUTIONS

Alpine Club Library Londres, p.16 centre, p.16 right, p.19 below, p.26 below / **Patrimoine della Fondazione Cassin, Lecco**, p.38, p.39 left.

TRANSLATED FROM FRENCH BY AUBREY LAWRENCE
AND REVISED BY GEOFF BIRTLES AND IAN SMITH

—

GRAPHIC DESIGNER: ÉLÉONORE GERBIER

—

FIRST EDITION OCTOBER 2015
PRINTED BY NUEVA IMPRENTA, ALCOBENDAS, SPAIN
LEGAL DEPOSIT SEPTEMBER 2015